YESTERDAY'S GLOVEMEN

YESTERDAY'S GLOVEMEN

The Golden Days of Ulster Boxing

Brian Madden

THE BREHON PRESS
BELFAST

First published 2006 by The Brehon Press Ltd
1A Bryson Street, Belfast BT5 4ES, Northern Ireland

ISBN: 1 905474 02 4

Design: December Publications
Printed and bound by J.H. Haynes & Co Ltd

CONTENTS

For Brigid

INTRODUCTION

"Made it, Ma! Top of the world!"

Anyone who has ever watched James Cagney utter those memorable worlds at the explosive finale to the classic gangster movie *White Heat* won't forget them in a hurry.

With the exception of Rinty Monaghan and Johnny Caldwell, none of the courageous little scrappers featured in this book quite made it to the "top of the world". Of course, some did win major trophies and titles, but that is not the overriding concern of *Yesterday's Glovemen*.

The principal object of the pages that follow is not merely to detail which fighters won or lost whatever championships. No, the main intention is to resurrect the names of many of the battlers featured, the majority of whom have passed on, and in some cases have almost been forgotten. They are all boxers who gave so much joy for so little remuneration to fight fans down through the years.

The idea for the book first struck me when, while heading into the centre of Belfast in a taxi, I spotted the great Johnny Caldwell from the car window.

"There's Johnny Caldwell," I said to the driver, a man in his forties.

"Who's he?" he replied.

"You obviously have no interest in boxing," I remarked.

"But I have," said he, and he proceeded to rhyme off the names of the Brunos, the Eubanks, and the McGuigans of this world. When tested further on other homegrown pugilists from yesteryear, he continued to show his ignorance in such matters.

This gave me food for thought, and I decided to put together a volume about Caldwell and his "band of brothers" who defined the golden days of boxing in Ulster. These were men who stepped between the ropes and into the squared circle with frightening regularity when compared to the contestants of today. Many times, they were expected to don the mitts at merely a moment's notice. They were all local heroes, whose names were consistently gracing the sports pages of the local press, and it struck me as unjust that they seemed to be fading from the collective memory.

So, here it is: the lives and times of a (personal) selection of gladiators who hailed from our own home turf. I hope you enjoy it.

Brian Madden

ACKNOWLEDGEMENTS

I would like to thank most sincerely all of the ex-boxers who permitted me to interview them for this book, and the relatives of deceased boxers, who kindly gave of their time to speak to me. A special word of thanks to Harold Alderman and Derek O'Dell in England for all the boxing records which they sent me, and it is important that I mention my friend, the late Philip Rooney, who gave me information about his brother Jimmy Rooney (Ike Weir), and who also sent me photographs. Others who deserve mention are Al Gibson, Paddy Graham, Jimmy Wilkinson, Sean Canavan, Wilgar Graham and Fred Heatley. I would also like to thank the staff of the newspaper library in Library Street for their courtesy and friendliness, and Hugh Russell, Brendan Murphy and Kathleen Bell of the *Irish News*. Thanks also to the *Belfast Telegraph*, the *News Letter*, the *Boxing News*, the *Derry Journal*, and to that excellent researcher Vivien Burgess in London. Extra special thanks are extended to Henry Morgan, who made many personal sacrifices in the course of this book's long journey into print, and who tirelessly advised on its design; also to Henry's charming wife, Marion, for the numerous tasty meals she served up during my visits to her husband's studio. I am deeply indebted.

In the gathering of illustrations for this book, the author has been overwhelmed by the kindness shown by the fighters and their families in allowing him to reproduce many of the images included within these pages. Wilgar Graham has shown that same generosity, as has Jack Magowan of the Belfast Telegraph. Additional photographs are reproduced by kind permission of the Gardenia Press and the Irish News. The front cover image, which is also featured in the Rinty Monaghan chapter, is included thanks to kind permission from Getty Images. Every reasonable effort has been made to contact the copyright holders of photographs; if any involuntary infringement of copyright has occurred, sincere apologies are offered and the owners of such copyright are requested to contact the publisher.

Mickey Lavery

Reports of his death were greatly exaggerated

The consultant looked sternly at Mickey Lavery and said: "Mr Lavery, you've been in hospital in England for a year and you've cheated the Grim Reaper at Neuve Chapelle. So far, you've had eleven operations, your left leg has been severely injured, there's shrapnel so close to your heart that it would be absolute folly to try to remove it – and you're asking me if you can box again. Forget about it, son. You're going to find it difficult enough to walk, never mind get into a boxing ring. And there's every likelihood that you will experience bouts of pain and depression throughout your life."

He was absolutely right. Lavery was seriously injured and would suffer frequently from unbearable pain. Mickey's wounds were a result of his part in the First World War battle to take the village of Neuve Chapelle, which had raged between 10 and 13 March 1915. It had been announced in bulletins and newspapers that Mickey was one of the fatalities. There were actually two reports circulated about him. The first, on 3 April 1915, read: "Mick Lavery, the clever little Belfast boxer, who fought at The Star and Alexandra Theatre, was killed in action at Neuve Chapelle at the age of nineteen. Lavery had many contests and twice beat Young Crowe."

The second report, a week later, could have been penned by Mark Twain for reports of young Lavery's death had been "greatly exaggerated": "Mick Lavery, the Belfast boxer, previously reported killed at Neuve Chapelle, lives to fight another day. We can now report that he is actually in hospital in England. Although seriously wounded, we all hope that he makes a full recovery and apologise to his family for any distress caused by our earlier report." Unfortunately, Mickey's brother, James, who was with the First Battalion Connaught Rangers, was later killed in action in Mesopotamia on 17 April 1916.

Mickey was born on 19 April 1893 at Institution Place in Belfast, later moving to Welsh Street in the Markets area. His father, James Lavery, was from the Falls Road and his mother Catherine hailed from Donegal. He had three brothers, James, Joseph and Hugh, and he attended Eliza Street School. When young Lavery left school he became something of a DIY expert, so getting work wasn't too much of a problem. He later became an expert tailor, making garments with the minimum of material. In the early 1900s, when parents found it difficult to clothe both their children and themselves, Mickey was always ready and willing to give a helping hand without asking for anything in return.

Although he was interested in most sports, it was the toughest of all sports the boy from the Markets constantly dreamed about – professional boxing. He didn't waste any time in making his dream a reality. On 12 May 1911, he got the feel of things inside the hem-pen strands with a no contest bout against J McKee.

Mickey's fledgling career was slow in taking off. When it did make a move on Friday, 8 November 1912 in The Star on Church Street in Belfast, in what was described as "the best fight of the night", Mickey defeated Belfast boy Young Norney in a real thriller. Lavery's right hand was a punishing weapon while his left hand was seldom idle. Both boys mixed it and there was never a dull moment over six enthralling rounds. One week after his fine performance against Norney, Mickey drew with Young Weir and exactly one month later he out-pointed Young Cullen over the novice journey of four rounds.

On 3 January 1913, Mickey had a date in The Star with Barney Murray, which he won comfortably. On his next visit to The Star, Mickey was beaten by Young Nixon. After a ten-month break from the game, he was in fantastic form against Curly Megarrity, whom he knocked out in the second round in the Victoria Athletic Club, Portadown.

In 1914, Mickey took his career a step further when he stopped Jack Weir in the second round. The little bantamweight was particularly impressive when, on his first trip over ten rounds, he out-pointed Taylor Brady.

On his next outing, on 27 March, Mickey had a fine win over Young Crowe. It was a short but exciting affair. In the opening round, Lavery was dropped for eight by a well-timed right to the jaw. In the second, he completely turned the tables on Crowe, boring in with heavy rights and lefts to the body and jaw. At the end of the round Crowe was groggy. A heavy right sent Crowe down and out in the third. This was a good win for Mickey because Crowe went on to be Featherweight Champion of the Black Watch, in which he was a private.

Mickey Lavery (left) in a publicity shot with an unnamed referee and opponent

Crowe used to tell a story about the time he was in Dundee and went to see Jack Johnson, who was giving an exhibition on stage in the King's Theatre. Jack asked if anyone in the audience would like to take the opportunity to spar with him. Crowe volunteered and in the second round he drew blood from Johnson. Jack asked the squaddie if he would spar with him for the rest of that week, and on receiving permission from his commanding officer, Crowe agreed. The Black Watch boxer described Johnson as "a real gentleman".

Mickey proved his superiority over Crowe when they met for a second time on 1 May at the Belfast Palladium. The proceeds were going to well-known referee, Mr Jim Warner. Unfortunately for Mr Warner, there was a

Mickey in his older years with a younger member of the Lavery clan

poor attendance. It had been a pretty level contest up to the seventh with Crowe just shading it. However, the Black Watch boxer wasn't doing enough watching and Lavery's right hand came like a thief in the night, catching Crowe on the jaw and it was all over. It was a fine win for Mickey.

The gutsy little Belfast bantamweight's career, while not exactly over, would never be the same again after his horrible war wounds. Mickey was discharged from the hospital and the army, and returned home determined not to let his injuries destroy his quality of life. Every day was an uphill struggle. His leg hurt like hell and the shrapnel residing in his body, dangerously close to his heart, increased his discomfort ten-fold. He was shunted from hospital to hospital and when he was released the doctor was a frequent visitor to his home. Still, he would box again even though he accepted that he could never be the same fighter.

Mickey tried to put his chronic pain to the back of his mind for his big day when he married his lovely bride, May McArdle, from Belfast, in St Malachy's Church in July 1917. Their marriage would produce five boys and eight girls.

On his return to the ring on 17 January 1918, Mickey unbelievably took a fight at short notice in Derry's Guildhall against Dubliner, Joe Meehan. Mickey, who was standing in for Billy Padden from Glasgow, was ill-prepared for this contest and took a lot of punishment before being stopped in the fifth.

He rested for six months and when he returned for action on 22 June he had a splendid win over Jack Hughes, whom he knocked out in the first round. The usual opening sparring was in progress when Lavery jumped in and swung a desperate right with great force to the chin. The blow was so powerful that it lifted Hughes clean off his feet and his head struck the boards with a thud before he was counted out.

This tremendous win increased Mickey's confidence when he stepped into the ring on 6 July to meet Corporal Swingler from the Somersets army regiment. The corporal was a clever boxer and far too fleet-of-foot for the local boy. Swingler opened well, connecting with his right in great style and forcing matters. Mickey tried in vain to connect with his deadly right hand but the soldier was too wary and his speedy footwork kept him out of danger.

The second stanza was similar to the first. Although Swingler did have a few narrow shaves from Lavery's right, he proved altogether too fast for the Belfast boy. Lavery was dead game, taking punishment galore while endeavouring to keep his opponent at bay with his left. In the fourth round, it was obvious that Lavery was up against it but he was not in severe difficulties. However, one of his seconds threw in the towel at the end of the round, an action that nearly led to a scene as Lavery wanted to continue.

Mickey didn't fight again until 21 March 1921, when he was knocked out after three rounds by Willie Woods in Glasgow. In the last fight of his career, he was knocked out by Rab O'Reilly after four rounds in Belfast. They didn't come any braver than Mickey Lavery: he survived the battle of Neuve Chapelle and he came out of his ring battles unscathed. Bravery and gentlemanly conduct were his trademarks. He died on 3 January 1973.

PROFESSIONAL CAREER
1911–1922: 16 traced contests: won 9, lost 5, drew 1, no-contest 1.

Jack Garland

Had little love for professional boxing

The 1928 Amsterdam Olympics were the first games in which women competitors were allowed to take part in certain track and field events. It was also the first time the Olympic flame continued to burn throughout the games, and the first time that doves were released at the opening ceremony.

Other highlights that year included Irishman Patrick O'Callaghan taking the gold in the hammer throw; Johnny Weissmuller ending his Olympic career, before going to Hollywood to star in the *Tarzan* movies, with two more gold swimming medals; and Buster Crabbe, who would also play Tarzan, as well as Buck Rogers and Flash Gordon, winning a bronze medal in the 1500 metres freestyle and a gold in the 4 x 200 metres freestyle relay.

Belfast's Jack Garland also attended the games, representing Britain in the boxing events. He was part of a team that included Fred Mallin, later the ABA Middleweight Champion from 1928 to 1932, whose older brother Harry not only held the same ABA title from 1919 to 1923 but was Olympic Middleweight Champion at the 1920 Antwerp Games, and again in Paris in 1924.

Jack got off to a great start in his quest for Olympic glory when he had a narrow victory over Ernest Mignard from France. In his next bout, despite doing exceptionally well, he was beaten by Vittorio Tamagnini, who, on turning professional, would go on to beat the World Bantamweight Champion, "Panama" Al Brown. Jack had to give ground in the first round against the compact and ferociously active little Italian and he was caught by a wild swing which forced him to take a short count.

In the second round, Garland seemed to realise

that if he didn't step up a gear, defeat was inevitable, so he went in and scored heavily with both hands. This, unfortunately, gave the Belfast man the false impression that all was going well, enabling Tamagnini to gain in confidence and rush in, scoring all the time. This was a contest that Garland could, and should, have won but bad tactics cost him the fight. The Italian went on to win the gold medal, John Daley (USA) won the silver, and Harry Isaacs (South Africa) won the bronze.

Many years later, Jack Garland would say, "I regretted leaving the amateurs. Among the amateurs one found real sporting organisers out to help the boys, not men bent simply on taking all they could from promising boxers, giving practically nothing in return. Professional boxing, as I found it, is not a game, but simply a racket in which the boxer invariably comes off second best."

During his career as a professional, Jack struck up a friendship with his London trainer, Jack Goodwin. Goodwin later trained Larry Gains, the former British Empire Heavyweight Champion, in whose corner he collapsed during a promotion at the Royal

Jack Goodwin

Albert Hall. Goodwin passed away soon afterwards in the dressing room. Commenting on Goodwin's death, Garland said, "I lost my best sporting friend when he died."

Garland was born in Lincoln Street, Belfast, on 2 January 1908, to mother Agnes, a native of Castlewellan, and father John, a crane driver from the city. Jack would have two sisters, Kathleen and Maureen, and a brother, Thomas. He went to the nearby Slate Street School but the family moved to Rockville Street, just off the Falls Road. With his education completed, Jack obtained work in the shipyard as a caulker. There wasn't much money for socialising and, rather than staying indoors after a hard day's work, Jack joined a local boxing club where he not only picked up the rudiments of the amateur code but also picked up a 7st 4lbs local title.

After being laid off from the shipyard, Jack joined the Second Battalion Gordon Highlanders, where he soon made a name for himself in the ring. In 1927, Private Jack Garland won the Imperial Services Championship and he retained this title in 1928, the year he also won his ABA title and participated in the Olympics.

He decided to turn professional, being trained by Jack Goodwin and managed by Syd Hulls. He was bought out of the army by the Falls Road publican, Jack Hynes, a friend of Jack's grandfather.

In January 1929, Garland made his debut at Premierland in London, getting off to a good start with a points win over fifteen rounds against Con Lewis (Bethnal Green).

This was a great fillip for young Garland's confidence, which was evident in his performance six weeks later when he stopped Sheffield's Tiny Smith, again at Premierland, in five rounds. Jack's third successive win came when he beat Gideon Pottean from France. His fine form continued with points victories over Young Jackie Brown (Bethnal Green), Kid Socks (Bethnal Green), Andre Regis (France), George Williams (Treherbert) and Con Lewis.

Jack's run of eight consecutive wins ended when he lost narrowly to sixteen-year-old Londoner "Nipper" Pat Daly on 6 June. Daly repeated his win with more conviction over Garland on 11 August. The London boy opened up with some lefts to the face but Garland, although on the defensive, countered the majority of blows. He was first to land a hard punch, a left hook, which connected with Daly's jaw in the second round.

Daly scored to the body in the third, though in this round there was a lot of holding, which didn't please the referee. Daly was always working with both hands and never allowed Garland to get settled. He caught the Irishman with a right in the fourth and, in the next, he had the former amateur champion against the ropes, punishing him with lefts and rights to the head.

Garland did better as the bout progressed. He landed a neat uppercut in the sixth and three times in this round he scored with left swings to the body. Daly continued to force the fight and took the seventh, eighth and ninth rounds with comparative ease. Garland bravely stood his ground against an onslaught of blows, but was unable to make any impression on his young opponent.

The tenth and eleventh rounds were keenly contested, Garland taking the honours for the first time with some well-timed lefts to the jaw. The last round also went to Garland who appeared to have left his challenge rather late since he was certainly as strong as Daly when the final bell sounded.

In his next outing, Jack boxed a thrilling draw with Welshman Ginger Jones and, as the result would indicate, it was punch-for-punch all the way. Both boys gave their best with the closing stages so hotly contested that the majority of the three thousand fans were off their seats. Garland began promisingly, punishing Jones with straight lefts to the face and it was not until the third round that Jones replied with a right. Garland's two-handed work gained him the points and an excellent left hook to the jaw midway through the fourth shook his opponent.

The bout progressed on an even keel. Then in the eighth, a hard right from Jones had Garland in serious trouble. Jones continued the onslaught with vicious lefts and rights and it looked odds-on that he would stop

Garland and Henri Machtens pose at their pre-fight weigh-in

Garland, who was tottering around the ring. The Irishman gave a plucky display in the last four rounds and his early points tally enabled him to share the honours. In his final contest of 1929, Jack had a points win over Lew Pinctus (Notting Hill).

Due to an ear injury, Jack was out of action for two months. When he made his reappearance on 8 January 1930, he had a comfortable points win over Frenchman Marcel Delobelle in the Stadium Club, London. The highlight of the evening was the closing stages of a heavyweight competition for the *Sporting Life* belt, plus a nice little prize of £250. The belt and the money were won by Birmingham's Jack Taylor, who knocked out Billy Hunt from King's Cross in the first round.

Garland was given an opportunity to get into the big-time when he was matched again with Ginger Jones on 29 January 1930 in the Ulster Hall in the eliminator for the British featherweight title. The first round was a cautious one, and there was little in it by the end of the fifth. Garland came out for the sixth looking more confident than he had previously and was shaping up well. His left hand shot out time and time again, although there was little sting in the blows. Jones was clever in getting under his opponent's attack and countering with both hands. In the eleventh, Garland was performing brilliantly and staggered his man. He pressed home his attack in relentless fashion and Jones, whose defence was good at times, required all his skill to keep his tormentor at bay. There were periods when Garland more or less toyed with his man, notably in the thirteenth, but as the contest came to an end, Jones did show flashes of brilliance. The decision in favour of Jones was received by the Belfast crowd with a demonstration of dissent. The majority of the audience thought that their man should have got the decision and the referee, Mr Thomas Murphy from Newcastle-on-Tyne, was booed. Jack Goodwin loudly questioned the decision at ringside and many of the spectators left their seats to protest.

When the hubbub died down, Jones said, "I won easily. It was by no means my hardest fight. The crowd seemed to have overlooked how often I made Garland miss, and I scored in the in-fighting." Garland said, "It was a rotten decision. I feel sure that I won. The last five rounds were easily mine." Mr Murphy, the referee, asserted, "There was no doubt about the result. Jones won ten rounds, and if the fight had been over that distance it would have been an easy win for the Welshman. Garland missed a great deal and, in the finer points of the game, Jones was easily superior." Murphy's words proved prophetic because when Garland and Jones met for the final time in 1933, Jones won on points over ten rounds.

In London, Dominique di Cea, a rugged Frenchman, gave twenty-two-year-old Garland all the trouble he wanted, and when it seemed that defeat was inevitable, the gutsy Belfast lad rallied to snatch a draw. Di Cea, although crude in his methods, was very effective in his hitting to the body in the early rounds. He swung both hands wildly and Garland had to concentrate solely on defensive work.

Garland failed to stem the onslaught of the Frenchman in the second round and was dropped for a count of eight by a left hook to the jaw. Jack boxed cautiously in the third and failed to take advantage of the many openings presented to him. Di Cea continued to have the better of matters, penetrating Garland's guard and scoring heavily to the body. In the fifth, the Belfast boxer was groggy from further punishment to the body, yet he fought back strongly and, in the eighth, when the Frenchman held a comfortable points lead, Garland steadied his man with accurate left leads. Thereafter, the Irishman did better. He timed his lefts accurately and hit with more power. Di Cea gradually tired and Garland was able to gather points at such a rate that, when the final round opened, he was behind only by a very small margin. The boxing in the last round was spirited but it was Garland who held the upper hand and at the end the referee's verdict was a draw.

Another continental, in the form of Belgian Henri Machtens, was Jack's next assignment. The Belfast lad had a points win over fifteen rounds, the fight taking place in Grimsby. Next up was Con Lewis, who was bettered by Garland yet again, losing on points over fifteen rounds.

Jack had a date with Frank McAloran for the latter's Irish featherweight title in a contest, which was billed as "The Greatest Fight Ever Staged in Ireland". It took place in St Mary's Hall on Wednesday, 16 April 1930, and was promoted by Mr Tom Murphy. There was also the matter of £100 for the winner. Such was the intense interest in this fight that Murphy decided to hold back the contest until 10pm in order to facilitate those attending the greyhound racing at Celtic Park.

McAloran was four years older than Garland and had made his professional debut in 1923. Going into the fight, the vastly experienced champion, who had won thirty, lost nine and drew seven of his bouts, looked to be the hot favourite to retain the title. Frank had won his crown by knocking out George Kelly in May 1929.

Garland entered the ring first and was received with applause but the big ovation was reserved for McAloran. Before the fight commenced, Packy McFarland from Dublin challenged the winner, his father being present to lodge £50.

In the first round, Garland did the forcing; keeping to the centre of the ring he was boxing beautifully and his left leads were superb. Twice he connected with a right to the body without reply from McAloran. There were several bursts of in-fighting in which the exchanges were pretty even. In the second round, Garland went in and out as he liked in the opening stages. McAloran, however, came back and hung on like a terrier, using both hands to the body. He raised the hopes of his supporters, who cheered loudly, when he landed a hard right to the body just as the bell went.

In round three, McAloran rushed his man all over the ring and his head was giving Garland a great deal of trouble. Frank was cautioned twice to keep his head up. He certainly scored very well in the in-fighting. Garland clearly took the fourth as he scored repeatedly with left leads to the face, one of which drew blood from McAloran's mouth. In the fifth, McAloran was cautioned for holding. Garland continued to box beautifully and his left leads were a source of annoyance to McAloran, who received blows from them time and time again.

The sixth was a very hard session in which Garland scored frequently, though McAloran had his moments. In the seventh, McAloran had the crowd protesting when he caught Garland with a low blow. Garland replied with a succession of straight lefts. Just before the gong, McAloran scored in a bout of in-fighting.

In the eighth, Garland began by accepting McAloran's invitation to a toe-to-toe slam and ended it with a right to the face, which undoubtedly shook the champion. McAloran was being out-boxed and the feature of the round was the speed with which Garland closed up for in-fighting. The ninth was a fiercely fought round. McAloran went right in from the start and took all that Garland dished out in an effort to land a decisive body blow. In this he was not successful as Garland covered up with the art of a master. Towards the

Packy McFarland

end of the session Garland forced his man to the ropes where the latter's headwork was conspicuous.

The tenth was a good round of boxing. The fight had so far alternated between a round of boxing being succeeded by a round of in-fighting. Garland was short with two right leads and McAloran countered well. The exchanges in the eleventh were fairly even. Garland was still plying the left with good effect and once missed a nice attempt to uppercut. McAloran scored with both hands in the in-fighting.

The twelfth was a slam-bang affair from beginning to end, both boys attacking to the body. The thirteenth was fought amidst tremendous excitement. The noise was deafening and the action non-stop, neither giving nor asking for quarter and it was testimony to the fitness of both boys that they withstood such a gruelling pace. Garland's shoulders were spattered with blood from McAloran's face. The champ still fought back tenaciously, belting Garland's body with both hands.

In the fourteenth, McAloran did much better, landing his left much more frequently than at any time during the fight. The round lacked some of the fire of the previous ones. At the finish both came out looking surprisingly fresh. Garland did the forcing, while McAloran met his attacks with grim determination. Garland landed a lovely left to the jaw and McAloran responded with stiff body shots before he slipped to the boards. On rising, he was caught by a left that went perilously close to the point of the chin. Garland got the decision, which was a popular and deserved one.

The year 1930 hadn't been a particularly memorable one for Londoner Kid Pattenden, the former British Bantamweight Champion. He had dropped points decisions to Charlie Rowbottom, Dick Corbett, Frank Markey and Selwyn Davies, and when making his debut as a featherweight, he would drop another points decision to the new Irish Featherweight Champion, Jack Garland. After the contest, which took place at The Ring in Blackfriars, Syd Hulls, Garland's manager, issued a challenge not only to Johnny Cuthbert, the British Featherweight Champion, but to anyone else who would care to share a ring with his boy.

Boyo Rees (Abercwmboi) had not been stopped in thirty-eight fights. He lost this fine record of durability when he was stopped in round twelve by Garland in Liverpool Stadium. Garland was so much on top that the main feature of the fight was the gameness of the little Welshman. Boyo Rees would win the Welsh lightweight title and, in the course of his career, amassed more than 140 fights, winning about seventy-eight of them.

Jack retained his Irish title against Packy McFarland in nine rounds in the Ulster Hall. Sandwiched between two defeats by Newcastle's "Seaman" Tom Watson, who would go on to win the British featherweight title in 1932 by defeating Nel Tarleton, he had a points win over Belgium's François Machtens. Jack brought 1930 to a close with a points win over former opponent, Dominique di Cea.

Al Brown was born on 5 July 1902 in Panama. He not only grew in stature, peaking at 5 feet 11 inches, but also grew into a fine fighting machine. When he was twenty-one, he moved to New York where, in 1929, he participated in an eliminator for the vacant bantamweight title. He beat Videl Gregorio over fifteen stanzas in New York to become Panama's, and Latin America's, first world boxing champion. Instead of staying put to sort out the bantamweight situation, Al decided not only to take his version of the title – Bud Taylor was recognised by the NBA – to Europe, but to reside there as well. This was a decision that angered the powers-that-be in New York and they refused to recognise him as their bantamweight champion.

Brown defended against Knud Larsen, Eugene Haut (twice), Nick Bensa, Pete Sanstol, Kid Francis (twice), Young Perez (twice), Emile Pladner and Dom Bernasconi. Prior to these title defences Brown had knocked out Willie Farrell and Douglas Parker. His next opponent would be twenty-three-year-old Jack Garland.

This was a daunting task for Garland. However, if he was suffering from nerves in the Belle Vue Arena in Manchester that April evening in 1931, there was certainly no evidence of it. In the first round, after taking punishment to the head and body, he staggered Brown with a left to the body and followed up with a left to the head. In the second, Brown got in with a left to the face but when he tried to land to the body he found Garland's defence equal to the occasion. The Irishman then flashed in a left to the face in breaking away from a clinch. In the third, Brown stopped a left from Garland and the Panama boxer demonstrated that holding was not for him by raising his arms when Garland lay on.

In round four, Garland was holding a lot and it was obvious, at long range, he was no match for the Latin American, whose flashing arms moved like lightning. Garland rushed in and landed to the body, making his opponent back away. Then he slipped in a wicked left, putting Brown to the ropes. Garland's classy opponent scored with a terrific left to the stomach and a left to the head knocked the Belfast boy through the ropes for a count of seven. Garland rose to fight back strongly.

In the fifth, Garland rushed into a clinch when he missed with a left, while two rights to the head staggered him. The Irishman got in a right to the face but he took a lot of punches, including a stinging right to the head. Garland was warned for holding at this period. When Brown missed in the sixth round Garland landed two short lefts to the jaw. Brown was ripping home some deadly punches to the body, although he took a left to the jaw towards the close of the round. Garland looked to be spent and was glad to hang on.

In the seventh, Garland missed repeatedly but he lashed out with his left, catching Brown on the jaw. Brown continued to poke his long left into Garland's face almost at will and the Belfast boy was once again warned for holding. In the eighth, Garland fought pluckily, yet was outclassed. He continued to rush at his opponent but Brown punished him unmercifully to the body. The Irish champion got home with only two blows in the round, both lefts to the head, and he was always glad to run into a clinch when Brown threatened with his long left.

In the ninth, Brown slipped away cleverly from a swinging left and countered with a damaging blow to the body as Garland once again rushed in. The Irish boy was still doing a lot of holding, although he got in with a good right to the jaw. Garland was full of fight in the tenth and he staggered Brown with two successive lefts to the body. Another left to the head came from Garland. Brown was a master in dealing with his opponent's rushes, however, and he ducked a swinging punch to counter to the body.

In round eleven, Brown missed with a wicked right, which Garland was lucky to evade. Immediately afterwards the Irishman was down for seven from a beautiful left hook to the jaw. He was punched all around the ring and it was a marvel that he was on his feet at the end of the round. The Belfast boy was as brave as they come. The fight seemed all over at the beginning of the twelfth; Garland hung on for all he was worth and Brown landed a right to the head and ducked the counter. In the resulting clinch he rapped a tattoo on the Irishman's body. Excitement was at fever pitch as Garland flashed a left to the head, stopping Brown in his stride.

In the thirteenth, Garland scored with a left to the jaw and Brown was glad to hang on. The Irish boxer still had a lot of fight in him but his rushes were met with a superb defence. There was nothing of incident in this round. Brown continued to set a cracking pace in the fourteenth, while Garland had slowed down considerably. Two fierce lefts to the face sent Garland on to the ropes at the beginning of the round and only desperate holding saved him from a knockout. He took a left to the stomach but fought back with spirit. At the end of the round he was still on his feet.

In the last round, both boys battled fiercely. Garland had survived a gruelling fight and his courage was extraordinary. He lashed out with a good left and seemed to have a new lease of life, attacking relentlessly. The round ended with the boxers wrestling in a clinch close to the ropes. Brown, however, was a worthy victor.

Afterwards, Brown remarked, "It was a good fight. Garland is a very plucky fighter. I certainly think I won but it was a splendid tussle." Garland said, "It was a good, hard fight, but I don't think there was much in it."

Garland was not the only fighter that Brown met in England. He beat

George Kelly, official Lightweight Champion of Ireland

Teddy Baldock, Dick Burke, Johnny Peters, Tommy Hyman, Art Boddington, Dave Crowley and Johnny King. He lost on a foul to British Featherweight Champion, Johnny Cuthbert, and boxed a draw with Nel Tarleton. However, on 1 June 1935, Brown would no longer be recognised as champion after losing to Spaniard Baltazar Sangchilli in Valencia. When Hitler invaded France, "Panama" Al fled his Paris residence, leaving his hard-earned possessions behind. He returned to New York penniless and became addicted to drugs. He died from tuberculosis in April 1951.

Five weeks after his gutsy performance against Brown, Garland lost on points over twelve rounds to the skilful Nel Tarleton. Garland did his utmost to mix matters but the scientific Liverpudlian scored repeatedly with his left hand to win comfortably. This marvellous little fighter would win the British featherweight title on three different occasions and lose two world title bouts against American Freddie Miller.

In Croydon, Jack out-pointed Jules Bodson from Belgium. Then, on 15 June 1931 in London, he came unstuck against Italian Aldo Spoldi when he was knocked out in the first round. The fight had barely started when the Italian drove in a right that floored Garland. On rising, he took more punishment and a terrific punch sent him crashing heavily to the boards to be counted out. Spoldi would go on to win the European lightweight title in 1938, defeating Carl Andersen from Denmark, in Copenhagen.

Jack had a points win over Belgium's Joseph Pelemans but was out-pointed by Royton's Harold Ratchford, who had two wins over Spoldi. In the first of three meetings with Londoner Tommy Hyams, Jack won on points over fifteen rounds and, with 1931 rapidly coming to a close, he defeated Kid Lefevre (Belgium) (ko 3), Marcel Delobelle (France) (pts 12), Cuthbert

Taylor (Wales) (pts 10), and drew with Dominique di Cea.

Garland's fine sporting qualities would manifest in a contest against Scots champion Peter Cuthbertson at the Crystal Palace in January 1932. During the contest, which Garland won on points over twelve rounds, Cuthbertson frequently slipped to the boards. Jack, who could quite easily have taken advantage of these slips, stood back while his opponent rubbed his footwear in the resin. Cuthbertson appreciated the sporting action of his opponent and, at the end of each round, saluted him with raised glove. Earlier in the day, Cuthbertson had weighed in over the stipulated poundage. In another fine sporting gesture, Garland had waived his right to the full forfeit money of £10.

In his next job at The Ring in London, Jack again met Marcel Delobelle. The Frenchman was a thickset, short featherweight with rugged features, which left nobody in any doubt as to what his profession was. A thick ear and swollen nose suggested a rather open defence and this was capitalised on by Garland, who knocked out his opponent in the second round. Jack also won his next contest, beating Merthyr's Cuthbert Taylor for the second time.

At twenty-seven years of age, Jack's body was youthful and strong but his spirit for the fight game had deserted him. His career fragmented all around him. He had a habit of sullying his own abilities with frequent lacklustre performances that would characterise the rest of his career. He was knocked out in three rounds by Scot Jim Hunter and lost decisions to Brighton's Albert Heasman and the Canadian, Tommy Bland.

In a contest for the Irish lightweight title, vacated by Billy Gilmore, a packed St Mary's Hall witnessed an enthralling contest between Garland and fellow Belfast man Jack Flynn. The result, in favour of Flynn, was badly received by a noisy section of the crowd. The bout was level up to the end of the ninth but Flynn forged ahead in the last three and was a clever winner.

In his last two fights of 1932, Jack was out-pointed by Dubliner George Kelly and Leeds boxer Johnny Britton.

On 20 February 1933, Jack drew with Tommy Hyams, and in his third meeting with Ginger Jones, he was beaten on points. A points loss to South African Louis Botes was followed by a knockout by Hyams at the Crystal Palace when Garland was caught by a right to the jaw in the fourth. As he lay prone on the canvas, it was some time before he was revived by his seconds. Following defeats by Newcastle's Benny Sharkey (pts 12) and Liverpool's Peter Clarke (ko 6), Jack Garland was probably glad to see the back of 1933.

In 1934, Jack dropped points decisions to Leicester's Lynden Bennett, Belfast's Johnny Truesdale and Derry's "Spider" Kelly. When Garland was at his fighting best, many boxing aficionados, including one of the greatest fighters of all time, Jimmy Wilde (a boxing writer with a London Sunday newspaper), forecast that Jack would go far in the game. It is purely conjecture but if Garland had not lost an iffy decision to Ginger Jones in an eliminator for the British featherweight title in the Ulster Hall on 29 January

1930, the course of Irish boxing history may well have been altered.

Prior to the Kelly defeat, Jack had been knocked out in the first round by Northampton's Norman Snow, and on 19 May 1934, he was knocked out in two rounds by London's Harry Mizler, the British Lightweight Champion, who had won the title from Sheffield's Johnny Cuthbert. Mizler completely overwhelmed the Belfast boy, whom he dropped in the first round for a count of eight, and when Garland took another count of eight in the second stanza the referee stopped the one-sided contest.

Jack started 1935 with a points win over Bradford-based Jackie Quinn, who had been born in the Ardoyne district of Belfast. Two months later, Quinn avenged this defeat when he out-pointed Garland in Leeds. In Glasgow, Jack lost (pts 10) to Airdrie's Dan McGoldrick; in Dundee, he was knocked out in the tenth by local boy Gilbert Johnstone; and on 22 May in the Arena at Chapel Fields, in what was a thrilling fight, Jack lost to Belfast's Al Pedlar.

In June 1935, Jack married Ann McConnell in St John's Church on the Falls Road. The marriage would produce three girls and two boys.

Although Garland's name is unknown to today's generation of boxing fans, he was without doubt an outstanding amateur and professional fighter. He relinquished his Irish featherweight title in April 1936. After taking his final bow from the "fistic" stage with a points win over Jack Bernard from Carrickfergus, he retired as undefeated Featherweight Champion of Ireland. On 29 November 1985, he died suddenly in his home in Beechmount Parade, aged seventy-seven.

PROFESSIONAL CAREER
1929–1936: 61 (traced) contests: won 28, lost 29, drew 4.

Jim "Spider" Kelly

A magician of the squared circle

Born in Fahan Street, Derry, on 25 February 1912, Jim "Spider" Kelly was, at his peak, a class fighter, and his magic would manifest with slight, scarcely perceptible head shifts, rolling, ducking, weaving, side-stepping, cunning and inventiveness. Nailing him was like trying to thread a needle in a hurricane.

When Jimmy Kelly left Long Tower Primary School, work, like money, was as scarce as snow on a summer's day. Two years after he had his first professional fight at the tender age of sixteen there was still a dearth of coinage. When he was fighting in Scotland – which between 1930 and 1932 he did on a regular basis – he would go to Derry Quay and wait in the shadows until friends, who worked on the cattle boats, signalled that the coast was clear. This allowed Jimmy to nip in between the cattle to board the boat for the journey to Scotland. The reason for Jimmy's stowaway tactics was that the meagre purses, which were paid for six, eight or ten rounds of unbridled savagery, were not sufficient to enable him to travel as a paying passenger. He would be lucky to arrive home with a few pounds in his pocket. The largest purse that "Spider" Kelly would receive was £200 for defending his British and British Empire titles on 28 June 1939 in the King's Hall, Belfast against his nemesis, Johnny "Nipper" Cusick from Manchester.

Jimmy's career, which spanned almost two decades, began as a flyweight on 25 January 1928. Using the prefix "Young" before his surname, as so many fighters did in those days, he got off to a winning start (pts 6) in the Guildhall over a local lad, Young Stewart. Jimmy would occasionally be promoted by his manager, Joe Gilliland, as the "Derry Phantom" but with his exceptionally long arms and awkward, defensive style he would be forever known as "Spider" Kelly.

During a show promoted by Alderman P Meenan, who also acted as referee, the novice got a rude awakening in his second contest when he was put to sleep in the first round by Derry's Young Moran. He also lost his third contest (pts 6) when out-pointed over six rounds by

Belfast's Ted Rosbottom, again in the Guildhall.

Still, Kelly was made of sterner stuff and had wins over outstanding flyweights Hugh Britton (Derry) (rtd 3), Jim Sharpe (Belfast) (pts 10) and Jack McCleery (Belfast) (pts 10). Glasgow's Pete Curran was also added to the list (rtd 5). A week before Christmas, however, in a packed Derry Opera House, during a show promoted by Mr Jim Rice, Kelly lost (pts 10) to Dublin's Frank Traynor, who was making his professional debut. As an amateur, Traynor had won the All-Ireland bantamweight title in 1927, 1928 and 1929, and four days prior to his fight with Kelly he had boxed in the Ulster Hall for the Garda Siochana, beating West of Scotland Champion, Donald Lindsay.

On 1 February 1929 in Derry, Spider beat Glasgow's Young Taggart (pts 10). Then two weeks later, in St Mary's Hall in Belfast, as part of a show organised by Councillor Hugh McAlevey, he met a tough handful in Sheffield's Tom Winder, being counted out in the eighth of a scheduled twelve-rounder. He responded to this defeat three weeks later by stopping Glaswegian Jim McSorley in three rounds in Derry and, on 12 April, he won the vacant Flyweight Championship of Ireland by knocking out Jim Sharpe in the fourth in Derry's Guildhall. This was the first of five titles which Kelly would subsequently hold and it was the second time that he had beaten Sharpe. It was a good night for Kelly, but it was an even better night for the children's ward of Derry Infirmary with the proceeds of the tournament, which was promoted by Alderman Meenan, going to this worthy cause.

Spider's next outing was at Grosvenor Park where, in a dull contest, he lost to Belfast man Jackie Quinn. Following this defeat, Kelly had victories over Young Harden (Derry) (pts 10) in Derry, George Ballantyne (Glasgow) (pts 10) in the Scot's hometown, and Dickie Mack (Derry) (ko 2) in the North's maiden city, retaining the flyweight title. In his final contest of 1929, he out-pointed Belfast's Jack Bunting in a Derry promotion.

On 24 January 1930 in Belfast, Kelly boxed Ted Rosbottom for the second time, resulting in a draw. He went through the rest of that year undefeated, beating Blantyre's Dan Wyper (pts 10), Marleybone's Arthur Norton (pts 12), Airdrie's Alf Barrett (pts 10), and Edinburgh's Johnny Summers (ko 3).

There had been strong indications that Spider wasn't comfortable trying to make 112lbs and this speculation would bear fruit on 28 January 1931 in Derry when he was to have defended his Irish flyweight title against Jackie Quinn. When the Derry man weighed in at five pounds over the limit he forfeited his chance to retain his crown. A catchweight contest ensued and Quinn was completely outclassed. He took horrendous punishment and his corner threw in the towel in the third. Spider Kelly's days as a flyweight were over. He would, for a while at least, fight at bantamweight.

On a bill in the Ulster Hall, promoted by Hugh McAlevey and Mr John Connor, in which the proceeds went to charity, Kelly beat Sheffield's Percy

Dexter (pts 8). Then the Derry youngster had a setback when he travelled to Preston, where he was stopped in three rounds by Little Minor of Leeds.

Seven weeks later, Kelly accounted for Billy Warnock (pts 8) – one of four fighting brothers from the Shankill Road – at the Oval football ground. This was a tough, bruising battle but thanks to his longer reach, Kelly got home often on Warnock, who was clever enough to see that his best chance lay in in-fighting. Kelly was assertive throughout and deserved the points decision. In 1936 and 1937, Warnock's brother Jimmy had points wins over Benny Lynch, the British and World Flyweight Champion. On 15 June 1933, before Lynch won the world title, Billy himself went eleven rounds with the great Glaswegian.

Spider beat Glasgow's Johnny Grant (pts 10) and, in Strabane, he completed a double over Young Harden (pts 10). His other traced results for 1931 were: Jim Corbett (London) (won pts 10), Tug Wilson (Scotland) (won ko 5), Freddie Hughes (Glasgow) (won pts 10), Kid Markey (Blantyre) (no contest 2) and Dan McBride (Scotland) (won ko 5). All of these contests took place in Glasgow. The reason for the no contest decision in his bout with Markey was that both boxers received cut eyes in the second round, so the fight was called off.

In the latter half of 1931, Spider had been a regular visitor to that hotbed of professional boxing, Glasgow. Here he had earned the respect of its knowledgeable boxing citizens. In 1932, he practically resided in Glasgow. Out of approximately eighteen contests in which he participated that year, he boxed in the Scottish city thirteen times, notching up twelve victories in the process. His victories were against Johnny Grant (Glasgow), John Smallie (Scotland), Young McLeod (Scotland), Butcher Harper (Newcastle), Johnston Chambers (Edinburgh) (twice), Mickey Summers (Dundee), Joe Frame (Burnbank), Alf Barrett, and Kid Socks (Bethnal Green). All of these wins were on points. He also stopped Newcastle's Jim Haycock (rtd 1) and Bellshill's Willie Vint (rtd 8), and his sole defeat was against Blantyre's Arthur Grant (ko 5).

But there was one date in 1932 that Jimmy Kelly made sure that he was back home in Derry for – 21 April, the day that his son Billy was born. Billy would, like his dad, go on to win the British and British Empire featherweight titles. Jimmy and his wife Catherine would have a total of nine children – six girls and three boys. Another of Jimmy's sons, Paddy, would also be a professional fighter at featherweight boxing between 1957 and 1962, winning twenty-four of his thirty-seven contests.

Of course, Spider didn't fight exclusively in Scotland in 1932. At Belfast's Windsor Park on Friday, 3 June on the same bill that Primo Carnera boxed an exhibition bout against Cyril Woods from Plymouth before 12,000 spectators, Kelly was out-pointed by Jack Bunting. He also lost on points to Edinburgh's Peter McKinley in Belfast, drew with Shettleston's Fred Hardy in Belfast, beat Jack McCleery for the second time in Derry, and in the Ulster

Kelly and Carlin

Hall on a Jim Rice promotion he won every round against Bunting.

The year 1933 would be a busy one for the Derry lad and he threw his first punch of that year on 13 January against Pat Cassidy from Dublin, who, like himself, was a contender for the Irish featherweight title. Kelly weighed in at 8st 13¾ lbs, which was indicative that this was the division where his ambitions lay. Although it was a poor fight, with too much holding, Kelly was a worthy points winner. Less than a month later, Spider lost (pts 8) to Bunting, whom he met for the fourth time. On his next outing, in a packed St Mary's Hall, he boxed a draw with Merthyr's Fred Carpentier in a thrilling contest.

In the Ring Arena on 19 February 1933, the crowd rose to pay tribute to the memory of Jim Corbett, the former heavyweight champion of the world, who had just passed away. The tribute had barely ended when twenty-one-year-old Spider Kelly lay unconscious on the canvas after being hit on the chin by his Liverpudlian opponent, Bert Cantor. Ordinarily, this would have been a great result for Bert; unfortunately, it wasn't his fist that did the damage – it was his head. The bout, up to its sensational ending, had been a quiet affair with Cantor doing most of the leading and Kelly boxing brilliantly on the retreat.

Early in the second round Cantor rushed Kelly into his own corner and, in a furious mix-up, Kelly dropped heavily below the lower rope caught, seemingly, on the point of the chin by Cantor's head. For a few seconds the referee, Mr Joe Green, stood in bewilderment over Kelly's outstretched body, looking appealingly at the timekeeper. Ultimately, amidst a clamour of protests from a packed house, he started with the count and Spider was still on the floor at its termination. Cantor denied the allegation that he had hit Kelly with his head: "I got him with a left jab, my head did not touch him." His pleas were in vain and he was disqualified. Exactly one week later the pair

Dan McAllister

met again and Cantor lost once more in the second round – on a disqualification.

In St Mary's Hall on 11 March, in what was undoubtedly the survival of the fittest, Spider was beaten by Maesteg's Stan Jehu, who just edged home by the narrowest of margins. At the same venue on April Fool's Day, Bolton's Nipper McFarlane, who had taken the fight at short notice in place of fellow townsman Joe Croft, proved no match for Kelly. The Irishman lacked only one asset in a fight in which he won every round – a punch that would have ended the bout without it being allowed to last the full six rounds. Joe Croft did get to meet Spider, but in the Ring Arena he fared no better than Nipper McFarlane had and, like his Bolton compatriot, was completely outclassed. This was an excellent performance by Kelly as the tough Bolton fighter had, a few months previously, knocked out Jackie Quinn in the same arena.

Spider's next outing was against Blantyre's Frank Markey, a former bantamweight champion of Scotland; the Derry man was out-pointed over eight rounds. Before the year was out he would meet Markey on two more occasions. A week later, Kelly was back on the winning trail, beating Jackie Quinn in a Nat Josephs promotion in The Ring. In this fight Spider took a count of nine in the fourth round but made a remarkable recovery to get the referee's decision in a thrilling contest. The two men would meet for the final time two weeks later in the same arena in scorching June heat, with referee Mick Brennan deciding that a draw was a fair result.

Spider Kelly had another ten contests in 1933, in the course of which he beat Jim Driscoll (Glasgow), Arthur Killeen (Bolton), Frank Markey, Battling Croft (Sheffield) and Andy Byrne (Manchester). All these victories were on points and took place in Belfast. He had a points win over Young Gibbons (Belfast) in Killyclogher, drew with Frank Markey and beat Johnny Regan (Rotherham) (rsc 4). On the downside, he lost to Ted Sullivan (rsc 6) and Albert Lindley (Sheffield) (rtd 6).

From 14 January 1934 until 9 July 1936, the young but ring-wise campaigner had approximately thirty-one contests with an amazing twenty-seven victories. He had points wins over Jack Bunting, Albert Lindley (Sheffield), Jim Travers (Middlesbrough), Billy Smith (Belfast), Jack Garland (Belfast), Frank Barron (Sheffield), Stan Jehu, Alex Alston (Preston), Jack Lillie (Congleton), Dan McGoldrick (Glasgow), Freddie Miller (Belfast), Johnny Truesdale (Belfast), Bob Croxton (Liverpool), Joe Gale (Belfast), Lynton O'Neill (Merthyr), Benny Thackeray (Leeds), and Fred Todkill (Reddish). All of these contests took place in Belfast. His other results for the same period were: Norman Milton (Warrington) (lost pts 8) in Belfast, Tommy Rogers (Willenhall) (lost pts 10) in Wolverhampton, Angus McGregor (Greenock) (won pts 10) in Glasgow, Jimmy Barr (Glasgow) (won disq 6) in Belfast, Al Pedlar (Belfast) (won ko 6) in Belfast, Kid McLean (Glasgow) (won rtd 6) in Belfast, Chuck Flanagan (Belfast) (won pts 10) in Derry, Jerry Costello (Liverpool) (won pts 10) in Coleraine, Kid Dawson (Belfast) (won pts 8) in Omagh, Dan Gallagher (Derry) (won pts 8) in Ballybofey, Joe Doyle (Middlesbrough) (won ko 1) in Belfast and Spike Robinson (Belfast) (won rtd 7) in Belfast. Spider also drew with Newcastle's Benny Sharkey, and Spike Robinson in Belfast.

On 2 September 1936, Spider Kelly lifted the vacant Irish Featherweight Championship when he outclassed Frank McAloran (Belfast) in the King's Hall. Early in the fight McAloran suffered a serious eye injury but battled on gamely against one of the craftiest performers in Britain. In the tenth and eleventh rounds he put everything into a last gasp effort to retrieve the situation and the crowd rose to its feet in expectation. However, the eye injury was too severe and referee Jim Edgar called a halt to the proceedings in round fourteen.

As the Champion of Ireland, Spider beat tough Italian Gustaco Ansini in the Ulster Hall. Ansini, unlike Kelly, had little finesse and threw wild punches from all angles in the hope that one might land. It was a contest in which craft overcame brawn and Kelly won with something to spare.

In Spider's final contest of 1936 he had a clear-cut victory over the West Indian Ventura Hernandez. Kelly was now at his peak and better things lay ahead.

He opened his 1937 campaign on 11 January with an uninspiring draw against Ginger Roberts (Whitley Bay). On 22 February in the Ulster Hall, he gave an absolutely brilliant display, beating Liverpool's Nel Tarleton, the former British Featherweight Champion on points over ten rounds. Tarleton had, on two occasions, fought Cincinnati's Freddie Miller for the World featherweight title, losing both times over fifteen rounds.

The scenes at the end of the Tarleton fight were on a parallel with those that greeted Jimmy Warnock's King's Hall victory over Benny Lynch on 12 March 1936. Cheers rolled around the hall with newspapers fluttering into the ring from the balcony and a contingent of Derry men shouting themselves hoarse as a blood-soaked Kelly proudly made his way to the dressing room. Kelly's manager, Joe Gilliland, stated after the fight that he

Benny Caplan

would, on behalf of Kelly, challenge Johnny McGrory for the Glasgow boxer's British and Empire titles.

The fight with Tarleton was a magnificent exhibition of boxing with Kelly's speed, fitness and freehanded hitting astonishing the crowd. He was hardly ever in trouble during the fight and a cut eye sustained in the last round was due to his eagerness to give the audience a grandstand finish. This did not deter him and he kept firing away to earn the major points for the round. Referee Fred Blakeborough, from Bradford, walked over to the Derry man without totting up the score and raised his hand in victory.

For his next outing, in the King's Hall, Spider added another formidable scalp to his collection – that of Bethnall Green's Dick Corbett, the former British and British Empire Bantamweight Champion. Corbett had won his Empire title from South Africa's Dick Smith and the vacant British title when he beat Manchester's Johnny King.

On the same bill that Jimmy Warnock beat World Flyweight Champion Benny Lynch in Glasgow, Spider lost a close decision to Liverpool's Ginger Foran. However, in a contest against Consett's Jim Palmer, the Southern Area Champion, at Grosvenor Park, Kelly had the easiest of victories, winning every one of the eight rounds.

Spider got the chance to put himself in line for a title shot when he met Johnny McGrory, the British and British Empire Featherweight Champion, at Celtic Park. On this occasion, he failed – but only just – to take his opportunity, losing on points over ten rounds. Another title opportunity went a-begging six weeks later in the King's Hall, against Manchester's Johnny Cusick in an eliminator for the British Featherweight title. In a programme where a percentage of the proceeds went to various hospitals, eight thousand people watched Spider gave a below-par performance, losing on points over fifteen rounds.

Spider's last two contests of 1937 were also in the King's Hall. He had victories over Gateshead's Billy Charlton (pts 10) and Treherbert's George Williams, who had been down six times in the first round and wisely didn't come out for the second.

Kelly, now a professional for ten years, received a lovely twenty-sixth birthday present on 25 February 1938, when he knocked out former amateur champion Nipper Dan McAllister from Belfast. McAllister had been described in the press as a "fistic sensation", but was dealt with in the third in the King's Hall, enabling Kelly to become the first holder of the vacant Northern Ireland Area Featherweight Championship.

KELLY v. CUSICK		ARMOUR v. ROCHE
1		1
2		2
3		3
4		4
5		5
6		6
7		7
8		8

CONTESTS

THIS PROGRAMME IS SUBJECT TO ALTERATION.

15 (3-min.) Rounds CHAMPIONSHIP CONTEST FOR THE BRITISH and EMPIRE FEATHERWEIGHT TITLE	8 (3-min.) Rounds WELTERWEIGHT CONTEST at 10st. 8lbs.
SPIDER **KELLY** (LONDONDERRY). CHAMPION.	TOMMY **ARMOUR** (BELFAST). WELTERWEIGHT CHAMPION N.I. AREA.
v.	v.
JOHNNY **CUSICK** (MANCHESTER). CHALLENGER.	PADDY **ROCHE** (CORK).

8 (3-min.) Rounds BANTAMWEIGHT CONTEST at 8st. 8lbs.	8 (3-min.) Rounds FLYWEIGHT CONTEST at 8st. 3lbs.	6 (3-min.) Rounds HEAVYWEIGHT CONTEST
JACK MUSSEN (BELFAST)	TOMMY **STEWART** (BELFAST)	CHRIS **COLE** (MULLINGAR)
v.	v.	v.
CHARLIE **BROWN** (BELFAST).	RINTY **MONAGHAN** (BELFAST)	AL. **ROBINSON** (LEEDS)

MUSSEN v. BROWN		STEWART v. MON'AN
1		1
2		2
3		3
4		4
5		5
6		6
7		7
8		8

KELLY v. CUSICK: 1-15

COLE v. ROBINSON: 1-6

From the start Kelly had the measure of his opponent, whose youthful fire was no match for experience and superior boxing tactics. The new champion adopted a waiting role in the first round and showed splendid judgement, scoring with left and right leads. He was more active in the second period, throwing off his usual caution by forcing the fight and he paved the way to victory with two rights to the head and a left hook which knocked McAllister down for a count of eight.

Kelly tore into his man in the third, raining punches on McAllister at amazing speed. He floored the Belfast boy for nine and, when McAllister rose, landed a terrific left hook to the stomach. McAllister slid to the canvas for the full count. Kelly's aggressiveness was a surprise to all. A past master in ring-craft, his policy had usually been to allow his opponent to do the leading, but on this occasion he took the initiative himself. He revealed a terrific right and his left was no less damaging. Never before had Belfast seen Kelly in such a fighting mood; he hadn't had too many knockouts to his credit. It was, indeed, a "Happy Birthday" for the Derry man.

On 13 October 1937 at Parkhead, home of Celtic Football Club, Spider had given champion Johnny McGrory a run for his money. When they met again in the King's Hall on 30 March 1938, Kelly made no mistake and clearly out-pointed the champion from Scotland.

Slowly but surely, Spider Kelly was deservedly inching towards a title shot, and he rubber-stamped this entitlement with points victories over South Shields man Norman Denny in Belfast, Glasgow's Frank McCrudden in

Paisley, and London's Tony Hyams in Belfast. However, Johnny Cusick almost scuppered the Derry man's title chances when he beat Spider for the second time, the contest taking place at Tolka Park in Dublin.

With victories over outstanding glovemen like Tarleton, Corbett and McGrory, the Northern Ireland Featherweight Champion deservedly got his chance at glory on Wednesday, 23 November 1938. He faced the Londoner Benny Caplan in the King's Hall for the vacant British and British Empire Featherweight titles in a Mr John Sholdis promotion. History would also be made, as it was the first time that a Lonsdale belt contest had ever been held in Ireland.

On the morning of the big fight both boys were up early and went for a long walk. After breakfast, they were interviewed on radio. Kelly said modestly, "I hope it will be a good fight, and may the better man win." Caplan added a bit of humour to the interview by saying, "And I hope that man will be me." Such was the interest in this contest that many sporting events, such as greyhound racing, were called off.

Both boys received a great ovation on entering the ring and Kelly seemed just a little bit nervous. This was the chance for which he had been striving for years. Could he grasp it with both hands?

As the ring cleared for action, the lithe, tanned Derry man danced excitedly. When the bell sounded, he charged from his corner and opened up immediately with a swishing left that grazed Caplan's head and drove him on the defensive. With Kelly in pursuit, Caplan moved around the ring, forking out his left to hold the eager Derry man at bay and ducking under Kelly's swinging punches to the head. As Kelly attacked, Caplan whipped over a sharp right, which had a steadying effect and brought blood to Kelly's eye. Spider astonished his fans by his two-fisted attacking because everyone expected him to fight in the fashion that had earned him the sobriquet "Spider" Kelly. Instead, he was charging in, carrying the fight to his man and slinging punches recklessly.

In the second round, Kelly slowed down somewhat in his attack and commenced using his left hand. His eye, from which there was a small trickle of blood, made matters look serious for him, yet it did not slow up his aggressiveness, and he refused to switch over to defensive fighting. Caplan was waiting for Kelly to lead and endeavouring to collect points with counters but in this he found the Derry man elusive.

Caplan's left hand in the third round began to connect more frequently and Spider, with the counter popping into his face, could not get within punching range. His eye was bloodshot and Caplan's flicking left, although light, was a constant menace to it.

In the fourth round, Kelly looked more confident and he fought coolly with a complete change of tactics. He began waiting on leads from the Londoner and then countering, mainly to the body. Caplan refused to carry the fight to the Derry man and Kelly again took up the offensive with flailing arms and short rushes. In the fifth, he again tried to coax the elusive Caplan into leading or, at least, trading punches, but there was nothing doing. Benny had started in reverse and he had no intention of changing gears. As he was backing away from one of Kelly's attacks, Caplan dropped his guard to cover a left to the stomach. The speedy Spider, seizing his opportunity, whipped up the left that clipped Caplan on the chin. However, his body sway had taken the real power from the punch. Kelly followed up with a crashing right to the body that flung Caplan to the ropes and out again into a flurry of punches. Caplan seemed shaky but Kelly could not steady himself and his wild swings from all angles didn't have the effect that cooler punching would have attained. Caplan, falling gratefully into a clinch, rested. This was Kelly's best round so far, although his eye seemed to be troubling him.

In the sixth, Kelly, who was leading to the head and body, tried a long left to the stomach. Caplan cracked over a right that landed flush on Kelly's eye and drew blood. The eye was half closed and Caplan made it a target for his left that often brought the impetuous Kelly to a halt. Kelly could not get the range for his left hook to the head.

In the seventh, Caplan improved with his left hand and, moving around the ring, connected frequently to Kelly's face. In this round Caplan was spoken to by the referee owing to an incident in the break, and again for wrestling and flinging Kelly to the canvas.

In the eighth, Caplan took the initiative and connected with some good left and right crosses to the head, several of which landed on Kelly's damaged eye. Kelly was missing badly with his hooks. The ninth was a round in which defences were outstanding, but Kelly took the honours for aggressiveness and heavier hitting. Honours were level in the tenth, both men missing widely. In the eleventh, Kelly got in some snappy punches by hotly following up the back-pedalling Caplan.

In the twelfth, Kelly dug well to the body but Caplan came out on top in a two-fisted, close-quarter mill, snapping forceful rights and lefts to the Derry man's head. The thirteenth and fourteenth rounds were bruising affairs, with both men going for glory. Kelly was the more effective puncher and Caplan didn't relish his opponent's body punches, falling to his knees in one of the mêlées. The last round was a thriller, being fought out during indescribable pandemonium. Kelly knew he had to clinch the issue and got a good start by bending Caplan double with a fierce right to the body. There was no stopping him now and he thumped Caplan around the ring amid frenzied cheering. A couple of hard uppercuts from Caplan did not quench the fiery flame burning inside Spider and Caplan was more severely punished in this round than in any other.

When the referee raised Kelly's hand in victory a great roar of acclamation from eight thousand throats greeted the decision. Kelly danced with joy and, as Caplan sat disconsolate in his corner, police surrounded the ring to keep enthusiastic well-wishers from mobbing the winner. The Lonsdale belt was placed around Spider's waist by the Duke of Abercorn and at the request of the crowd Spider, his voice quivering with emotion, said, "I wish to thank you for giving me such support. I am a very proud man tonight, happy to go home to my wife and five children as British champion." When Spider arrived back home there were, needless to say, scenes of great jubilation as over five thousand people welcomed the new champ.

On the same bill that Spider achieved his well-deserved moment of glory, Tommy Stewart became the first Northern Ireland Flyweight Champion when he stopped fellow Belfastman Jim McStravick in the tenth. Freddie Warnock (Belfast) drew with Glasgow's Frank Kenny; Dan McAllister (Belfast) drew with Len Beynon (Wales); and Charlie Brown (Belfast) had a points win over Alex Knight (South Africa).

Spider was fighting again on Boxing Day, a month after being crowned champ. In the King's Hall he out-pointed Londoner Jackie Hurst over ten rounds, thus bringing a memorable 1938 to a close.

Spider's reign as champion would last seven months. He had his first fight of 1939 when he boxed a draw with Sunderland's Tom Smith. Spider arrived in Newcastle a short time before the fight was due to start. He had followed the remains of his two-year-old son to their final resting place in Derry Cemetery the day before and, a few hours afterwards, he left his home in order to fulfil this engagement. Under such circumstances, it is quite remarkable how Spider Kelly even managed to get a draw against Smith.

On his first visit to London he had a points win over Gateshead's Billy Charlton in Earl's Court and, on his second visit, he proved that his victory over Benny Caplan was no fluke when he beat him again in the Albert Hall. Loud booing lasting for several minutes greeted the result in favour of Kelly. It was difficult to see why, since he looked to have won with a fair margin to spare. Spider lost on points to Len Beynon on the Swansea man's home turf; in Liverpool, he was most unlucky to lose to Scouser Nel Tarleton, whom he had beaten in February 1937. Tarleton was conceding six years to Spider and was in front after eight rounds, but from that point onwards Kelly took command. He attacked fiercely and, in the ninth, Tarleton was down for eight. On rising, however, he caught the champion with a right to the chin and Kelly took a short count. In the eleventh, Tarleton was down for nine, but defended cleverly to survive.

On 13 October 1937, Johnny "Nipper" Cusick had beaten Spider on points in the King's Hall. On 4 August 1938, in Dublin's Tolka Park, he had repeated the dose with a points win over ten rounds. Then, on 28 June 1939, Cusick took Spider's titles in the King's Hall before ten thousand people.

From the outset, Kelly attacked immediately, missed with a left, and a bout of in-fighting followed with both men hitting hard to the body. Kelly was jerked back by a stiff right to the face but he retaliated with a jolting right and left, evading a hard right to the head. In the second, Kelly landed twice with his left and ducked a return. He was defending well, although several times he was caught with flicking lefts to the jaw. Both were taking turns to attack, but no damaging punches were landed and the pace was hectic.

Kelly cut loose in the third, slamming hard rights to the head, driving Cusick across the ring. The crowd was roaring as Kelly attacked. He punched Cusick a dozen times without reply, staggering him. Near the end of the round Cusick came at the champion, clipping him with crisp rights. Excitement was at fever pitch as both boys slogged in mid-ring and Cusick's nose was bleeding. Kelly was avoiding cleverly.

In the fourth round, both were engaged in a close-range mêlée on the ropes and Kelly emerged with blood coming from an old wound above the left eye. A gasp of dismay arose from the crowd. Cusick came after the champion, aiming for the injury, but Kelly surprised him with a sudden attack and forced him back across the ring. Both were using their lefts, trying to create openings for their rights. Things looked bad for Kelly as several stinging lefts sneaked through his defence to aggravate his eye injury.

In the fifth, Cusick swung a wicked right that just missed Kelly's eye. He followed this up with stabbing left leads, which were successfully parried by the champion who came back with a snappy left and right to the head. Kelly was waiting for Cusick to come in to enable him to counter-punch, but Cusick covered well and absorbed most of Kelly's counters on his arms. Both men were boxing cautiously until, in a burst of punching, Cusick sent the champion staggering across the ring. Cusick was fighting coolly and making Kelly's injured eye his target. At the end of the round Kelly's eye was treated by his seconds and the bleeding stopped.

As he came out for the sixth, Cusick connected with two lefts to the head and neatly slipped the champion's retaliation to catch him with a hard right to the jaw, followed quickly by another. Cusick was doing well with left leads and, near the end of the round, despite a flurry of punches, he caught Kelly with a left lead, an uppercut and a right hook to the head as the champion danced away. In his corner, Kelly's eye was again treated. The bleeding had stopped and the injury did not seem to be troubling him, although he took care to protect it from Cusick's rights.

Cusick launched a fast attack at the beginning of the seventh but it was neatly smothered by the champion, who followed up with speedy right and left hooks to the body. Kelly began to carry the fight, shooting lefts to the body and clipping Cusick to the head with short, right-arm crosses. A hefty left swing to the head was neatly foiled by Cusick's darting left. The Manchester boxer kept cool despite the champion's attacks and scored with a sharp right which had Kelly down for a second. Kelly was shooting out his lefts to the face, while the challenger avoided cleverly to let them slide over his shoulder. Kelly's timing was not so good and Cusick looked confident.

In the eighth, Cusick forced Kelly into his own corner but had to retreat before a two-handed barrage of punches. Kelly showed speed in getting under the challenger's left leads, but several times he was caught with a chopping right as he was coming up. The champion's defence was excellent and, at close range, he was connecting with rapid, short punches to the head. Just before the bell, he shook Cusick with a left to the jaw.

In the ninth, Kelly began to throw his right and forced the challenger to the ropes with a swinging punch to the head while Cusick's left hand was still jabbing at the champion's face. Kelly was scoring to the body as the challenger attacked. He seemed to be trying to connect with a KO punch, yet the Mancunian was too crafty and defended well. Both were engaged in a slog on the ropes when a crisp left sent Kelly down for five. He rose groggily to meet the rush of Cusick and instead of covering he began to trade punches. The crowd was on its feet as Kelly, practically out, staggered around the ring, still fighting. Cusick, with the championship almost in his grasp, threw punches from all angles while Kelly crouched on the ropes. The bell sounded for the end of the round.

Kelly came up fresh for the tenth and, as Cusick rushed in, he pulled him up with a sharp right to the jaw which he followed with three short punches to the head at close range. The blows did not seem to affect Cusick, who attacked strongly, and, feinting with his left, he smashed over a hard right that sent Kelly staggering across the ring. As Cusick followed, Kelly stopped him with a neat right to the head. The champion was jabbing with his left and following with a right but he was jolted by three stiff rights to the head from the challenger.

In the eleventh, Kelly was fighting well, with his left jab keeping Cusick at a distance. He suddenly changed to attack and the challenger, fighting coolly, scored to the body as Kelly came in. The pace of the fight had slowed up both men but the exchanges were rapid. Cusick, who was advancing with his left extended, seemed to be measuring the champion for a right, but Kelly beat him to the punch to connect with a left to the head and body.

The champion had not fully recovered from the effects of that right when he came out for the twelfth and he looked distressed. Cusick glided in and snapped a sharp right to the head. Kelly backed to the ropes, jabbing with his left, while Cusick dodged under it and swung a wicked right that landed flush on the jaw. The champion sagged. A second, third, fourth and fifth right smashed home on his unprotected jaw and Spider dropped heavily to the canvas. He was trying to raise himself at the count of four when referee Jack Hart stopped the fight and awarded it to Cusick.

Cusick fought like the champion he was and deserved to win. It was his short, chopping rights to the head that weakened Spider and led to his defeat. Without detracting from the magnificent display put up by the Manchester lad there is no doubt that Kelly was not fighting in the form that had won him the championship seven months previously. Up to the fifth round there was little between the boys but, as Cusick found the range with a short right, which floored Kelly in the seventh, he began to edge ahead. Although he forged attack after attack, Kelly could not penetrate Cusick's defence to land

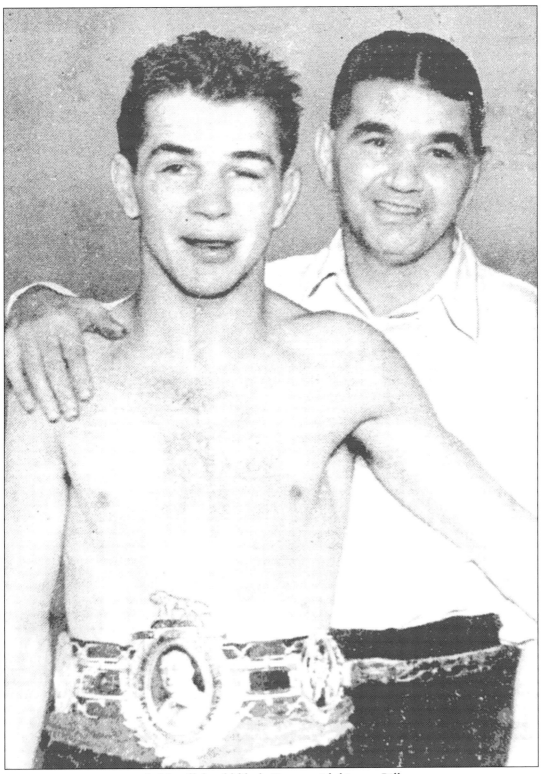

A chip off the old block: Jimmy with his son, Billy

a finishing punch and, when the battle reached the tenth round, it was obvious that only a KO could win Spider the fight. Afterwards, Mr Hart, speaking into the microphone, said, "It was a great title fight and I had to stop it to prevent Kelly getting greater punishment."

Spider next saw ring action – on the same bill that Jim McCann won the Bantamweight Championship of Northern Ireland from Jack Mussen – in the Ulster Hall on 4 March 1940. The former champion, weighing in at ten stone, showed plenty of his old artistry against the Featherweight Champion of Scotland, Frank Kenny, and won on points over eight rounds.

Just over six weeks later, Spider proved that he had been training hard when he came well inside the featherweight limit for a fifteen-round local title clash in the King's Hall against Jim Keery from Lisburn. Keery, however, came in at 9st 8oz and the contest, much to the disappointment of the capacity crowd, was reduced to a ten-round catchweight fight. Spider's ring-craft had him well in front until he received an eye injury in the fourth and the London referee, Moss Devong, stopped the fight.

Spider had points wins over Billy Baxter (London), Taffy Davies (Wales), Dennis Cahill (Dundee), Tommy Cullen (Dublin) and "Nipper" Fred Morris (Stepney). He beat Vic Andrews (Leeds) (rsc 8) and Billy Baxter (rsc 6), but lost to Al Lyttle (Belfast) (rtd 5).

Spider's career was gradually winding down. Although he was occasionally well overweight in his fights, he continued to entertain the crowds with the skills he had exhibited throughout his boxing life.

In 1941 he had two victories over Vic Andrews, making it three times in all that he had beaten the Leeds boxer. When he met "Gunner" Angus McGregor from Greenock for the second time, after having already beaten him, Kelly was disqualified for the first time in his illustrious fourteen-year career. Spider, the most cool and unruffled of boxers, lost his temper twice during the seven rounds. He had protested to referee Jack Hinds about McGregor's hitting and pushing him with the heel of the glove. Then, in the seventh round, McGregor pushed in a clinch and both boxers fell to the canvas. Kelly was rattled and started hitting while both were on the ground. He continued to hit out, even after the referee tried to intervene, and was disqualified for his transgression. McGregor was declared the winner. In September and October respectively, Spider had wins over Belfast's Mick Magee (pts 10) and Lurgan's Ken Seeley (pts 10) in Derry contests.

Spider kicked off 1942 by stopping Dublin boy Mickey Quinn in three rounds in the Rialto. Two more fights in Belfast saw him defeat Jim Hamilton (Carrick) (pts 10) and draw with Jimmy Smith (Clonmel). In the last of his four fights in 1942 he beat Jim McCann on points over eight rounds in Derry.

On 29 May 1943 Spider, coming in at 10st 7lbs for a match made at 9st 13lbs, gave a superb boxing display in an eight round duel with Jimmy Smith, the Eire Lightweight Champion, in the Ulster Stadium. At the end of an interesting contest the referee opted for a draw, which flattered Smith, who the majority of spectators felt had been out-boxed and out-thought by the former champ. It was the second time that Smith had drawn with Kelly.

In June, Spider completed a double (pts 8) over Mick Magee in Belfast and, at the Brandywell, he lost on points to Dublin's Jimmy Ingle.

Spider had only one fight in 1944, losing (rtd 4) to Dublin's Freddie Price in Derry, and, in 1945, he was inactive. It was the first time in seventeen years that this amazing man did not fight, and during his absence from the ring he worked at the Belfast docks, his residence being Annie McHugh's in Fleet Street.

Spider was now thirty-four and second-tier fighters, who had nothing to offer except the odd dash of bravado, would give the old master plenty of trouble. However, on 16 May 1946 in Newcastle, Spider met a really useful fighter from North Shields called Stan Hawthorne. Hawthorne, who was eleven years younger than Kelly, had lost only one of his last nineteen fights, fifteen of which he had won inside the distance. The North Shields man was probably thinking that the scalp of a former British and British Empire Champion would look well dangling from his belt. The fight lasted only ninety seconds, during which Spider visited the boards twice, once for a six count and the other for nine. Spider tried his best to avoid the dangerous punches but his feet weren't working. Hawthorne quickly followed up his advantage with a hard right to the ribs, then a right to the jaw, which sent Spider down for the full count. A few months later, Hawthorne would lift the vacant Northern Area lightweight title, in a fight that was also an eliminator for the British Lightweight crown, by beating Billy Thompson from Liverpool. However, when he did get a crack at the title, he was beaten by Thompson in three rounds.

Perhaps Spider should have quit after the Hawthorne fight, but he carried on and, in a Bob Gardiner promotion at the Guildhall, he beat Dubliner Nick Weldridge (rtd 4), following this up with a one-round win over Belfast's Joe Scott.

No matter where Spider Kelly fought, as his career neared closure, the smoke-filled arenas were always packed, for his name was still magic. Still, it wasn't the Spider Kelly of old that his fans saw, just an old Spider Kelly.

In 1947, Spider had nine contests: he beat Jim Coates (Lisburn) (pts 8), Dempsey Brady (Lurgan) (pts 8), Gerry Smyth (Belfast) (disq 4) and Frankie Brown (Liverpool) (ko 2). He lost to Jim Coates (Lisburn) (rtd 4), Jackie King (Belfast) (rtd 4) and Paddy Dowdall (Dublin) (rtd 6). In Derry, he lost to Tommy McMenamy (Belfast) (pts 8) and drew with Jackie King (Belfast).

On 10 February 1948, in a tournament organised by Mr Frank Skelton at the Town Hall, Ballymoney, Spider was knocked out in the second round by Paddy Trainor from Belfast. It was an inglorious finish to a glorious career, though I'm sure that Trainor would have agreed that he didn't beat the ex-champion – he beat the ghost of a champion past. The boxing magician from

Derry would fight no more and those fans in the Town Hall witnessed the exit of a pugilistic hero.

Jimmy Kelly fought in an era when a boxer had to fight scores of times before a promoter learned how to spell his name. With opposition like Rosbottom, Britton, Sharpe and McCleery, Spider was fighting and beating some of the best flyweights in the country. In his retirement Spider coached other boxers, paying particular attention to his son Billy. Jim "Spider" Kelly, the first Irishman to win British and Empire Championships, died on 23 March 1988 at his home in Derry.

PROFESSIONAL CAREER
1928–1948: 167 traced contests: won 119, lost 35, drew 12, no contest 1.

Pat "Maurice" Marrinan

Fist of iron, heart of gold

Maurice Marrinan was a tough, handsome, Belfast heavyweight fighter who had wanderlust in his veins, iron in his gloved fists and a heart of gold. He boxed professionally between 1935 and 1939 in venues such as the Ulster Hall, the King's Hall, the Albert Hall, Wembley, Earl's Court, and that famous old octagonal-shaped boxing venue, The Ring on Blackfriars Road in London. While living in Australia in 1938, he boxed under the name of Maurice Costello and won two of his three fights there.

Maurice was born on 11 March 1913. His father was Patrick Marrinan, CBE, Barrister-at-Law, a County Louth man who had been an amateur heavyweight champion. His mother Sarah was a Ballymoney-born lady, the sister of Canon Patrick Boyle. Maurice had two brothers, Desmond and Patrick, both of whom were barristers, and three sisters, Pauline, Gabrielle and May.

He was brought up in Portstewart, where he attended Coleraine Academical Institution, and from there he went to Belfast Royal Academical Institution. He then attended Queen's, where he represented the university at boxing. Even from an early age Maurice had demonstrated true grit and remarkable courage, a prime example being when he dived into the sea at Portstewart and, with the assistance of his sister Gabrielle, rescued three people.

Another instance of his "derring-do" was when he jumped ship in Turkey, after sailing from Australia, and was promptly arrested and imprisoned for having no documentation. Inside the grim Turkish prison, conditions were so inhumane that Maurice hatched an audacious plan to gain freedom. The prison guards brought food to the cells at exactly the same time every day and Maurice decided to feign a suicide attempt and be found "hanging" at the precise moment that they entered his cell. He very nearly paid the price with his life because the guards weren't as punctual as usual and Maurice, close to death, had to be cut down. He was removed to hospital where, as well as his neck injuries, he was discovered to have peritonitis too. As he lay seriously ill in a foreign land, his father died back home in Belfast.

Boxing for Queen's, Maurice used the ring name "Pat". He had about sixty-five amateur contests, the highlights of which were his lifting of the Irish Varsities heavy and cruiser titles in 1932 and the Ulster Senior light-heavyweight title, which he won in the Ulster Hall on 19 January 1933. On this occasion, he defeated Constable Nelson of the Royal Ulster Constabulary in highly controversial circumstances. Even though Pat had been the aggressor throughout the contest, he seemed to be a long way behind at the start of the third round when he jumped in with a right to the body that touched the borderline. Nelson dropped in apparent pain and, while he lay writhing on the canvas, no effort was made to take up the count. The officials were non-plussed and after a spell, Nelson's seconds jumped into the ring and carried him to his corner. After a lot of indecision, the MC announced that neither the judges nor the referee saw a low blow and the fight continued with sixty seconds remaining. In the thrilling exchanges which followed, Nelson kept the Queen's boxer at bay by sheer pluck and still seemed to have enough in reserve to win on points. The decision in favour of Marrinan had a mixed reception and the large audience showed its disapproval by loudly protesting. For a brief spell things looked ugly.

The urge to travel got the better of Pat and he joined the Palestine Police Force, where it didn't take him too long to make his presence felt, winning the Inter-Services and Police Cruiser Championship. He capped this by also taking the heavyweight title. Pat Marrinan was a man of principle and was so disgusted at the treatment meted out to local Arabs by the police that he resigned from the force to live the life of a Bedouin in the Negev Desert.

However, when desert storms, blazing sunshine and political unrest lost their appeal, the young Irishman headed for the cooler and damper climes of London. Here, he was introduced to professional boxing by George Cook, a five-foot nine-inch former Australian Heavyweight Champion. Cook had boxed in Australia, New Zealand, the United States, Canada, Argentina, England, Italy, South Africa, Scotland, Germany, France and Sweden, among other countries. He had fought, and lost to, such notables as Jack Sharkey, Primo Carnera, Young Stribling, Jack Petersen, Larry Gains and Phil Scott. Cook became Pat's manager, but died at the comparatively young age of forty-five. The big Irishman was then managed by Ted Broadcribb who, boxing under the name of "Young" Snowball, was the only Englishman to take the scalp off the "Orchid Man", Georges Carpentier. When Pat returned to Belfast in 1937, he trained with the former Irish Featherweight Champion, Frank McAloran.

HEAVYWEIGHT CONTEST
6x (6-minute) Rounds
DOM LYDON v **IVOR MALCOLM**

Green Corner   Red Corner

ROUNDS	1	2	3	4	5	TOTAL	WINNER
LYDON							
MALCOLM							

FEATHERWEIGHT CONTEST
Ten (3-minute) Rounds
SPIDER **KELLY** v. GEORGE **WILLIAMS**

Green Corner   Red Corner

ROUNDS	1	2	3	4	5	6	7	8	9	10	TOTAL	WINNER
KELLY												
WILLIAMS												

INTERNATIONAL FLYWEIGHT CONTEST
Ten (3-minute) Rounds
JIMMY WARNOCK v. MICKEY O'NEILL

Green Corner   Red Corner

ROUNDS	1	2	3	4	5	6	7	8	9	10	TOTAL	WINNER
WARNOCK												
O'NEILL												

HEAVYWEIGHT CONTEST
Eight (3-minute) Rounds
PAT MARRINAN v. JEFF **WILSON**

Green Corner   Red Corner

ROUNDS	1	2	3	4	5	6	7	8	TOTAL	WINNER
MARRINAN										
WILSON										

FEATHERWEIGHT CONTEST
Ten (3-minute) Rounds
DAN M'ALLISTER v. **KID OLIEVERA**

Green Corner   Red Corner

ROUNDS	1	2	3	4	5	6	7	8	9	10	TOTAL	WINNER
M'ALLISTER												
OLIEVERA												

Pat Marrinan made his professional debut on 1 April 1935 in the Albert Hall and knocked Albert Inwards from Watford backwards and out for the count in the first round. Six days later he scored his second one-round victory, halting Bill Perry of Marleybone at The Ring. In the first sixty seconds, Pat landed three terrific punches on Perry's jaw and the referee intervened to save the Londoner from further punishment.

Pat's apprenticeship continued with wins over Mayfair's Jack Grant (pts 6) in Horsham, Jim Hayton from Berkhamstead (ko 1) in Rochester, Jack Marshall (pts 8) in St John's Wood, and Jack Langford (rsc 2) in Lowestoft. He lost to George Brown (pts 8) in Holborn and Kid Scott from Sheffield (disq 1) in Sheffield, and drew with Dagenham's Len Rowlands in Lowestoft. Pat would be disqualified a few more times in his career and George Cook remarked that he feared they might be "charged with manslaughter" if his protégé did not learn to pull his punches.

On 8 October 1935 in Wembley, in the first series of a £1,000 Open Heavyweight competition *Search for a Star*, the best fight of the night was between Marrinan and Billy Roberts from Cornwall. The Cornish motor mechanic was stopped in the second round to save him from serious injury in a contest that was an absolute thriller. During one extraordinary exchange, over thirty blows to the jaw were landed by both men, who took them unflinchingly.

Three weeks after his win over Roberts, Pat returned to his hometown to fight Egyptian Salah El Din in the Ulster Hall. He didn't let his fans down, stopping his swarthy opponent in a couple of rounds. Marrinan's ferocity and his absolute imperviousness to punishment knocked the heart out of El Din, who must have known that the sands of time were running out when Marrinan left him sagging with a fierce right to the stomach halfway through the second round.

Marrinan opened with all the tearaway aggressiveness of his amateur days and there was just no stopping him. Taking all the vicious left and right uppercuts the Egyptian could throw at him, Pat crowded his man all over the ring, disdaining punishment, and the round ended in a series of wicked exchanges that El Din did not relish. To everyone's surprise, the Egyptian indicated to his corner that two rounds with Marrinan were more than enough for him.

In the quarterfinals of the Open Heavyweight Competition in Wembley on 12 November, Pat beat Archie Norman from Harrow on points over four rounds. Norman, who was giving away a stone to the hard-punching Belfast boxer, took tremendous punishment throughout but gamely held on to the end. On the same evening, Pat reached the final of the competition with a points win over West Norwood's Eddie Steele. Jack London from West Hartlepool won his two contests, setting up an encounter with Pat in the final, which would not be staged until the following year.

Pat's last fight of 1938 was on a Jim Rice promotion in the King's Hall in front of ten thousand boxing enthusiasts. His opponent was Eddie Wenstob, a cowboy from Viking, who was the idol of Alberta. Wenstob's fans were hoping that he would be the first fighter to bring a world crown to their province. Marrinan gave his best but failed to outgun the cowboy and was stopped in the fifth of a twelve-round contest, prevented from continuing after sustaining two badly damaged eyebrows.

In a fast opening, Wenstob, who had the advantage of a longer reach, twice shot out his left to Pat's chin. He was nearly always the first to lead, being quicker with both hands, and easily won the first round. At the start of the second, Wenstob caught Marrinan with a left and right but Marrinan wouldn't give ground. The Canadian hit him from every angle but his blows, though punishing, lacked finishing power and Marrinan was doing well inside.

Wenstob again out-boxed his man in the third, but lack of strength told against him. Time after time he crashed his right to Marrinan's chin yet could not shake the game Belfast boy. Ultimately, Wenstob's left hand marked Marrinan's right eye but the cowboy still could not keep Pat at bay. Nevertheless, Marrinan was well mastered in the finer points of the game.

Wenstob was well on top in the fourth while Marrinan, fighting desperately and half-blinded, crowded his man into a corner and scored heavily to the body. Wenstob's superior boxing skill got him out of trouble and he renewed his persistent attack. In the final round, Marrinan was still strong and willing. Even so, when patches of blood began to show on the referee's white shirt and the Canadian danced around the Belfast boy, jabbing

Pat (third from left) with family and friends in Montreal

and upper cutting, it was obvious that the fight could only have one ending. To save Pat from unnecessary punishment, the referee refused to allow him to come out for the sixth.

Pat's 1936 campaign didn't get under way until 25 May, his opponent being Gunnar Barlund from Finland, a heavyweight gold medal winner at the 1934 European Championships in Budapest, who had lost only one of his sixteen professional fights. The Finn continued his winning run, stopping the Irishman in the second round when Marrinan sustained a badly-cut right eye. In the first minute, Barlund punished Marrinan with hard rights to the jaw and, with a heavy left, he soon opened a cut under Marrinan's right eyebrow. Blood streamed from the wound, yet Pat was able to come out for the second round. No sooner had the boxers met in the centre of the ring than Marrinan received a cut over the left eye and by the end of the round his face was a mass of red. The referee had no hesitation in declaring Barlund the winner. The blond Finn had displayed good footwork and feinted beautifully before bringing his powerful right into action. Marrinan needed two stitches in his damaged eye when he reached his dressing room.

On 9 November 1936 in Wembley, Pat boxed Jack London (real name Jack Harper) from West Hartlepool, in the final of the Open Heavyweight Competition. He lost his third fight in a row when he was disqualified in the sixth for an alleged low blow. The decision wasn't too popular and the crowd booed for over five minutes. The Belfast boy was unlucky, as he had won every round comfortably before the incident. On 15 September 1944, London would win the vacant British and British Empire heavyweight titles when he out-pointed Freddie Mills in Manchester. His son Brian would win the same titles when he knocked out Cardiff's Joe Erskine in eight rounds at the White City in London in June 1958.

Pat got back on the winning trail in what was his last fight of 1936 when he knocked out Harry Briars from St Helens in the sixth round at The Ring. When Briars fell to the boards from a body punch there was an appeal from his seconds for a foul but the referee went on to count him out and award the verdict to Marrinan. Immediately, one of Briar's seconds rushed across to Marrinan's corner and began protesting vigorously. For some moments Marrinan and the opposing second were involved in a heated argument until officials had to climb into the ring to restore order. As Briars was being carried from the ring there were cries of "Fetch a doctor".

Pat had only three contests in 1937, which took place in his native Belfast. His first contest was on 29 April against Manchester's George Bennett at Grosvenor Park on a Jim Rice promotion. Marrinan described the fight as a "comeback" as he had not boxed since the previous November. The lay-off proved to be an irrelevancy as Pat gave a crisp display of hard hitting to stop the Manchester boy in the fifth of a scheduled six-rounder in which the result was never in doubt. Bennett did all that he could with a stabbing left hand to hold off Marrinan's attack, yet the writing was on the wall early in the fourth when the Mancunian was shaken with a hard right to the face.

Another right early in the fifth opened a gaping wound over Bennett's left eye and the referee had no option but to stop the contest. Although Marrinan was the heavier by nearly a stone, the Englishman towered over him and had a longer reach. He was also at times quicker with his left hand, which drew blood from Marrinan's face as early as the second round. Pat, however, punched with venom and, after rocking his man with a hard right to the temple towards the end of the second stanza, he went all out in the third, refusing to be stopped by Bennett's stabbing left. Bennett was tired yet game and willing. He kept poking his left to Marrinan's face, seldom missing, but in the close-quarter battles Pat was well on top.

There was always menace in Marrinan's punches and, early in the fifth, he brought over a crashing right, almost from the hip. Bennett reeled back with blood spurting from a nasty injury. The wound was so severe that the referee stopped the fight. On a Nat Joseph/Joe McAllister promotion in the King's Hall on 20 October, Bert Ikon from Stoke looked a winner against Pat when the local boy's left eyebrow showed a nasty gash in the third round. Pat boxed cautiously in the fourth and, halfway through the round, knocked the Potteries man out of the ring. Marrinan discarded his storming recklessness and opened with good judgement. He found Ikon such an easy target that, after weakening the Englishman with sledgehammer blows, he was able to land five times without reply to Ikon's head towards the end of the first round. Ikon was not distressed and Pat had nothing to spare in a gruelling second round. He was too prone to a right swing and, at each attempted delivery, Ikon beat him to the punch with a stabbing left. Marrinan, who was still wide open for a straight left and a right hook, forgot his early caution in the third and paid for it when his right eyebrow was opened by a chopping right.

Pat was on the retreat in the fourth for a minute or so, then got Ikon where he wanted him and nearly carried the head off his man with a right that had all the force of his body behind it. Ikon crumpled against the ropes and Marrinan went berserk, hooking and jabbing until Ikon went over the ropes, bringing a couple of newspapermen to the floor with him.

Pat Marrinan had, in his last fight in his hometown, a convincing win over Windsor's Jeff Wilson in the King's Hall. Wilson was on the canvas so often that it became monotonous, yet he received a tremendous ovation for being a game competitor.

In his first contest of 1938, Pat was out-pointed by the Londoner "Seaman" Harry Rowles at the National Sporting Club in London. Pat, with a seven-pound advantage, was up against rugged bodywork. Both boys were cautioned and had to be parted after the bell had sounded in one round. Marrinan often forced Rowles to the ropes and found his opponent a determined boxer on the defensive. In the last two rounds, Rowles was the aggressor and, despite the result bringing howls of derision from a section of the crowd, he just about deserved the decision.

Pat would have his last fight, at least in this part of the world, on 10 March 1938 in West Ham. He was out-pointed by Canadian Larry Gains, the former Empire Heavyweight Champion, who had won the title by knocking out Phil Scot in June 1931. It was a splendid performance by Marrinan over twelve hard-fought rounds against an opponent who, even though his best days were behind him, still oozed class.

Pat was on the canvas in the second round but was up before the count started. In an action-packed third round he sustained damage to his nose. The injury was not serious and the next two rounds produced toe-to-toe exchanges. In the closing stages, Marrinan fought in vain to close the gap.

Pat returned home to Belfast for a while, before moving to Australia, where he lived in Sydney and was employed by a shipping company. Under the name of Maurice Costello, he won two out of three fights before calling it a day. On 21 March 1938, he was stopped in the fifth round by Sydney fighter, Young Campbell. Eight months later, he had his first win on Australian soil when he stopped Jack Oliver in five rounds. The big Irishman brought his career to a close on 30 December 1939 with a points win over Jack Mitchell.

If Pat had harboured any thoughts of making a ring comeback, they were well and truly scuppered when he was badly injured aboard a Canadian ship, which was destined for the Antarctic. A large beam fell on him, resulting in a serious back and heel injury which saw him hospitalised in Montreal.

On his release from hospital, Pat devoted much of his time to writing his memoirs and helping the homeless and needy. He used to wander round the poorer areas of Montreal looking for people who were hungry and needed a roof over their heads for the night. On one occasion, Pat came across a former priest who was penniless and homeless, and whose faith had lapsed. With Pat's help he recovered his former dignity and returned to the Church.

Pat Marrinan was a tough, fearless, hard-punching fighter who lived life to the full. He died in a Montreal hospital on 30 January 1983, aged seventy. At his funeral, the priest who had been helped by the kindly Belfast man when he had fallen on hard times said, "Without Maurice Marrinan I wouldn't be a priest today."

He was truly an extraordinary man who lived an extraordinary life.

PROFESSIONAL CAREER
1935–1939: 26 traced contests: won 16, lost 9, drew 1.

Ike Weir
(Jimmy Rooney)

The little man with the big heart

He was short in stature and short of vital pounds and ounces, but what Jimmy Rooney lacked in size he more than compensated for with a heart like a lion, indomitable courage and a personality that only a corpse could fail to warm to.

Born on Friday, 13 February 1920 to Isobella Rooney (née Gallagher) and her electrician husband, James Joseph, affectionately known as "JJ", Jimmy resided at 28 Foundry Street in the Short Strand area of the east of the city. His arrival on the scene was against a background of social turmoil in Belfast, which was in the middle of a dispute between the National Union of Dockers and the city's coal merchants, resulting in over six hundred shipyard workers being locked out. Thousands of ill-clad women and children with wheelbarrows and makeshift carts queued for hours at the Queen's Quay and along the Queen's Road, where the largest of the coal depots was situated, hoping to get enough fuel to heat their homes. One newspaper described how a woman pathetically shrieked, "I would the happiest woman in Belfast if I could get some coal."

At the same time and on the sporting front, Welshman Jim Driscoll, one of the greatest scientific boxers of all time, although retired and his hair tinged with grey, boxed an exhibition with Glasgow's Mick McAdam in a packed Ulster Hall. Driscoll also refereed all the other fights, including a top of the bill encounter between local lad Pat McAllister and Glaswegian Bob Docherty. McAllister won on points over fifteen rounds. Five years later, "Peerless Jim" was dead from consumption at the age of forty-five.

Isobella and "JJ" would have twelve more children – four girls, including Edna, who is local fighter Damaen Kelly's mother, and eight boys, including Leo, who is Damaen's assistant coach.

Like the majority of the Short Strand populace, Jimmy was educated at St Matthew's School, formerly the Bridge End National School, in Seaforde Street, formerly Chapel Lane. On leaving school, he worked as a house repairer, proving so competent that, when he got the boxing bug, he transformed an old dilapidated store in Foundry Street into a first-class boxing gym for all the local fighters.

Jimmy was also a first-class footballer, playing on the wing for Albert Star in the Lisburn and District League, where he was spotted by the late Johnnie "Toby" Mercer, who persuaded him to sign for Glentoran. In his playing days, Toby had worn the colours of Linfield, Distillery, Brighton, Preston and Derby County. He had also been capped eleven times for Ireland, was a director of Glentoran for twenty years, as well as being chairman for both Distillery and the Irish League. Jimmy, however, decided not to pursue his football career and concentrated instead on his boxing.

As a teenager, Jimmy won titles with the Red Triangle Club on the Ravenhill Road and the Albert Boxing Club in Anderson Street, run by the popular Jim "JB" Brady. Around this period, he became aware of the life and times of Isaac "Ike" O'Neill Weir. Weir had been born on 5 February 1867 in Castle Lane, Lurgan. His father "Jakey" had worked at the coal quay in Belfast and Isaac himself had spent his boyhood in Ballymacarrett. Reared by the Nixon family, who had a fowl-dealing emporium in Middlepath Street, he acquired the *ring de plume*, the "Belfast Spider", because of his awkward but clever fighting style. When Weir went to England, he successfully participated in tournaments in Manchester, where he beat three opponents in one night, as well as Preston and Liverpool, before setting sail for Boston, Massachusetts.

What most impressed Jimmy about the man was that, within two years of beating William Snee (pts 4) in his debut American fight in Boston on 28 May 1886, Weir had notched up fifteen wins and four draws. He had also earned himself a crack at the vacant world featherweight title against Birmingham-born Frank Murphy.

The title had become vacant when Dal Hawkins, who was recognised in the States as the rightful claimant to the featherweight crown, retired. Hawkins had knocked out Freddy Brogan after ninety-one rounds for the title in San Francisco in June 1889. Due to bad light, the bout had taken two days to complete, with the initial seventy-five rounds being fought on the first day.

On 31 March 1889, Murphy and Weir fought each other to a standstill over eighty savage rounds in Kouts, Indiana. In the end, all that these brave men got for their endeavours was a draw and a purse of $1,500. They would probably have continued for another eighty rounds if the police hadn't interrupted the proceedings. Less than a year later, Ike was matched with Billy "Torpedo" Murphy from Auckland, New Zealand. The "Torpedo" sank the "Belfast Spider" in round fourteen in San Francisco and the New Zealander claimed the featherweight title.

"Torpedo" Murphy lost his title to Young Griffo (real name Albert Griffiths), who hailed from Sydney, Australia, and was described by boxing aficionados as a "genius of the ring". Griffo, an alcoholic, died penniless in 1927.

On 8 July 1890, Ike prepared to do battle with featherweight, Jimmy Connors. When Ike smashed him to the canvas in the third round, it was game, set and match to the Belfast scrapper. The following April, Ike boxed Johnny Griffin in Nantucket. Griffin considered himself to be the rightful champion but when the fight was stopped by police after four rounds, with the outcome a draw, the so-called "title fight" became a non-event. It was, however, a decent performance by Ike. Griffin would, on two occasions, go the distance with George Dixon, who was the first boxer to be recognised as Bantamweight Champion of the World when he beat Nunc Wallace at the Pelican Club, London, in June 1890. When Dixon moved up a weight, he claimed the featherweight title by knocking out Carl McCarthy in March 1891 in New York.

Ike had one more fight in 1891. He withered a boxer called the "Kentucky Rosebud" in three

Ike Weir, Jimmy's hero

rounds in Philadelphia, but the "Rosebud" blossomed sufficiently to enable him to go four rounds with Ike in a return bout eight months later, the result being a no decision. Ike went on to beat Frank Steele (ko 12) in New Bedford, drew with Tommy White over ten rounds in Minneapolis, and stopped Joe Flahery in the second.

In 1893, he had three great results: he stopped Joe Hopkins in four rounds in Hoboken, avenged his defeat by "Torpedo" Murphy with a sixth round knockout and, two days before Christmas, saw Eddie Loeber off in the fourth during their Boston bout.

On 17 March 1894, Ike was blown away in the third by Young Griffo in the "Windy City" of Chicago. This proved to be Ike's swansong, as he never fought again. He was twenty-seven years of age. He died on 24 September 1908, and his remains are interred in Holy Cross Cemetery, Malden, Massachusetts.

He may have died but Ike's name would live on in the capable hands of Jimmy Rooney. Jimmy assumed the name on joining the professional ranks, and the "Ike Weir Part Two" bandwagon started to roll on 11 September 1940. In the Ulster Hall, on a Ma Copley promotion, the new incarnation of

OPENING FLYWEIGHT CONTEST

8 Three-Minute Rounds at 8 st. 1 lb.

Ike Weir

(BELFAST)

One of Ireland's cleverest flyweights, Ike's handicap has always been weight. Never weighing more than around the 7 stone 10 lb. mark, he is always set to concede weight to his opponents.

versus

Eddie Fitzsimmons

(LIVERPOOL)

This boy boxed in Belfast during the past few weeks against Frank McCoy (Portadown) and conceded almost a stone in weight for that match. Tonight he meets an opponent similar in weight to himself, so it should be a match on the scales.

BE YOUR OWN REFEREE

ROUNDS	1	2	3	4	5	6	7	8
Weir								
Fitzsimmons								

Ike Weir must have been as nervous as a kitten in a dog's kennel. This was not because of a lack in confidence at beating his opponent, Joe Harvey, but because he was using for the first time the name of the fighter for whom he had so much respect. His sister Molly had sewn a simple "IW" on to her brother's shorts for the occasion. Ike overcame any nerves he might have had to knock Harvey out in the fourth round.

One week after this demolition job, Sam Smith took a terrible pounding from the Short Strand man. From the opening bell, Ike was aggressive and his southpaw stance puzzled Smith. Weir found it easy to land with a right lead and his tornado-like tactics, coupled with a heavy left hook, proved a bridge too far for Smith, who retired in the fourth of a scheduled six-rounder.

In Ike's third fight, he was giving away eleven pounds to hard-hitting Al Graham. Graham stalked Weir throughout the six-rounder but Ike's cleverness in eluding Al's powerful punches earned him a draw and the admiration of the crowd.

On 16 October 1940, Ike, coming in at 7st 11lbs, knocked Billy Nash out in the third round of a contest that had "early finish" written all over it. After punishing Nash with vicious body shots, Weir switched tactics, and the knockout came via a short left cross to the chin. Top of the bill that night was a thriller between Tommy Armour, the Northern Ireland Welterweight Champion, and Joe Buxton, with Armour winning on points.

Exactly one month later, Ike beat Jimmy Quinn (the younger brother of Jackie Quinn from Sailortown) in the third round of a scheduled six-rounder.

Veterans Jimmy and Popeye Rooney square off in a Short Strand derby

Quinn slapped his smaller opponent all around the ring in the first two rounds but, in the third, Weir brought over a right cross and Quinn dropped for a long count. When he rose, Ike went after him like a newly graduated surgeon goes after his first sack of gallstones. Blows rained on the courageous but hapless Quinn until his defence crumbled. The referee wisely called a halt to the one-sided affair. Ike would meet Jimmy four more times, winning two, losing one, and drawing one. It has been remarked that Ike Weir and Jimmy Quinn fought each other so many times that they were thinking of getting engaged. This quip could be applied equally to Ike's five encounters with Joe Meikle and, to a lesser extent, to the four bouts that Ike had with Jackie Rooney and Joe McCarthy. Neither of the last two ever managed a victory over the Short Strand southpaw.

On 20 November, Ike tasted defeat for the first time at the hands of Derry's Harry Rodgers, who had been a class amateur. So impressive was Rodgers' performance that he was being touted as a future champion.

In 1941, Ike won seven, lost one and drew one of his nine contests. His hand was raised in victory against Jack Garlow (pts 6), Tommy Taylor (Cornwall) (ko 5), John Cosgrove (ko 2), Tiny Croxton (Preston) (ko 1), Joe Meikle (pts 6), Jim McNulty (rtd 4), and Sam Ramsey (pts 6). His loss was against Jimmy Quinn (pts 6) and he drew with Joe Meikle over six stanzas.

On 26 December 1941, Ike had another win. He won the hand of his sweetheart, Ann McAllister, in a marriage that was to produce three children.

1942 proved to be a year of transition for the local boxing scene. On 25 May, Bob Gardiner promoted his first professional bill with a first-class show at the Rialto in Peter's Hill. Then, on 29 August 1942, the "Grand Old Lady of Ulster Boxing", Ma Copley, promoted her last card in the Ulster Hall, which was being taken over by the military. Ma Copley had formerly promoted in the Chapel Fields in the Markets district of Belfast. Boxing fans

Jimmy with his brother Philip

paid tribute to Ma on her departure from the sport by presenting her with a silver fruit dish. She had been the pioneer of boxing in the city, staging over eight thousand contests. The next time a promoter's licence would be granted to a woman by the British Board of Boxing Control would be in 1969 when the recipient was Mrs Beryl Gibbons from Bermondsey.

1942 was also a key year for Ike Weir. Between 4 February and 14 November, he participated in twenty-one contests, winning sixteen, drawing two and losing three. He beat Jackie Rooney four times, all inside the distance; Joe McCarthy four times, all on points; Dave McAllister (ko 3); Jim Hogg (ko 1); Bert Robinson (ko 1); Joe McNulty (ko 2) and Jim Kelly (pts 4). He also fought Jimmy Quinn three times that year, garnering two wins and a draw; lost to Joe Meikle twice inside the distance; fell to Tommy Madine (pts 6); and boxed Jim Blair twice (one win and a draw). One of the fights with Jimmy Quinn (won pts 4) was part of Bob Gardiner's promotional debut, and the win over Jim Hogg occurred during Ma Copley's final promotion.

In 1943, he fought Tommy Madine twice (winning one and losing one), Joe McNulty (won ko 1), Jim Kelly (won pts 4), and Boyo McIntosh (Blantyre) (won rsc 3). As part of a Bob Gardiner promotion on 13 July at Solitude, Ike beat Rinty Monaghan in an eliminator for the Northern Ireland flyweight title. On his next outing, however, Ike was stopped by old foe Joe Meikle and, on 18 September, in his last contest of the year, he lost to Dublin's Joe Collins (rtd 4).

Ike attempted to relieve Bunty Doran of his Northern Ireland flyweight title at the Ulster Stadium on 19 February 1944, but was knocked out in the third. Three months after this setback, Ike knocked out Belfast's Davy McAllister in the second. His next fight was in October, when he stopped another Belfast fighter, Jim Knowles, in four, and he finished the year off with a points victory over Dublin's Mickey Stewart.

Ike received a personal body blow when his mother died in 1944, but thanks to the support of his close-knit family, he managed to weather the storm.

He travelled to Liverpool on 31 May 1945, where he beat Belfast's Jack McKenzie on points over eight rounds. It was the only contest that Ike had that year. In 1946 he suffered losses at the hands of Al Hutt (Burma) (ko 1), Alf Hughes (West Hartlepool) (rtd 7) and Jimmy Thompson (Nottingham) (ko 6). However, he did beat Gilbert Hughes (Merthyr) (pts 8) and Tommy Farricker (Manchester) (pts 8), while managing a draw with Billy Hazelgrove (Brighton). Within a week of being knocked out by Thompson in Skegness, Ike was not only back on the winning trail but went through 1947 undefeated. His victims were Chick Ferris (Dublin) (ko 2); Frank McCoy (Portadown), three times on points; Tim Molloy (Dublin) (rsc 3); Les Johnson (Finsbury Park) (pts 8); Jackie Swann (Glasgow) (pts 8); and Billy Birch (Belfast) (pts 8).

Ike's first contest in 1948 was against Eddie Carson from Edinburgh in the Belfast Hippodrome. Carson was one tough little fighter whose record was dotted with knockout victories. Five weeks earlier, he had stopped Jackie Briers in five rounds in Glasgow. Ike was giving away eight pounds, and against a belter like Carson this was verging on the suicidal. Weir took a lot of punishment and the towel came to his rescue in the fourth.

On 20 March, he had a win over Eddie Fitzsimmons (Liverpool) (pts 8) in Belfast. This was a good confidence booster since he was hoping to get another shot at the Northern Ireland flyweight title, which had no tenant. First, however, he would have to participate in an eliminator against Jackie Briers.

This was staged at the Ulster Hall on 7 August before a sell-out crowd. Although Ike was well beaten, he received a thunderous ovation for a brave performance. In the third round, he took a count of nine, was down for four in the fourth, and for eight in the eighth. He soaked up punishment like blotting paper soaks up ink but Briers, hard though he tried, just couldn't finish him off. On 26 November, Briers won the local title when he beat Portadown's Frank McCoy in six rounds.

At the age of twenty-eight and with the sun about to set on his career, Ike had four more contests in 1948. He beat Belfast's Mickey McLaughlin (pts 8), repeated a win over the Liverpudlian Eddie Fitzsimmons (pts 8), lost to Pat McNally from Belfast (pts 8) and was knocked out by Glasgow's Vic Herman in the third round in Belfast. After a year of inactivity, he met Belfast man Jimmy Orr on 24 December 1949. Weighing in at a meagre 7st 5lbs, he was conceding more than ten pounds to the Shankill Road fighter. This weight difference, along with some ring rust, didn't help Ike's cause and he retired in the second round. The fight also marked his overall retirement from a sport that he had graced with dignity and courage.

Unlike the original Ike Weir, who had died at the age of forty-one, Jimmy Rooney lived to more than three score and ten. He died at his daughter Patsy's residence in Newtownards on 19 August 1991.

PROFESSIONAL CAREER
1940-1949: 71 traced contests: won 49, drew 5, lost 17.

Rinty Monaghan

When he died, Irish eyes weren't smiling

John Joseph Monaghan was born on Saturday, 21 August 1921 at 13 Thomas Street, off Lancaster Street in Belfast, to parents Thomas and Martha. John Joseph would be one of nine children, with five sisters and three brothers. Like most kids, young Monaghan had boundless energy and was always getting into mischief. At that time, a German Shepherd dog by the name of Rin Tin Tin was the rage of the silver screen, so John's granny Margaret, who doted on her grandson, began calling him after the celebrity canine. This handle was too long, however, and was shortened to "Rinty", a nickname that stuck like superglue.

Rinty was educated in St Patrick's School in Donegall Street and when any argument or a fight occurred, the finger of suspicion was more often than not pointed in his direction. He used to take the cane even when he was innocent but invariably got his revenge on the real culprit after school, with the "set-to" usually taking place up some entry. In these after-school fights, there was only one winner – Rinty Monaghan.

Rinty's first job was with Roden Bros Ltd, Flax and Tow Waste Merchants, in Great George's Street, not far from his home, where his father was foreman. This was where Rinty met his future wife, Frances Thompson. The couple had three daughters and a son. Frances didn't like to watch her husband box and was too nervous to even listen to his fights on the radio. Rinty once said of

her that "She was the best 'second' a man could ever have, and her smile when I returned home from a fight was worth more than any promoter's cheque."

One day at work, Rinty had an accident that very nearly ended his boxing career before it got started. While painting a roof, the ladder, which had not been properly secured, gave way and he went crashing to the ground. He was very fortunate to sustain nothing more serious than a broken ankle. As a result, Rinty would box with his ankle bandaged.

The Independent Labour Party (ILP) Hall in Belfast's York Street ran boxing shows in those days. Rinty used to go along the queue with his mates, asking punters if they would bring him in with them. One chap, who was much bigger than him, jumped the queue, provoking Rinty to punch him on the chin. Bedlam broke out and Rinty was ushered into the hall by an official. Before he knew it he was matched with "Pimple" McKee. Between them, the two boys barely weighed ten stone and were announced to the amusement of the crowd as a "special heavyweight attraction". After that, "Pimple" and Rinty were on ILP bills quite often and the outcome was consistently a draw.

Rinty always sang Gracie Field's "Sally", which was very popular at that time and was frequently requested by fight fans in the hall. His singing delighted the audience, who would throw pennies into the ring.

Rinty claimed to have had over one hundred fights but we will tune into his career from 1934 when he drew with Belfast's Sam Ramsey and out-pointed Jim Pedlow from Whitehouse.

In 1935, Monaghan out-pointed Young Finnegan and, on a bill in aid of charity at The Ring in Thomas Street, he knocked out Vic Large with a neat right hook in the fourth round. Rinty had a much busier schedule in 1936, boxing Sam Ramsey to two wins and a draw. He had the same result when he faced Carrickfergus boxer, Young Josephs, over three fights that year, and also took on Young Kelly, Jack McKenzie and Joe Duffy.

In 1937, he was out-pointed by Lisburn's Jim Keery. The seventeen-year-old was improving all the time and had wins over Belfast boxers Mick Gibbons (twice), Frank Benson and Sam Ramsey. Cross-channel boxers who lost to the classy Monaghan were Manchester's Tommy Allen, Glasgow's George Lang and Liverpool's Paddy O'Toole. Rinty described the contest against O'Toole as his "miracle fight", saying that he didn't even know that he had got the decision until informed by his manager, Frank McAloran. He had been down for seven in the second round and remembered nothing after this as he had hit his head on the boards, resulting in concussion.

McAloran was in no doubt that his boy would make the grade, describing Rinty as "Belfast's Jimmy Wilde" because of his "hard-hitting propensities". Monaghan definitely produced the goods between January and July of 1938 against Alf Hughes (West Hartlepool) (ko 9), Joe Kiely (Limerick) (ko 2), Pat Murphy (Jarrow) (rtd 4), Spider Allen (West Hartlepool) (ko 2), Peter Peters (Glasgow) (ko 1) and Ivor Neill (Glasgow) (ko 1). Rinty also had points victories over Cyclone Kelly (Manchester) (twice) and Joe McCluskey (Glasgow). His first fight against Cyclone Kelly (real name Con O'Kelly) in Liverpool Stadium was the Belfast lad's first trip away from home. Rinty gave the crowd a song at the end, as was his trademark, and they simply loved him.

However, on 23 July 1938 at The Oval, home of Glentoran Football Club, Glaswegian southpaw, Jackie Paterson, smashed Rinty to the floor in the fifth round in front of five thousand fight fans. The army of local supporters were shell-shocked by the knockout. Just over a decade later, Rinty said, "I jumped into the ring as cocky as you like, clad in a jazzy dressing-gown – a gladiator ready for the kill. This was a pushover, it won't be long now [was what] I managed to convey to the fans with a series of grins, bows, gesticulations and general clowning. They roared their heads off in anticipation. Boys-a-boys, if they and I had known what was coming – not to them, but to me! Frank, unlike his usual shrewd self, thought it would be easy, too; so easy that, early in the bout, he left my corner and took a ringside seat to discuss some other business with a friend. It was the only time in my life that he had ever left my corner.

Rinty training hard at McAloran's gym

"Things were going all right. There was no great action but one of Jackie's eyes was puffed. I was kidding around, dropping my hands now and again, sticking out my chin and inviting Paterson to come and get me. The crowd enjoyed this but were impatient. 'Hurry up, Rinty,' they cried. 'Hurry up. Polish him off and give us a song.' So, to oblige, I dashed out at the sound of the bell for the fifth but was soon back on my heels as Jackie met me with a flurry of rights and lefts.

"In the twinkling of an eye I was on my back. I had asked for it – and I got it. Frank sprang from his seat to the ropes. 'Keep down! Keep down!' he yelled, hoping that, by waiting, I would shake off the effects of the attack.

"When I got up at eight, however, I was still groggy and wide open. Paterson charged me immediately and landed again. The blow knocked me against the ropes and I rebounded to the other side of the ring, falling plump on the canvas for nine. I rose by instinct, but a left hook quickly sent me down once more and, as the referee tolled the dreaded 'one . . . two . . . three', right up to ten, Frank, seeing my glassy eyes, knew that I had had it and flung in the towel.

"As Frank and his brother, Jimmy, were taking me to the dressing room I was not too sure what it was all about, but I do recall hearing some fair-weather friends shouting, 'What about a song now, Rinty?'"

Rinty's bad day at the office was far from over as he had to contend with the razor-sharp tongue of Frank McAloran. Rinty said, "He nearly scared the life out of me. If Frank hit as fast and as hard in his day in the ring as his tongue wagged and cut that afternoon at The Oval, then thank goodness he was before my time and that I was not a featherweight." Rinty would meet Paterson twice more, with their final meeting seeing the world flyweight crown being transferred from Scotland to Ireland.

After the Paterson incident, Rinty made his second visit to Liverpool, where by cool and confident two-handed boxing he had a comfortable win over Joe Curran. After the fight, he gave his version of that old favourite, "Umbrella Man". In the eyes of promoter Johnny Best, Monaghan was not only an outstanding, value-for-money fighter, but also a brilliant entertainer.

He ended his 1938 campaign on 2 September at The Oval, losing to a gallant little battler from York Street called Tommy Stewart. The fight was an eliminator for the vacant Northern Ireland flyweight title.

On 27 February 1939 in Newcastle, Rinty weighed in at two o'clock in the afternoon for his second fight with Liverpool's Joe Curran on a charity bill promoted by Fred Charlton. There was a great atmosphere about the place and Rinty, as usual, was in good form. He attracted some strange looks as he sang and danced around the hall as if he hadn't a care in the world.

He had plenty of time on his hands before climbing into the ring and took himself off to see the Bing Crosby film *Paris Honeymoon*. He was enjoying it so much that he completely forgot about the time. It was exactly 7pm when to his absolute horror a notice flashed on the screen: RINTY MONAGHAN WANTED IMMEDIATELY. Rinty dashed out to find Frank McAloran almost demented. Not knowing which cinema Monaghan had gone to, Frank had searched for him all over town and was on the verge of giving up when his fighter appeared. With no time for a light tea before the bout, Rinty had to be content with a raw egg and a glass of sherry. When he did eventually enter the ring, the fans were stomping their feet with impatience.

Rinty was unfazed by the racket and as he listened to the referee's final instructions he looked very fit indeed. It was obvious that his power walking from York Street to the Cave Hill, together with a diet of raw eggs, brandy and goat's milk had stood him in good stead.

When the contest got under way the Liverpudlian did well for three rounds but took a lot of punishment in the fourth. In the fifth, Rinty feinted with his left and then let go with a powerful right and it was all over. While Joe Curran was wondering what had hit him, Rinty sang "Solitude".

Monaghan had to settle for points victories over his next four opponents: Sammy Reynolds (Wolverhampton), Tommy Stewart (Belfast), Billy Ashton (Wigan) and Seaman Chetty (South Africa).

Frank McAloran oversees Rinty's training

He had four fights in 1940, two of which he lost. On 10 January in Newcastle he gave a lacklustre performance against Manchester's Paddy Ryan, losing on points over ten rounds. He won his next contest against Tommy Stewart but when he topped the bill in Newcastle he was out-pointed by Nottingham's Jimmy Gill. Gill took full advantage of his greater height and reach and was aggressive throughout the fight. Rinty, however, made himself a difficult target and, in addition to good work at close quarters, he twice floored Gill with right-hand punches. He was doing so well that he had a chance of securing the verdict. Unfortunately, in the later rounds, he visibly tired as a result of Gill's relentless body attacks. A terrific right to the jaw sent the Belfast boy to his knees in the tenth, wrecking his chance of being declared winner. Rinty closed the year with a points win over Belfast's Joe Meikle.

Monaghan didn't see any ring action in 1941 and 1942. Instead, he had all the action he wanted on the high seas. He joined the Merchant Navy and his ship was torpedoed. Returning home he joined the Civil Defence as an ambulance driver. He once described being an ambulance driver at the time of the Belfast Blitz as an "unenviable experience".

The war didn't prevent Rinty from entertaining and he formed The Three Hillbillies with two mates. As well as being the lead singer he also did impressions, including a brilliant Popeye. The trio got on very well and eventually came to the attention of a talent spotter from the Entertainments National Service Association (or ENSA). The trio's first assignment was a three-month tour among the troops and civilians in the London area. Rinty was full of praise for the people of London and said, "To live with Londoners at that grim period was a wonderful experience."

The trio was sent to Normandy, where they did four shows a day before returning to England. On a short holiday back home, Rinty resumed training in Frank McAloran's gym. He wanted to fight but Frank was not interested. "You're not fit," he advised, but Rinty had a way of winning people over, even Frank McAloran. Contests were arranged with Harry Rodgers from Derry and the Short Strand's Ike Weir. Rinty and Rodgers boxed to a draw, and at Cliftonville football ground on 13 July 1943, Monaghan lost to Weir over ten rounds.

Rinty rejoined ENSA but was straining at the leash to get his boxing career back on track. With Hitler about to throw in the towel Frank McAloran was informed that his star pupil was coming home. The boxer who had the doubtful privilege of welcoming Rinty home was Joe Meikle, who was knocked out in the first round. Rinty then accounted for Joe "Boy" Collins in the Theatre Royal, Dublin, before visiting Liverpool Stadium, where he out-pointed local boxer Tommy Burney. When Rinty returned to Liverpool the following October, however, he lost to Joe Curran on their third encounter. Rinty still sang for the fans at the end of the bout, despite their being on the side of the victorious local boy.

On 6 November, Rinty was set to challenge Bunty Doran for the latter's Northern Ireland flyweight title. Doran was both a good friend and a relative through marriage, and had won the vacant title from Harry Rodgers, successfully defending it against Ike Weir. When Rinty stepped into the ring in the Ulster Hall he was in great shape, thanks to vigorous sparring sessions with Eddie McCullough, Peter Robinson and Jim Campbell. Belfast's Andy Smyth, a former amateur boxer, who was recognised as one of the best referees in the world, was the third man on the night. Even Smyth must have been surprised at the brevity of the contest – Bunty was knocked out in the fourth round. He had been doing well up to this point when, scorning the finer arts, he rushed in and was caught with a short right that put him down for eight. He rose on unsteady pins and Rinty completed his night's work with a powerful right-hand punch. As he left the famous boxing venue Monaghan's supporters hoisted him shoulder-high and carried him in triumph all the way to his home in Little Corporation Street, where an amplifier was rigged up and the new Northern Ireland Flyweight Champion sang well into the night.

It was April of 1946 before Rinty saw action again, travelling to Liverpool to beat Tommy Burney convincingly on points over eight rounds.

Since Jackie Paterson had knocked Rinty out at The Oval, the Scot had won fifty-two of his sixty-six contests, capturing the British, British Empire,

Rinty signs for the Paterson fight watched by McAloran and Bob Gardiner

World and European flyweight titles. Paterson was due to defend his titles against Joe Curran in Glasgow on 26 June 1946 but was persuaded by promoter Bob Gardiner to fight Rinty in an overweight fight in the King's Hall on 7 June. Monaghan had waited eight years to avenge his humiliation at The Oval and there was no way that he was going to let this chance slip by. The evening was given an added edge by the likelihood that Rinty would get a crack at Paterson's titles if the Glaswegian went on to beat Joe Curran.

On the night it could have been all over early had Rinty connected with a right hand. In the third, the referee called both boys over and hinted that they should provide more action. They contented themselves with sparring around, seeking an opening and indulging in some in-fighting, with Rinty collecting the majority of the points. Following a further appeal from the referee the men stepped up a few gears. Paterson caught Monaghan with a good right and the Belfast boy took a short count but he was not seriously troubled. Paterson was cut in the seventh and shortly before the round ended Rinty caught the champion with a terrific right hook to the jaw. Proceedings were halted to a deafening applause and, at the request of the spectators, Rinty sang "Broken-Hearted Clown".

Three months later, Rinty fought Alec Murphy at the Kelvin Hall in Glasgow, where the fans recalled that Monaghan had beaten their world champion and crooned "Broken-Hearted Clown". Rinty took a lot of flak because of this during his fight with Murphy. Nevertheless, he didn't allow the hostile crowd and the tense atmosphere to prevent him from winning with rounds to spare. At the finish, he made a move to sing but was shouted down, and he and his entourage moved under police escort to the dressing room. Rinty later said that he "never had any intentions of hurting Paterson's feelings".

Paterson's defence against Joe Curran was put back until 10 July due to the eye injury picked up in the Monaghan bout. When the fight eventually took place at Hampden Park the champion retained his title, winning on points over the distance of fifteen rounds.

In his final contest of 1946, Rinty beat Sammy Reynolds from Wolverhampton at the King's Hall. Reynolds was disqualified for hitting below the borderline in the eighth round.

Rinty made his London debut in the Seymour Hall on 11 March 1947 against Terry Allen (real name Albert Edward Govier), a barrow boy from Islington. Allen had won his first thirty contests since making his debut on 3 September 1942, before being knocked out in the sixth by Alec Murphy on 14 May 1946. Murphy was to die from injuries sustained during a bout with French flyweight Emile Famechon on 9 December 1946. Although Allen was a substitute for Famechon on the Seymour Hall card, and it had the makings of a first-class contest, Rinty's London debut proved to be a brief affair when he knocked out the barrow boy in the first round.

The bout had hardly begun when Allen was put down for a count of seven from a left hook and he staggered to his feet in a dazed condition. A second left hook landed on Allen's jaw and sent him down for eight. He rose pluckily, only to take a similar punch that sent him sprawling for a third time. The Islington boy got up at seven but Monaghan easily penetrated his defence with a right hook, putting the twenty-three-year-old on the deck for a nine count. Although he managed to beat the count, the referee stopped the contest. As usual, Rinty was in fine voice after the fight.

Rinty went on to out-point Emile Famechon at Olympia. Although the Frenchman looked dangerous with his wild swings, Rinty was the better ring general, causing a lot of damage to Famechon's eyes in the fifth and sixth rounds. Monaghan was a clear winner and his fine form was worthy of a world title contender. After the fight, Rinty not only gave his customary song, he also did a little jig.

At a rain-soaked Hampden Park on 16 July 1947, before 25,000 people, Rinty was disqualified in the ninth round for persistent holding against Dado Marino, a thirty-one-year-old from Honolulu. The defeat did not jeopardise Monaghan's world title aspirations. He had come in as a late substitute for Jackie Paterson, who was to have defended his title against Marino. Paterson

took ill and failed to appear at the weigh-in, and was deprived of the titles he had won from Peter Kane in June 1943.

Rinty met Marino for a second time on 20 October 1947 at Harringay in London. The fight, which was billed as being for the Flyweight Championship of the World, was recognised by the NBA and the Eire Boxing Board of Control. Paterson, however, had taken legal action against the British Board of Boxing Control, which prevented them from recognising the fight as being for the title. Paterson's appeal was successful and the title was returned to him.

The Monaghan-Marino fight was a poor affair with few thrills or spills and the crowd showed their displeasure by booing and catcalling. Nevertheless, it was of the utmost importance that Rinty won. If the NBA version of the title had gone to the States things would have become bogged down in complicated boxing politics and Rinty could have been easily left out

in the cold. Rinty got the decision and it was now time to prepare for his challenge for the lineal world flyweight title, which had been returned to Paterson. Years later, Rinty revealed that throughout the Marino fight he had had great difficulty with his breathing.

On the same evening that Rinty had beaten Marino, Paterson successfully defended his British and Empire bantamweight titles at Harringay, knocking out Norman Lewis in the fifth round. Paterson was obviously strong at bantamweight but would he be comfortable at eight stone against Monaghan?

Paterson was due to arrive in Belfast on the eve of his world title defence against Rinty, and promoter Bob Gardiner must have had palpitations when the world champion failed to show. However, in the event that Paterson was unable to make the weight, as had been rumoured, Maurice Sandeyron, the French European Flyweight Champion, would deputise. Jackie did turn up but not until 2pm on the day of the fight, at exactly the time he was due on the scales.

An almighty roar greeted the champion when he walked in and the roar multiplied ten-fold when Jackie's weight was announced as 7st 13³/₄lbs. The world champion had made it by the thickness of a five-pound note. Rinty's weight was 7st 12³/₄lbs. Those present noted that there was no clowning around this time by the challenger. Rinty had vowed that he would only do his celebrating after his fights.

And celebrate the little man did after knocking Paterson out in the seventh round. As Rinty came in, Paterson caught him with a right to the jaw but when he was following up his attack Monaghan caught him with a powerful right and the champion was down for a count of nine. Paterson was dazed when he got to his feet and Monaghan chased him into a corner, belting him with lefts and rights until the champion sank into a sitting position in Monaghan's corner. He was counted out amid scenes of wild excitement. Rinty sang "When Irish Eyes Are Smiling" followed by a Judy Garland song, "Chasing Rainbows".

Ireland's Flyweight Champion had his next contest in Birmingham and easily accounted for Coventry's Charlie Squire in the seventh round. Rinty was so much on top that he asked the referee to "stop the fight". He had had to pay a forfeit of £50 as he came in well over the limit.

It was eight months before Rinty boxed again, losing to Terry Allen. In the course of the fight Rinty took four counts, though he took his defeat well and

Allen versus Monaghan

said, "I have been without a fight for nearly eight months and I wasn't timing my punches very well. Allen didn't worry me at all."

Rinty was back to his best in the King's Hall on 5 April 1949 when he defended his world crown and attempted to wrest the European title from France's Maurice Sandeyron, who had beaten Raoul Degryse for the prize in Brussels on 21 May 1947.

Displaying real championship class, Rinty had the upper hand for most of the fight with the exception of three shared rounds. At the end of the contest, referee Mr C B Thomas raised the champion's hand in a token of victory without the slightest hesitation. It was a hard and fast fifteen rounds and towards the end both boxers tired. While the fight wasn't exactly an epic it did prove that the Belfast man was a worthy holder of the crown.

In the penultimate contest of the singing boxer's career, he out-pointed Otello Belardenelli, the Italian Flyweight Champion, at The Hippodrome in Belfast.

By 30 September 1949, Rinty's scheduled fight against Terry Allen in the King's Hall had created interest of unprecedented proportions. Those without tickets had to sweat it out for the result since Rinty's defence of his four coveted titles – the British, European, Commonwealth and World

flyweight crowns – was not being broadcast live on the radio. Throngs of men, women and children made their way to the *Irish News* office in Donegall Street, not too far from Rinty's home, to wait for news of how the fight was progressing. A round-by-round account of the fight came over the teleprinter and was relayed by a member of staff to the anxious fans outside. At one stage, the street was so jammed that the police came on the scene to make a passage for traffic, which was finding it impossible to get through.

From the opening bell, Rinty went at Allen, determined to show him who was boss. He drove his opponent to the ropes but missed with two left hooks. Rinty tried a wild swing, aimed at the side of Allen's face, and missed by the proverbial mile. Allen looked worried and back-pedalled his way out of trouble. It was a good round for Rinty, despite missing a lot with wild swings.

In the second, Rinty continued to force the issue but Allen's defence was standing the test well. Rinty was still badly out of range and his wild, reckless swings left him open to a succession of Allen's jabs. Allen then caught Rinty flush on the jaw and the champion's fans were stunned as he went down for a count of eight. He was kneeling on one knee but he seemed to have his wits about him. When the bell sounded to conclude the round, Rinty grinned and ruffled Allen's hair.

At the beginning of the third, Monaghan went at Allen, intending to make it a short fight. He was boxing well and his left hand was darting out like a cobra's tongue. Allen tried to retaliate with right crosses but Rinty seemed to read his opponent's mind and kept out of trouble. The boxers were in a clinch in the centre of the ring when, for some inexplicable reason, Rinty went down for a count of five. He was not hurt, however, and the bell rang to end the round. To regular fight fans, it was obvious that all was not well with Rinty and it later emerged that he went through the contest having great discomfort with his breathing.

In the fourth, Allen was boxing with more confidence and seemed to sense that all was not right with his opponent. Time and time again, he put the champ on the defensive and, when Rinty did respond with his own artillery, Allen took most of the flak on the gloves and elbows. So far the fight was anything but a classic, yet the crowd didn't seem to notice too much.

At the beginning of the fifth, Allen went immediately on the attack and Rinty was definitely not showing the form that had won him the title eighteen months previously. Allen was warned by the referee for something he did in a clinch and Rinty, true to form, didn't complain, grinning that infectious Monaghan grin.

The sixth round looked to be something of a damp squib when Allen was caught with a terrific right swing. He went down but, incredibly, only took a count of one. The crowd went wild, thinking the tide was beginning to turn in Monaghan's favour. Allen smiled as the bell went.

In the seventh, Rinty continued to pressurise the Londoner, throwing lefts and rights with venom, and Allen scampered around the ring like a cat being chased by a Rottweiler. In the eighth, both men missed time after time with right and left hooks, seemingly cancelling each other out. At times the champion was extremely economic in his use of the right hand that had in previous contests proved such a potent and reliable weapon.

Rinty tried some vicious punches early in the ninth, one of which was near enough to make Allen blink and back away. The speed of the champion's swings was like lightning, though they were nearly always inclined to be wild. Both men, in turn, landed good punches to the side of the head but Monaghan appeared to be just a little faster with his deliveries.

Round ten and Rinty scored with three left jabs to Allen's nose. He was definitely boxing better now. Allen, however, was still strong and fast and fought back whenever the opportunity arose. Round eleven saw both boxers bobbing and weaving and hardly a decent punch was thrown. The fight was now uninteresting and the crowd outside the *Irish News* were probably having a better time than those in the King's Hall. Round twelve saw Rinty throw

The Champ is laid to rest in 1984 some very wild punches and Allen had no difficulty at all in avoiding them, yet he was not taking advantage of the openings Monaghan was generously leaving him.

The thirteenth opened promisingly for Rinty. Allen was flushed as a barrage of punches engulfed him but when the round ended he looked unconcerned. In the penultimate round, Allen looked a little stronger than Rinty. The contest was so close than Monaghan's fans must have been more than a little worried about the outcome. Rinty was now giving his all to retain his hard-won titles. Tension reigned as the final round neared.

"Seconds out, fifteenth and last round!" Would the popular little Belfast man retain his titles? The crowd roared and Rinty was the first to score with a short right to the chin. Allen retaliated and both fighters went at it hammer-and-tongs. They were head-to-head, throwing punches from all angles with no thought of defence. Rinty tried for a knockout in the closing stages and was hammering away at Allen when the final bell went. When referee Sam Russell held up both men's hands to signal a draw, the crowd was incensed. They had no need to get angry because Rinty had retained his titles.

Allen's supporters in the crowd thought that their man had won but Monaghan was content. Despite just having been through fifteen rounds of world championship boxing with serious breathing difficulties, he gave the fans a rendering of "How Can You Buy Killarney?"

Rinty was due to fight again but for health reasons packed the fight game in, relinquishing his titles on 30 March 1950. On 25 April he announced his retirement from the ring due to chronic bronchitis. Rinty departed this world on 3 March 1984, aged sixty-three. It was a day when, to quote from his signature tune, "When Irish Eyes Are Smiling": "There's a tear in your eye, and I'm wondering why, for it should never be there at all."

PROFESSIONAL CAREER
1934–1949: 66 traced contests: won 51, lost 9, drew 6.

Bunty Doran

Doran or Dornan, he was a class act

By the time Edward Dornan had knocked "Young" Row out in the second round of his debut fight at the Belfast Arena in Alfred Street, he had been transformed into "Bunty Doran". "Bunty" was a handle he had already acquired as a child when, while wearing a different type of glove, baby mittens, somebody had commented, "What a bunty wee lad." "Doran" came about when the *n* from his name had been mistakenly dropped in the programme for that 1938 encounter with Row. Dornan was now Doran, and a legend was born.

Bunty himself was born on 16 December 1921 in Nelson Street, Belfast, in the heart of "Little Italy" to father Edward and mother Sarah. The area, comprising the likes of Frederick Street, Great Patrick Street and York Street, was home for many Italians who had settled and successfully blended into Northern Ireland life. Dornan senior, who was to lose a leg during the Belfast Blitz, worked as a school caretaker. Bunty had two sisters and five brothers, and attended St Patrick's School, later driving a lorry for the waste-paper company, Cooks.

He first became involved in boxing in the Newsboys' Boxing Club in Frederick Street and, by the age of seventeen, was fighting out of The Star. His original mentors were Harry Fulton and Minty Rose, but he later teamed up with Liverpool brothers Dom and Tony Vairo. Among their fighters were: Stan Hawthorne (North Shields); Jim Brady (Dundee), who won the vacant British Empire bantamweight title by beating Kid Tanner (British Guiana) on 1 January 1941 at Dens Park, Dundee; Bert Jackson (Fleetwood); Dan McAllister (Belfast); Willie Whyte (Glasgow); Billy Stevens (Glasgow); Gerry Smyth (Belfast); Jimmy O'Brien (Sidmouth); Bobby Boland (Dundee), Bert Hornby (Bolton); Eddie Dumazell (Cardiff); Kid Tanner and his brother, Jack Johnson (British Guiana).

After dealing successfully with Young Row, Bunty's next outing

The contract for the Doran versus Monaghan fight

was against Young Joseph (Carrick). The result was a draw and, apart from a defeat at the hands of Belfast man Johnny Cosgrove (rtd 5 with a cut eye), whom he had beaten four months earlier, he sailed through 1938 with points wins over local boxers Tommy Wilson (twice), Billy Grimmason, Jim O'Brien (twice) and Dick Frame. Wins, via the short route, over George Maynes (rtd 1), Ted Campbell (rsc 1), Sam Ramsey (rsc 6), Young McAloran (rsc 7) and Al Bryson (ko 5) also characterised the year.

On a full-house Ma Copley promotion in the Ulster Hall at the start of 1939, Bunty threw what was considered to be one of the best knockout blows ever seen at that venue and flattened local boy Frank Benson in the sixth round. Less than a fortnight later, he defeated Dick Frame for the second time. Both boys mixed it from the bell and, in the second round, Frame went down from a left hook. He got to his feet only to be confronted by another Doran explosion. Frame rose gamely once more but, when he visited the canvas yet again, the referee counted him out.

Bunty next met Alf Hughes, a clever little fighter from West Hartlepool. Despite losing the bout, Hughes earned thunderous applause from the audience because of the excellence of his boxing. Using his five-pound advantage, Bunty looked menacing as he stalked Hughes throughout the fight. A scientific *rat-tat-tat* from Hughes continually stopped Bunty from unleashing his weapons of mass destruction. Nevertheless, he ran out a narrow winner.

In the Ulster Hall on 15 March, Bunty met Angel Garcia, a game little Spaniard. Although Garcia had courage in abundance, he fell prey to innumerable rights to the jaw. The tough-as-teak Angel soaked up punishment like a sun-worshipper soaks up the sun. Referee Neilly Thompson eventually intervened to prevent him taking any more punishment by stopping the fight in the seventh round, much to the relief of the compassionate Belfast fans.

Garcia was in action in the Ulster Hall again two weeks later, losing on points to local lad, Ted Meikle. Top of the bill was Bunty, who faced Nottingham's Jimmy Gill. Gill was also a jockey and had lost only two of his thirty-three fights, but he couldn't raise a gallop and was stopped in the seventh of the ten-round contest.

On a beautiful summer's evening in 1939, at a major Hugh McAlevey promotion in aid of Distillery Football Club, five thousand souls crammed into Grosvenor Park to witness Tommy Armour, the Northern Ireland Welterweight Champion, out-point Patsy Quinn. Across town, in a packed Ulster Hall, Bunty Doran and Ted Meikle served up another thriller. From the first gong, neither boy took a backward step. Doran scored heavily to the face and head but Meikle was connecting to the body. In the third, both connected with rights and lefts to the jaw. Meikle was dropped but, though dazed, got to his feet and went in to have a go. His eye was cut in the fourth and Bunty's straight and accurate left was doing untold damage. The sixth had excitement in abundance and it was remarkable how both lads stood up to the punishment. A right to the jaw dropped Meikle but he would not take a count. It was furious in the seventh with Doran connecting with wicked punches to the body. Meikle, however, was more than willing to trade punches and Doran went back to his corner at the end of the round with his left eye puffed and closed. The referee inspected Bunty at the end of the eighth and it looked like he was facing defeat. In the ninth and tenth rounds, Bunty realised he would have to finish the job and went in with both hands working overtime. Meikle could not cope with the onslaught and was dropped for nine. He was practically out on his feet and, once again, went down for nine. Bunty was now well on top, although Meikle was still making a fight of it. He rocked Doran with a right hand but Bunty was not to be halted and put his opponent down for eight. Meikle was groggy and just about survived the round. After this fine victory, the boxing pundits forecast a bright future for Bunty Doran.

Four weeks later, Bunty stopped former amateur flyweight champion Bobby Campbell (Glasgow) in seven rounds in the Ulster Hall, with Campbell sustaining a damaged nose. Doran also had a brace of wins over Belfast's Jack McKenzie. When Bunty met Joe Kiely, the Limerick boxer was disqualified for persistent low blows. The referee probably did Kiely a favour as he was taking too much punishment.

On 28 September 1939, Bunty debuted in an English ring as a substitute for Hanley's Tiny Bostock and took on Joe Curran in the famous Liverpool Stadium. A professional since 1932, Curran was seven years older than Bunty and had won thirty-eight of his seventy-four contests. In the space of nine days in August 1938, Curran had twice beaten Jackie Paterson. On 10 July 1946, at Glasgow's Hampden Park, Joe got a crack at Paterson's British, British Empire and world flyweight titles but lost on points over fifteen rounds.

Bunty performed courageously against Curran and his loss was met with a storm of protest. There was nail-biting action in every round. Doran was on the floor in the first but later bossed the exchanges. Curran took two counts of eight in the fourth and eighth rounds and, by clever ring-craft, only just managed to evade a knockout defeat. Even in defeat, Bunty's performance had enhanced his title aspirations.

On the day of his eighteenth birthday, Doran knocked out Dublin's Mick Byrne in the second round at The Ring in Thomas Street. Another Dubliner,

Billy Phelan, also had an early night when he was knocked out by Jackie Mussen in the first round of a scheduled ten-rounder.

Bunty then renewed hostilities with Alf Hughes, once again winning on points over ten rounds. Four weeks later in the Ulster Hall, he wasted no time in disposing of Billy Clinton, a Scot based in Croydon. Seven days earlier, Clinton had given Jim McCann, who was due to fight for the area title, all the trouble he wanted over six rounds.

Still the fights kept coming and, within the space of ten days, Bunty was twice out-pointed by Jimmy Stewart from Edinburgh. These defeats were put behind him and, in a tough, brutal fight with Hanley's Tut Whalley he won on points over ten rounds. Good sportsmanship was not on the menu in the Ulster Hall that night and referee Billy Gilmour had his work cut out to make sure that both boys boxed within the rules. Bunty's win over Tommy Ensor brought 1940 to a jubilant close, when he stopped the Mancunian in six rounds. That was the year he also married his girlfriend, Margaret Brownlee, in St John's Church. The union would produce five sons and a daughter.

Bunty tried to pull rank on Lieutenant Jack Kiley from Swansea in his first fight of 1941 but lost his way, and the soldier was awarded the decision. He fought on five more occasions that year, beating Harry Cullinan (Armagh) (rsc 6), Chick Ferris (Manchester) (rtd 8), Dixie McCall (Belfast) (rtd 4) and Jeff Smith (Wellingborough) (twice).

York Street's Tommy Stewart, who had won the vacant Northern Ireland flyweight crown after stopping Jim McStravick in ten rounds at the King's Hall in November 1938, was no longer involved in the fight game. When Bunty safely negotiated three hurdles in the shapes of Belfast men Charlie Brown (rtd 6), Billy Docherty (pts 8) and Joe Meikle (rtd 1), he was given a crack at the vacant title in the Rialto. His opponent was Derry's Harry Rodgers. When the boy from the Maiden City went down in the first round for a count of eight it looked to be all over. However, Rodgers made a surprising comeback and took the second and third rounds by the sheer ferocity of his attacks.

From the fourth round, Doran's rasping body shots told and, once more, Rodgers touched down for a count of eight. Half a minute later he went down again and it was obvious he wasn't going to make it. The flyweight title was now in different hands. In a division that was heavily populated and fiercely competitive, holding an area title was a step in the right direction towards inclusion in the British eliminators.

On 10 March 1943 in Derry's Guildhall, Harry Rodgers once again fell to the devastating punches of Doran, taking the full count in the third. In the Queensberry Club in Soho, Bunty stopped Billy Hazelgrove in six. The Brighton lad was hounded from rope to rope and was completely out of his depth. Hazelgrove was down for six in the second round and for two more counts in the third when the bell saved him. He continued to absorb punishment and it was no surprise when the referee intervened.

Less than two weeks later, the pair met again, this time in Hazelgrove's own backyard. If Billy thought that the Brighton sea air would help his cause against Doran, he was wrong. The Belfast lad knocked him out in the third round on a charity bill organised by Tommy Farr, the former British and British Empire Light-Heavyweight Champion. Farr will always be remembered for his gallant performance against Joe Louis on 8 August 1937 in New York.

Bunty returned to the Queensberry Club to extinguish the flame of Edinburgh's Johnny Summers with a second-round knockout. Such was the power of the body punch that brought the contest to a quick conclusion that the unfortunate Summers, after receiving treatment in his corner, had to be carried from the ring. At the same venue a week later, Bunty was out-pointed by Sammy Reynolds from Wolverhampton.

On a bill in Birmingham, in which Irishman Martin Thornton out-pointed Canadian Arnold Hayes, and Nel Tarleton, the British Featherweight Champion, lost to Len Davies from Swansea, Bunty defeated Scotsman Jack Mackenzie by a clear margin.

Bob Gardiner

Whenever or wherever Bunty Doran was fighting, he never failed to grab the headlines. Descriptions of Doran's performances appeared in the local press with monotonous regularity. There was one occasion when, despite Bunty giving an outstanding performance in knocking out Jack Mussen in the third, he did fail to grab the sporting headlines. On 13 July 1943 at Solitude, the home of Cliftonville Football Club, Tommy Armour, the Northern Ireland Welterweight Champion, knocked out Eric Boon (Chatteris), the British Lightweight Champion, in the fifth round. Controversy raged after the fight when Jack Solomons, Boon's manager, said that he was "disgusted with what had happened in the ring". He believed that Armour should have been disqualified for hitting low and protested in vain to the British Board of Boxing Control. On the same bill, Ike Weir defeated Rinty Monaghan on points in a local flyweight title eliminator.

It wasn't long before Bunty was back in the headlines with two fights. He stopped Dublin boxer Billy Phelan in two rounds, while another Dubliner, Joe Collins, also succumbed to Doran's heavy punches, being stopped in round two.

Bunty's first fight of 1944 was in defence of his Northern Ireland flyweight title. His opponent was Ike Weir and the fight took place in the Stadium, Peter's Hill. It was obvious from the outset that Doran was going for a quick finish. Sure enough, the end came in the third round. Bunty was punching Weir in a neutral corner and the referee separated them. Immediately, Doran was at his opponent again, hitting him with a left hook and Weir went down for the full count.

Bunty won only two more fights in 1944. He knocked out Con Caffrey from Dublin in five rounds and, in a magnificent performance, which the papers described as "a notable win", Bunty defeated Glasgow's Hugh Cameron, the Scottish Flyweight Champion, on points over ten rounds. It was only the remarkable courage and pluck of the Glaswegian that enabled him to hang around long enough to see Doran's hand being raised in victory. In the course of the fight Cameron had taken five counts and frequently seemed to be out on his feet.

Jimmy Warnock, one of four fighting brothers from the Shankill Road, is best remembered for his two points wins in 1936 and 1937 over Benny Lynch, the reigning World and British Flyweight Champion. When Warnock stepped into the ring in The Hippodrome to meet Bunty Doran on 15 March 1945, he was giving away nine years. Jimmy had been inactive in 1944 but in his last two contests had scored points wins over Gibraltar's Dick Dyer and Con Caffrey; Bunty had won his last seven fights. For the first five rounds it was a pretty even contest until the supreme boxing and heavier punching of the younger man began to take its toll. In the seventh, Warnock was caught with a left hook; he went down but the bell sounded before a count was taken. In the eighth, Doran went for the kill and landed with both hands but the referee halted the proceedings.

Bunty's next job was in Wolverhampton against Norman Lewis, the Welsh Bantamweight Champion, who had lost only seven of his last fifty-three fights. Among these defeats was a knockout by Liverpool's Joe Curran in a final eliminator for the British flyweight title eight months previously. After some keen exchanges Bunty took an eight count in the third round. Lewis was later caught by a good right-hand punch and was floored for four. Doran was down again for eight in the fourth, but he fought back and forced the Welshman to retire at the end of the sixth session. Doran had performed well, considering that he had pulled a muscle in his left arm during the first round.

Two weeks after the Lewis bout, Bunty was in action in the Royal Albert Hall against Glasgow's Alec Murphy. Murphy, who was number three in the British flyweight ratings (three places above Bunty), had been a brilliant amateur, winning the Scottish ABA flyweight title in 1940, bantamweight title in 1941 and 1942, and both titles in 1943. However, he was knocked out in the second round by the Belfast man's speciality powerful left hook.

Bunty, by now a leading challenger for the British title, made it a hat-trick of wins in the space of five weeks when he defeated Southend's Mickey Jones, sinking the Royal Navy man in the seventh when Jones sustained a hand injury. He then renewed his acquaintance with Sammy Reynolds in a ten-round contest at Willenhall, resulting in a draw.

In Hamilton, Bunty doubled his victories against Hugh Cameron with a points win over ten rounds. On his return to action in the Ulster Hall, Bunty's many fans witnessed leading Welsh flyweight Ronnie Bishop being put to the sword by their hero. Bishop was knocked out in the fourth round.

Less than a week later in Leicester, Bunty defeated Mabelthorpe's Jimmy

Gill with a points win over eight rounds. Bunty, who was four-and-a-half pounds heavier, was fast and aggressive from the start. He found Gill willing to mix it, and there were some fast and furious exchanges in which both meted out a lot of punishment. The crowd applauded Gill for some smart work, but the Belfast lad kept on attacking and had the better of the exchanges.

On 6 November 1945, as part of a Bob Gardiner promotion in the Ulster Hall, came the eagerly awaited fight between Rinty Monaghan and Doran for the latter's Northern Ireland flyweight title. Fight fans were divided as to what the outcome would be, although Bunty was perhaps the slight favourite. The fight was of monumental importance to both men, who were vying for a shot at Jackie Paterson's world title. Monaghan created a sensation when he knocked Doran out in the fourth round. It was Bunty's impetuousness and carelessness in rushing around the ring that lost him the fight. Had he kept at a safe distance and allowed Monaghan to go on the offensive occasionally, the result might have been different. Instead, he kept rushing after Monaghan, discarding the boxing skills that made him one of the cleverest flyweights in Britain.

Doran scored most of his points with left-hand punches to Monaghan's face. It was during one of his rushes at Rinty that he took the right hook which put him down for a count of eight. It was a strong punch and it weakened Doran considerably. When he beat the count he was practically out on his feet. Monaghan had very little trouble in finishing the contest with a terrific right-hand punch that put a completely unguarded Doran down for the final count.

Rinty's jubilant supporters jumped to their feet, shouting and cheering so loudly that the MC's appeal for order was useless. Gradually, order was restored and Monaghan left the Ulster Hall after a song and with the first of his many titles.

After the loss of his flyweight title, Bunty got on with the job of earning a living. In London, he stopped Tommy Burney from Liverpool in three rounds and brought 1945 to a close in the King's Hall with a points win over Jimmy Gill.

He started his 1946 campaign in spectacular fashion, catapulting himself not only into the world's boxing headlines but, more importantly, into world title reckoning. In a non-title fight, he beat Jackie Paterson on points over ten rounds in the Theatre Royal, Dublin. Paterson had won his British, British Empire and world flyweight titles when, in June 1943, he knocked out Peter Kane from Golborne at Hampden Park in Glasgow. Eleven days after his defeat by Doran, Paterson would win the vacant European title by beating Frenchman Theo Medina.

Amazing scenes followed Bunty's victory. The majority of the four thousand people in the hall were on their feet, cheering vociferously and flinging papers and hats into the air. Inside a few seconds, the ring was flooded with Doran supporters as they attempted to embrace him and carry him around the ring. Gardaí rushed in and tried to keep the excited crowd at bay. At one corner of the ring, two enthusiastic fans had to be forcibly removed by police. Bunty had given a superb display of boxing, at times completely outclassing the champion.

The first two rounds were uneventful, with both boys exercising the utmost caution, although there were spasmodic bouts of in-fighting. Paterson was very fast and at times attempted to catch Doran with his famous left hook. However, the Belfast flyweight was far too clever. He kept at a safe distance, came in when the time was opportune and manoeuvred in such a fashion as to puzzle the champion. In the third round, Doran landed a solid right hook to Paterson's face and followed with a strong left to the body, which slowed the champion down. A vicious left swing by Paterson hit the air due to Doran's clever evasive tactics. The fourth round opened with Doran forcing the pace and catching his opponent occasionally with left swings. Paterson came back very strongly and landed a few body punches, but the Belfast man was undaunted. He eventually fought his man out into the centre of the ring, forcing him against the ropes where vicious in-fighting took place.

In the fifth, Doran continued his aggressiveness and struck Paterson two heavy blows to the head that drove him back against the ropes. In the sixth, Paterson came out very strongly and aimed at landing a knockout punch. He forced Doran into a corner where both of them mixed it hot and heavy. Doran moved out, made a swing with his left and Paterson countered with a right, which Doran luckily caught with an open glove. From this to the end, Doran was the stronger and kept forcing his man around the ring. He missed occasionally but was dangerous with heavy body punches. In the last round, not one of Doran's supporters had a palm that wasn't sweating. They had nothing to worry about because Paterson, intent on going the distance, kept moving away from Doran's full-blooded attack and the Scot was relieved to hear the bell.

Bunty then met Theo Medina in the King's Hall. He gave another outstanding performance, coming back from two knockdowns in the second round to stop the Frenchman, who sustained a badly injured eye in the sixth round. Four months later, Medina would avenge a European title defeat at the hands of Paterson when he regained his title after knocking Jackie out in the fourth.

Twenty-four-year-old Doran was now at the peak of his profession. In Brighton, he stopped Jimmy Webster from Canning Town in six rounds. He had a points win in Glasgow over Teddy O'Neill, the Scottish Bantamweight Champion; beat the Welsh Bantamweight Champion, Norman Lewis, for the second time in Port Talbot; and drew with Stratford's Johnny Boom.

Sports writers were full of praise for Doran and several of them expressed surprise when his name was omitted from the list of eliminators. One pointed out that Bunty had beaten all the champions – English, Scottish, Welsh and

Danny O'Sullivan

French – in the bantamweight division. The Boxing Board of Control replied that Doran was not an area titleholder. This incensed Bunty's manager, Tony Vairo, who applied to the Northern Ireland Board of Control demanding that Bunty be included in the eliminating series.

Two weeks into 1947, Bunty accounted for Georges Mousse, who as an amateur had been champion of Paris in 1944. He had won thirty-eight of his fifty-one fights wearing the vest. As a professional he would go on to lift the French bantamweight and featherweight titles. However, clever though he was, he was clearly out-pointed by Bunty in London's Seymour Hall.

In January 1947, the British Board of Boxing Control issued a statement saying that boxing booths were out of bounds to all their licensed members. A month later, Bunty met Peter Kane, who was not only a former booth fighter, but also an ex-World Flyweight Champion. Kane was four years Bunty's senior and boxing aficionados agreed that he was one of the hardest hitters the flyweight division had ever seen.

For his first crack at the British and World flyweight titles, Kane was knocked out by Benny Lynch in the thirteenth round at Glasgow's Shawfield Park. A year later, he captured the vacant title from the USA's Jackie Jurich at Anfield football grounds. He held the title from 1938 to 1943 until Jackie Paterson seized it from him. Going into the Kane fight, Bunty had won sixty-three of his seventy-four fights, while Kane had lost only four out of eighty-five contests. The former blacksmith had fought Belfast boxers before, having beaten Jimmy Stewart (rsc 10) in Belfast, Jimmy Warnock (rsc 4) in Liverpool and Tommy Madine (ko 4) in Nottingham.

The contest was staged in Belle Vue, Manchester. After a real thriller, the decision in favour of Kane was met with a mixed reception. Many thought that a draw would have been a fairer result. In the early rounds, it was nearly all Kane. He put Bunty down for a count of eight in the second from a right uppercut. Several times after that, Doran was in trouble but he stuck to his task and was never afraid to mix it. So well executed were his bobbing, weaving and swinging punches that, in the fifth round, Kane was a worried man.

Nevertheless, Kane carried the heavier punch and, in the sixth, he brought Doran up short with a right chop to the jaw. Bunty was now fully recovered from the earlier punches and seemed capable of absorbing punishment, always coming back for more. He landed twice in succession on Kane's jaw in the sixth and was actually forcing matters at the end of the round. The fight continued at the same killing pace in the seventh, both boys standing toe-to-toe and swapping punches with a will. There was little boxing skill and no quarter was asked for or given. The fight was fought first to one man's advantage and then to the other's with Doran doing slightly more forcing. The last round saw both fighters striving for a decisive blow. Both landed heavy punches to the head and body and at the conclusion it was difficult to say which of the two were ahead. Seven months later, Kane won the European bantamweight title, beating Theo Medina over fifteen hard-fought rounds.

Bunty cemented his claims to be included in British title eliminators. Within six weeks, he won the Northern Ireland bantamweight title by knocking out Belfast's Tommy Madine in four rounds and the All-Ireland bantamweight title when he knocked out Joe "Boy" Collins in one round, both in the Ulster Hall.

Despite having a broken bone in his right wrist and a disjointed knuckle, Bunty went the extra mile on a Bob Gardiner promotion in the King's Hall and scored a meritorious victory over Jean Jouas, a contender for the French bantamweight title. It was a brilliant display of defensive boxing by Doran, especially in the last two rounds when he was in apparent agony. Bunty claimed to have received his injuries in the first round when he had landed a right-hand punch on the Frenchman's head. Up to the seventh round the pain was merely troublesome. By the end of the eighth, it was so intense that he pleaded with his manager, Tony Vairo, to be allowed to retire. No one in the hall at that point was aware of how serious the injuries were. On the advice of his handlers, but with obvious reluctance, Bunty came out for the ninth, and it was in that particular round that he gave one of the most brilliant demonstrations of defensive boxing ever seen at a Belfast tournament. He scarcely allowed the Frenchman, who pursued him relentlessly, to lay a glove on him. Bunty received a tremendous ovation at the end of the round. The tenth round was practically a repetition of the previous one with Doran bobbing and weaving to steer out of trouble.

In his next outing, he was stopped by Joe Cornelius, the Bantamweight Champion of Belgium, when he received a cut eyebrow after a clash of heads. Up to that point, Bunty had provided the fans with an impressive display.

On 26 December, Doran met Manchester's Billy Tansey, but did not fight with his usual brilliance. Nevertheless, he proved too strong for Tansey and won on points over eight rounds.

Bunty had to wait ten years, during which time he accumulated sixty-seven wins, nine losses and four draws, before he was even involved in a British title eliminator. This was against Liverpool's Stan Rowan on 18 March 1948. Stan went into the fight with thirty-five wins, four losses and three draws under his belt.

Doran lost this eliminator yet gave a splendid performance, and his tearaway style had the crowd on its feet a number of times. He scored repeatedly in the early rounds with head and body blows, and in the fourth, he put Rowan down for six with a left to the head. Despite a cut on the left eye, picked up in the third round, he didn't let up and was ahead on points until the fifth. He was occasionally a bit wild in his swinging and this was probably the deciding factor in the verdict. Rowan was more methodical in his style and his well-timed blows gave him a slight edge. However the verdict in his favour was a narrow one.

Bunty's next fight couldn't have been any harder: a return, at four days notice, with Peter Kane. Kane had lost his European bantamweight title two months previously to Italian Guido Ferracin in Manchester. He dominated the fight from the start and Bunty retired in the eighth of their ten-round contest after being down for a count of four from a vicious right just above the heart. Walking to his corner, Bunty signalled his retirement and Kane was announced the winner, provoking an outburst of disapproval from the audience. Afterwards, Bunty said, "I only had four days to train for the fight. In the fourth round my right hand went. I tried to make a fight of it, but it was no use and I had to give up." It was the second time that Kane had beaten Bunty. In a return with Ferracin, three months after his win over Doran, Kane failed to regain his European title, being stopped when a clash of heads cut his eye.

Bunty next travelled to West Hartlepool to meet Teddy Gardner, but was beaten on points. Four months later in Belfast, Bunty would avenge his defeat by Gardner with a points victory. On St Patrick's Day in 1952 Teddy Gardner became British, British Empire and European Flyweight Champion when he beat Terry Allen in St James's Hall in Newcastle.

In between the two Gardner fights, Bunty showed splendid form in defeating the Belgian champion Gaston van den Bos in the Kelvin Hall, Glasgow.

In 1949 Bunty had five contests against quality opposition: Theo Medina; Georges Mousse, the French Featherweight Champion; Stan Rowan, the reigning British and Empire Bantamweight Champion; Guido Ferracin, the reigning European Champion; and last but not least, Danny O'Sullivan from London. O'Sullivan was a former amateur ABA champion, who did not turn professional until six months past his twenty-fourth birthday.

Bunty repeated his wins over the Frenchmen Medina and Mousse. Then, on 2 April 1949 at Dunmore Park, he once again shared a ring with Stan Rowan, who was now the holder of the bantamweight title.

Doran was after Rowan quicker than the greyhounds coming out of the traps at Dunmore. The second round was dominated by the ferocity of Doran's attacks. Rowan absorbed a steady beating from the Belfast man and took no fewer than six counts. From that point until he retired at the end of the sixth round, Rowan was no more than a chopping block. His defence was non-existent against Doran's full-blooded attacks to the head and body. Doran landed vicious right and left-hand punches forcefully and frequently. It looked like the biggest mismatch since the lions and the Christians.

When Rowan went down for the first count, the audience became so excited that hundreds rushed from the back towards the ring and the cheers were so loud that no one could hear the count. Officials had to race forward to stem the crowds. For the entire period of the second round excitement was at fever pitch with fans standing on seats, waving hats and cheering hysterically.

In the third, Doran scored repeatedly with head and body punches. Rowan seemed to be in a daze and made no effort to counter the avalanche of punches that came from all directions. Doran was looking for a knockout. He pursued the gritty Liverpool boy around the canvas jungle, landing rights and lefts. He did miss occasionally but not too often. Rowan's only refuge was to get into a clinch and the referee twice warned him for holding. He presented a pitiful sight towards the end of the round. He was completely exhausted and unable to lift a hand to fend off the shower of punches that landed to his face and body, and took two more counts of four. The fourth round again saw Doran fighting with ferocity, sweeping Rowan across the ring. The Englishman's legs buckled following a beautifully timed right to the head and it looked as if the British champion would go down again, but he got into several clinches and held on until the end of the round.

In the fifth, Doran looked as if he had punched himself out and seemed to ease up a little. He was still scoring and, at the end of the round, Rowan seemed to stagger a bit. When he came out for the sixth, Rowan's right eye was badly swollen and his face was in a state. He moved slowly around the ring, covering himself up as best he could against the torrent of Doran's blows, never once retaliating. Doran hit him where and when he pleased, yet Rowan remained on his feet to the amazement of all present. For his outstanding performance against Rowan, Bunty was awarded the *Boxing News* Certificate of Merit.

After Doran's great win, Bob Gardiner announced that he would be making arrangements for him to meet Guido Ferracin for the European bantamweight title. True to his word, the European champion was lined up to meet Bunty in the King's Hall for a non-title fight seven weeks later. However, Bunty didn't produce his best that night and, in a dull fight, he was out-pointed over ten rounds.

Although Rinty Monaghan retained his World, British, Empire and European flyweight titles at the King's Hall on 30 September 1949, Bunty was knocked out in the twelfth by Danny O'Sullivan in a final eliminator for the British bantamweight title. O'Sullivan had never found it easy to make the bantamweight limit and, while Bunty was strong at 118lbs, O'Sullivan just made it. Going into the last round, it was a toss-up as to who was in front. The bell sounded and O'Sullivan sprang from the stool like an arrow

Bunty in his later years

leaving the bow. He sailed into Bunty and punched with such venom and ferocity that Doran was taken by surprise. Powerful blows rained on the Belfast man and, under their impact, he was driven into the ropes and battered through the bottom strands, where he hung until counted out. It was a truly dramatic finish. Afterwards, Bunty was taken to the Mater hospital suffering from concussion. Three months later, O'Sullivan won the British bantamweight title when he stopped Teddy Gardner in nine rounds at the Albert Hall. He lost his title after Peter Keenan knocked him out in the sixth when they met in Glasgow.

In June 1950, Bunty beat Kid Francis from the Gold Coast on points over eight rounds in the Ulster Hall. He got a final chance for the big time when he travelled to Paisley to meet Peter Keenan in an eliminator for the British bantamweight title. Keenan, a professional since September 1948, had remained undefeated in twenty-two fights. His victims included Jackie Briers, Mickey McLaughlin, Raoul Degryse (the former European Boxing Union Flyweight Champion), Jean Sneyers – who would take the title from Degryse – and Maurice Sandeyron, who had also held the European flyweight title. Would Bunty avail of this final opportunity to get a shot at the title? The answer was no. Although the little man had beaten British champions Paterson and Gardner in non-title fights, he seemed to falter when it mattered most – in the eliminators.

Bunty was down in the first round, more from a push than a punch, and was up before a count started. He appeared stronger in the second but the Scot just shaded it. In the third, Keenan was warned for holding and a bruise appeared under both his eyes. Bunty seemed to be getting on top, while the fourth and fifth rounds were fairly level.

With his more precise punching and good left leads, the sixth went to Keenan. Then in the seventh, he found himself in trouble when, following his second warning for holding, Doran split Keenan's left eye. A further warning for holding came Peter's way in the eighth. Doran was out of luck in the ninth when a long right caught Keenan not quite on the point and the Scot, although slightly shaken, kept on the move. Bunty went all out in the final session but it was Keenan who landed what was almost a finishing punch – a vicious right hook – that shook Bunty to his foundations. He managed to finish the round through sheer instinct.

Doran had fought and beaten British, World and former European champions. In Durban in November 1950, he faced another world champion in the form of the South African Vic Toweel. Toweel had won the title when he beat Mexico's Manuel Ortiz in May 1950. Ortiz had won the title in 1942 when he beat Louis Salica from the USA in Los Angeles, and had defended it fifteen times before losing to American, Harold Dade. Ortiz regained the title from Dade and defended it a further four times before losing it to Toweel in Johannesburg. So this was a daunting task for the Belfast man, especially with the fight being in the South African's own backyard.

Bunty, who was four ounces over the stipulated nine stone, was completely outclassed in every department. He was hammered into submission in the ninth round of a ten-round non-title fight. Toweel, who had generously agreed to waive his right to the £50 forfeit by Doran for being overweight, dominated the fight in front of six thousand spectators. The ninth was only thirty seconds in when Doran, against the ropes in one corner, was severely punished with a succession of wicked blows to the head and body. The referee called a halt to the proceedings. Bunty had showed an amazing capacity for absorbing punishment. He was knocked down only once, and that was for a count of one in the third round. Even with his experience of ninety-three fights, Bunty was helpless before his twenty-two-year-old opponent, who was having his sixteenth fight in the paid ranks.

Bunty had only one fight in 1951, taking on Jackie Briers, the former Northern Ireland Flyweight Champion, on Boxing Day in the Ulster Hall. Much to the surprise of everyone, Bunty retained his Northern Ireland and All-Ireland bantamweight titles. The majority of fans believed that Bunty's lack of action and rumours about his weight problems made him vulnerable against Briers, who had won all six of his contests that year.

After the first two rounds, during which Briers did some damaging punching to the middle at close quarters, the fighting was stale until the seventh. Almost on the bell, Doran had his right eyelid badly gashed in a collision of heads. Blood poured from the wound but the seconds did a good job in staunching the flow. Briers went on the attack in the eighth and landed several damaging punches to the eye injury. Doran then seemed to go fighting-mad and shook Briers, punching heavily to the body and head. This was the most exciting round of the fight. Briers' punching seemed to weaken after this. In the twelfth, he crossed two rights to Doran's jaw that had little effect. Doran's eye started bleeding again in this round. A fighting finish in the final round probably gave Bunty his victory.

Bunty, now aged thirty, was coming to the end of his career. In his only contest of 1952, in February at the Royal Albert Hall, he lost to Ron Johnson from Bethnal Green on points over eight rounds.

It was almost a year before Bunty boxed again, losing clearly to Bobby Dodoo from the Gold Coast. Four weeks later, Bunty was in action against Andy Monahan from Preston. Although it wasn't the Bunty of old, he had enough savvy to edge home. A fortnight later, in the Ulster Hall, Bunty met the experienced Jackie Fairclough from Preston, who was also coming to the end of his career. It wasn't a bad night for the Irish champion; not only did beat Fairclough on points over eight rounds, but he weighed in at 8st 5^1/2lbs, half a pound inside the bantamweight limit. Bunty made it three wins in a row when he stopped the Liverpudlian Terry McHale in four rounds on a Dundalk card.

In the penultimate fight of Bunty Doran's career he was matched with Neville Tetlow from Manchester in the Ulster Hall. Tetlow had won sixteen of his last twenty-seven fights and had beaten George O'Neill (twice), Jackie Briers, Chic Brogan and Jimmy Cardew. However, he had succumbed to John Kelly in 1952. In the first two rounds it seemed that Tetlow would win quite easily. A couple of sharp right crosses had jolted Doran's head back, the first one almost putting him down. Doran had crowded his opponent and tried to fluster him out of his stride, but Tetlow did not appear to be unduly worried. In fact, he seemed so confident and dangerous that it looked like he would win inside the distance. By the third, it was quite clear that Doran's policy of bustling Tetlow around the ring was beginning to annoy and worry him. Bunty crowded in with his hooks and swings, yet Tetlow was the crisper puncher and deserved his points win.

On Saturday 27 June 1953, Bunty put his Northern Ireland and All-Ireland bantamweight titles on the line against up-and-coming-star John Kelly. Kelly was undefeated in eighteen contests and had been voted "Boxer of the Year" by the Dalzell Shield Committee. From the opening bell, it was obvious that Bunty would have to produce something extra special to remain champion. When he took a count of eight in the second, his crown began to tilt ever so slightly. Over the remaining rounds Bunty was punished by his young tormentor and, at the end of the eleventh, Minty Rose threw in the towel. There were warm handshakes all round and young Kelly appeared apologetic for dethroning the old warrior. These titles were bread and butter for Kelly. Four months later, in the King's Hall, he would beat Peter Keenan over fifteen rounds. Kelly accomplished in two years what Bunty had gamely striven to do over fifteen.

Bunty knew when it was time to quit. In his prime, he was always hovering on the periphery of the big time, but hard as he tried, he just could never clear the penultimate obstacles that were the title eliminators. He remains to this day one of the best little battlers never to win a major title.

Doran passed on to the great ring in the sky on 7 January 1996, taking the final count at the age of seventy-five.

PROFESSIONAL CAREER
1938–1953: 101 traced contests: won 77, lost 20, drew 4.

Al Gibson

Remnant of a forgotten era

David Brown, a youth of stocky build, who like his father was an avid fight fan, sat in the marquee in the Arena, Chapel Fields in Belfast. He was eagerly anticipating a good evening's boxing when his thoughts were suddenly interrupted by the voice of the matchmaker for the proceedings saying, "Hello son, my name's Alfie Kayes. I was wondering if you would be interested in putting on the gloves this evening and helping myself and Mrs Copley out?" The fifteen-year-old thought that Mr Kayes was joking and just smiled.

"Well, what do you think?" Kayes persisted, going on to explain that local boxer "Nutt" McKee was looking for an opponent. When Brown replied in the affirmative, Kayes was not in the least surprised. There was something about this kid. He had an air of confidence about him and displayed neither emotion nor nerves at the prospect of entering the squared circle. So, in August 1938, on a Ma Copley promotion, and clad in hand-me-down gear, Brown, using the name Al Gibson, made his entrance into the world of boxing by out-pointing "Nutt" McKee.

He chose the mantle that he did because he knew Al Gibson, the schoolboy soccer international, and it was the first name to enter his head. He did not want his parents, and in particular his mother, to know that he had risked life and limb by entering the world of pugilism for a few bob. As it happened, when he approached Ma Copley's caravan after the fight to ask for his money, the Grand Old Lady of Belfast Boxing told him, "Son, I have no money for you. The five shillings will do for your boxing licence."

David was born on 6 September 1922 in Joseph Street on the Shankill Road to Edward and Agnes Brown. Edward was a carter for the Belfast Corporation. David had three sisters and one brother and was educated in Deacon

The great Ma Copley

Memorial on McTier Street. He later obtained employment in White, Tomkins and Courage, a Henry Street company that produced oatmeal. The bulk of his working life, however, was spent as a plater in the Belfast shipyard. David could also read music as easily as he could the alphabet and was awarded a Certificate of Music for his outstanding ability as a drummer in the Burma Pipe Band.

On that fateful night at the Chapel Fields, David had deputised for Johnny Basham against "Nutt" McKee and came home penniless. Nevertheless, his victory over McKee made up his mind to forego a musical career for one in the ring. Permanently adopting Al Gibson as his fighting name, he joined the Corinthians Boxing Club in Tobergill Street in 1937, where he was looked after by professional fighter, Billy Armour. That year happened to be a good one for the club with Charlie Brown, a brilliant product of local amateur boxing, winning the Ulster flyweight title, before lifting the bantamweight title a year later. Another Corinthians lad, W S Jamison, won the Ulster lightweight title the same year. Perhaps the best-known Corinthians student at that time was twenty-one-year-old Tommy Armour who, since turning professional in 1936, had won thirteen out of fourteen fights, eleven via the short route. Armour would go on to win the Northern Ireland welterweight title in March 1939, when he stopped the

Al with his trainer, Harry Fulton

holder Jack Walsh in the third round. The greatest win of Tommy's career was when he knocked out the British Lightweight Champion, Eric Boon, at Cliftonville Football Ground on 13 July 1943.

Al trained hard and often at Corinthians, paying particular attention to his roadwork, which entailed covering six or more miles, morning and evening, several days a week on the Cavehill Road. Ten months after his victory over "Nutt" McKee, Al made his official debut on 20 June 1938. The men who sat on the eight thrones of British boxing on that day were: flyweight Benny Lynch (Glasgow); bantamweight Johnny King (Manchester); featherweight Johnny McGrory (Glasgow); lightweight Jimmy Walsh (Chester), who would lose his title to Dave Crowley three days later; welterweight Jack Kilrain (Bellshill); middleweight Jock McAvoy (Rochdale); light-heavyweight Len Harvey (Callington) and heavyweight Tommy Farr (Tonypandy). With such big names to contend with, Gibson still attracted a few lines in the local daily papers over his defeat of Young Cullen from Belfast on points in four rounds at Chapel Fields. Column inches notwithstanding, Al's main concern was to make as much money from boxing as possible for both himself and his family.

A month later, in a packed Arena, Young Warnock from Belfast out-pointed Preston's Cyril Maudsley in the main event of the evening. Further down the bill, Belfast's Jim Dunlop out-pointed Herbert Booth from Chesterfield, Jim Bryson stopped Jackie Donnelly in the fourth round of a Belfast derby bout, and the young apprentice Al Gibson out-pointed local boxer Billy Lester over four rounds.

Al was an extremely intelligent young man and knew that things would not always go to plan, that there would be hurdles at which he would falter. Two such hurdles came in the space of a month when he lost on points to Lisburn's Tommy Wilson and Jack Gillen from Belfast. On 12 September 1938, in what was Al's first trip over the eight-round journey, he avenged his defeat by Gillen with a points win. Although he would lose once again to Wilson, who had twice gone the distance with Bunty Doran, Al put up a splendid performance in his first Ulster Hall contest. There was plenty of in-fighting, with Wilson scoring with well-placed lefts and rights to the head and body.

Al contributed two outstanding performances to 1938. The first was

Al with Thomas "Hitman" Hearns in Belfast's City Hall, 2004

against Belfast man Bobby Spiers, whom he knocked out in the second round. In the second, he stopped another Belfast scrapper, Alex Meharg, in the sixth and final round at the Sports Stadium in Cuba Street.

Alongside a promising start to his sporting career, 1938 was also important for being the year that Al met his future wife, Thomasina McAteer, while attending Sunday school in the Joseph Street Mission Hall. The happy couple would marry on 29 August 1942. Two sons and a daughter would follow.

There were many exciting contests on the Ulster Hall bill for 1 February 1939. Just as the good wine is always kept to the last, the best fight of the evening, according to the local "scribblers", was the final one when Lisburn's Jim Thompson defeated Al Gibson on points over eight rounds.

From 25 February until 3 September 1939, Al Gibson had eight contests, winning three, losing four and drawing one. The details are as follows: Dixie McCall (Belfast) (lost pts 8), Jim Josephs (Carrickfergus) (won rtd 1), Jim Josephs (lost pts 8), Mick McAloran (Belfast) (lost pts 8), Jim Josephs (lost pts 6), Jim Farlow (Belfast) (won pts 6), Jim Bryson (Belfast) (drew 6), and

Jim Bryson (won pts 6). At the end of the year, Al had two defeats, dropping points decisions to Belfast boxers Sammy Wilson and Jim O'Brien.

In 1940, Al joined forces with Harry Fulton, who had founded the Star Boxing Club with his half-brother, "Akkie" Kelly. The club at that time was in Kent Street, just off Royal Avenue. On an Ulster Hall bill on 9 March, the principal contest was between Belfast's Jim McStravick and Ginger Murphy from Newry, with the former winning in round eight. That night also saw Al defeat Jim O'Brien on points, avenging his loss the previous year. Al would have three more contests that year, losing on points to Mick Gibbons, drawing with Private Johnny Dowling from Liverpool and, on 10 April in the Ulster Hall, knocking out Jim Farlow with a right hook to the solar plexus in the second round.

There were no Ulster or ABA championships in 1941 and 1942, and Al did not resume boxing until 1943. When he did return, he dropped decisions to Phil Milligan from Belfast, Tony McGowan from Derry, Jim Coates from Lisburn and Jack Dale from Cavan. In return fights with Dale and McGowan, however, he did manage to share the spoils. All of these fights took place at the Ulster Stadium.

In his first contest of 1944, Al met Lurgan's Max Brady on 29 January. Brady won on points that night and again, four months later, in Dungannon. When the pair met for a third time on 24 August 1946, it was Al's hand being held aloft by referee Andy Smyth after twelve rounds of boxing in the Ulster Hall. This contest should have decided who was to face Tommy Madine for the vacant Northern Ireland bantamweight title, but Al came in overweight and forfeited his big opportunity. Brady got a crack at the title on 24 March 1947 and lost to Madine. Eddie "Bunty" Doran was to seize the crown from Madine when he knocked him out on 5 May 1947.

1944 also saw Al beating Belfast's Tommy Gibbons (rtd 4), drawing with Bob McMillan from Lisburn and, in an exciting trilogy of fights with Belfast man Jackie Stephens, Gibson came out on top each time.

Al got off to a fine start in 1945 when, during a Michael Kelly promotion in Derry's Guildhall, on 31 January, he bored in from the opening bell, quickly connecting with two hard punches to Jim Girr's jaw and bringing the contest to an abrupt end.

In the Guildhall on 17 April that year, Ginger Watters from Lisburn was sent through the ropes by Jim Doran from Belfast in the second round. He was assisted back to the ring by spectators and the referee only took up the count on his return. Protesting at the interference by fans and at the fact that the count had not been started until his opponent had been assisted back through the ropes, Doran refused to continue and left the ring. Watters was declared the winner. On the same bill, Al drew with Dick Dyer from Gibraltar over eight rounds in a £25-a-side challenge fight. Recalling this fight, Al said, "Dyer caught me on the solar plexus and I went down in agony. Jim Creanor, the referee, took up the count and I got to my feet at eight. The

referee took a close look at me and asked, 'Are you all right?' I said to Jim Creanor, 'I wish I was.'" At the Ulster Hall on 19 September, in his last fight of the year, Al lost on points to local boy Jack Holland. He would meet Holland on three more occasions, losing twice, but earning a draw in their final encounter.

On 6 April 1946, Gibson renewed his acquaintance with Dick Dyer, and this time he made no mistake, winning on points over eight rounds in the Ulster Hall.

Pat Kelly, a rapidly improving local, had to pull out all he knew to get the better of a determined Gibson when the pair met over eight rounds in the main bout of the evening in the Ulster Hall on 4 May 1946. From the first ding to the last dong it was a terrific battle, keeping the crowd on tenterhooks throughout and when it was all over both boys got a terrific ovation. After this gallant effort, Al beat Derry's Paddy Harkin but lost his next two contests against Jackie Holland and Charlie Meikle respectively.

In the Ulster Hall on 19 April 1947, Jackie Holland beat Al for the third time, winning on points over eight rounds. Although there were bouts of heavy punching, try as they would, neither boxer was able to land a finishing blow. In the opening round, a right to the jaw shook Gibson and he was forced to hang on. As the referee shouted, "Break", Holland was caught with lefts and rights to the body. It was obvious that both boys were out for the kill, manoeuvring to land the pay-off punch, without success. When Holland was awarded the decision a section of the crowd loudly booed.

Al had not been near the gym for two weeks when he took a job at short notice against the talented Jim McCann. The touch of rust proved his downfall and he was stopped in the third round.

From August to December, Al had three contests, losing to Dublin's Jackie McGouran (pts 8) and drawing with Belfast's Jackie Holland. He gave himself a nice Christmas present when, in the Ulster Hall, he waded into Fred Wade from Halifax, halting him in the fourth round.

Al travelled to St Mungo's Hall in Glasgow on 7 January 1948 to face a formidable opponent in the shape of Jim Kenny from Polmont. Among the list of fighters who had fallen prey to Kenny's mighty punching were: Billy Whitelaw (ko 1), Frank McFarlane (ko 2), Basil Magee (rtd 3), Neilly McIntyre (ko 1), Owen Durkins (ko 1), Roy McGregor (ko 3), Joe Lynam (ko 5), Pat Cahill (ko 1), Bernard Pugh (rtd 3), Jackie Ryan (rtd 2), Sean Phillips (ko 2) and Jack Duffy (ko 1). Like these men, Al was unfortunate to meet Kenny on one of his good days and was knocked out in the first round. St Mungo's provided a bad night generally for Belfast boxers because, on the same bill, Clydebank's Johnny Smith knocked out Paddy Trainor, while Scottish champion Willie Whyte stopped Jim McFadden. In 1950, Kenny attempted to win the British featherweight title but was beaten by Ronnie Clayton at the Royal Albert Hall.

Al shrugged off the loss to Kenny and, in the Ulster Hall on 24 January, he stopped Dubliner Sean Tallon in the sixth round. In the same venue just over two weeks later, in what was easily the best fight of the night, he out-pointed Bernard Pugh from Liverpool. The night began with the crowd standing for a minute's silence in sympathy with Mrs Copley and her family on the death of her son, Percy. Al scaled at 9st 8lbs, while Pugh, the British Army Featherweight Champion, weighed in at 9st 5lbs. It was a hard-punching duel from the start and Al looked strong at the lightweight poundage. He surprised the Liverpool man, especially with the power of his right-handers. Pugh started to find his target in the third and fourth rounds, yet Gibson fought strongly to hold his winning margin in keen close-quarter exchanges. He had Pugh down for seven in the fifth heat, a powerful right swing to the jaw doing the damage. Pugh tried to turn the tables in the closing rounds but Gibson's supremacy proved outstanding and the referee's tally of the points was a mere formality. Next time out, however, in a fight that could have gone either way, Al lost to Billy Crapper from Warsop.

Gibson made his debut in the King's Hall on 28 September on a bill in which nine thousand fans witnessed a thrilling clash between Gerry Smyth and Jim Keery. Keery won in the fourth when Smyth sustained a cut eye. Unfortunately Al, despite giving one of the gamest performances of his career, was knocked out by Pat Kelly in an eliminator for the vacant Northern Ireland lightweight title. When he was sitting in the dressing room after the fight, Al blew his nose and was shocked when his eye almost came out. He went to the hospital with £175 in his pocket, the biggest purse of his career.

Gibson's boxing career was now winding down. Having blazed a merry trail in the local arenas for ten years, he was determined to go out the way he had come in – with a win. He did this in style when he gave Manchester's Jack Collins something of a going-over for five of the six rounds that their bout lasted. Collins was groggy in the third and took an eight count in the fourth. He was strong in the fifth but in the sixth Gibson attacked him like it was a matter of life or death. The Mancunian beat the count three times before his corner tossed in the towel. For his very last contest, in the Ulster Hall on 30 April 1949, Al out-pointed Mickey Foyle from Coatbridge.

With his ring days over, Al returned to work as a plater in the shipyard. On retirement he dedicated twenty years of his life to raising funds for the Northern Ireland Polio Fellowship on the Antrim Road; for one year, Al was the charity's chairman. From 1989 to 2005, he was Secretary of the Northern Ireland Ex-Boxers' Association, a role that he performed superbly. Sadly, Al was dealt a terrible blow on 23 February 1996, when he lost his beloved wife and best friend Thomasina.

Al had been a perpetual motion type of fighter throughout his career, buzzing and stinging with the best of them. Never less than entertaining in the ring, we can only be thankful that, in August 1937, he was around to step into Johnny Basham's boots at short notice.

PROFESSIONAL CAREER
1937–1947: 59 traced contests: won 25, lost 27, drew 7.

Paddy Slavin

Mixed it with some of the best in Britain

Despite making his home in Kircubbin, County Down, Gerald Patrick Slavin was actually born in Aughnacloy. The date was 9 January 1927, and his parents were Joseph Slavin, a shipyard worker from the County Tyrone town, and Mary Slavin (née Speers), a native of Ballygawley. Paddy attended the National School in Aughnacloy but when he was eight years old, he moved with his family to Huddersfield. After a lengthy spell in England, the family decided to return home, but Paddy – one of six boys and three girls in the Slavin clan – opted for a naval career. He joined the Huddersfield Sea Cadets and, during the war, was a seaman gunner on the battle cruiser *Nelson*. It was while at sea that the big Tyrone man served his boxing apprenticeship,

learning not only to roll with the waves, but to roll with the punches.

Paddy's professional career commenced in the Ulster Hall on 22 November 1947 with a win (rsc 5) over tough Mullingar boxer Chris Cole. The Westmeath man was all at sea against Slavin and was stopped in the fifth with a badly gashed left eyebrow.

It may be punctuated by losses, especially in the later years, but if Paddy's record were to be scrutinised fairly, it would be seen that he mixed it with the best in Britain. Among these opponents was Battersea's Don Cockell, who beat Paddy on points on 29 March 1949 over eight rounds in Earl's Court, London. Don would go on to win the vacant British light-heavyweight title when he knocked out Mark Hart from Croydon in the fourteenth round in October 1950. He also garnered the vacant European light-heavyweight title by stopping Frenchman Albert Yvel in six rounds in March 1951, and the British and British Empire

heavyweight titles when he beat Johnny Williams from Rugby on points over fifteen rounds in May 1953. What mature boxing fan could ever forget the bravery shown by Cockell in his fruitless quest for world title glory against Rocky Marciano in San Francisco in May 1955, when the referee mercifully stopped the slaughter in round nine? In October 1952, Cockell met Paddy for a second time, winning in two rounds.

Slavin also took on Johnny Williams, who stopped Paddy in three rounds at Birmingham City's football ground on 20 June 1949. Williams would go on to win the British and British Empire heavyweight titles when he beat the moustachioed Jack Gardner from Market Harborough on points in March 1952. This was always going to be a difficult hurdle for Paddy to clear as Williams had lost only twice in his previous thirty-nine contests – twenty-two inside the distance.

Welshman Dennis Powell would meet Paddy on three occasions, drawing one, winning one and losing one. Powell won the vacant British light-heavyweight title when he beat Stepney's George Walker in eleven rounds in March 1953.

Jamaica's Joe Bygraves defeated Paddy three times in the course of eight months, and went on to win the British Empire heavyweight title, beating Kitione Lave from Trinidad over fifteen rounds in June 1956.

And finally, Blackpool's Brian London stopped Paddy in two rounds on 11 July 1955, and would go on to win the British and British Empire heavyweight titles when he knocked out Joe Erskine in June 1958. London would unsuccessfully challenge for the world heavyweight crown on two occasions, being stopped by Floyd Patterson and Muhammad Ali.

With his maiden voyage into the professional ranks safely negotiated against Chris Cole, Paddy was managed by former Irish Featherweight Champion Frank McAloran. He sailed through his next six contests, torpedoing Battling Igo (Halifax) (rsc 4), Paddy Quirke (Dublin) (twice) (ko 1 on both occasions), Tommy Smythe (Mayo) (rtd 3), George Dawson (Wales) (rtd 3), and winning on points against Alex Woods (Randalstown). However, he ran into choppy waters in Birmingham when he was out-pointed by Tom Reddington from Salford, a boxer who would win sixty of his eighty-one fights.

Paddy got back into the winning habit when he knocked out Doug Mansfield from Derby in two rounds and, one month later in London, stopped Fulham's Frank Ronan in seven. Next time out, unfortunately, Johnny Barton from Lancaster halted Paddy in one round in a contest in Harringay Arena.

On 25 December 1948 in the Ulster Hall, Paddy gave himself and his fans a nice Christmas present when, in a fight that ended unexpectedly, he beat Alex Woods to win, at the age of twenty-one, the Northern Ireland heavyweight title. Woods, who had been severely punished in the opening round and was down for nine, twisted his ankle at the commencement of the second and his corner threw in the towel. It was the second time that Paddy had beaten Woods, a former Northern Ireland Light-Heavyweight Champion.

With ten wins out of twelve contests, Paddy was number six in the 1948 *Boxing News* Annual British Ratings for Bruce Woodcock's heavyweight title. Ahead of him were Charlie Collett from Watford, Reg Andrews from Deal, Alf Brown from Nuneaton, Jack London from West Hartlepool and Ken Shaw from Dundee. From 1948 to 1954 Paddy was never out of the top ten, his highest position being number five in 1952 when Johnny Williams was the heavyweight king.

One of Paddy Slavin's obituary notices read "He fought a good fight", and he certainly did in the King's Hall on 1 March 1949. As well as being the day that Joe Louis announced his retirement and relinquished his heavyweight

Paddy and his "Ma"

title, it was also the date on which Paddy came back from the brink of defeat against Sligo-born Gerry McDermott to win the All-Ireland heavyweight title on points over fifteen rounds.

Although Paddy started off in confident style, things looked black for him in the fourth round when he touched down for nine after taking a vicious punch to the body. He got himself up off the floor and only just managed to beat the fatal ten count, hanging on until the bell. Most of the fans at this stage were convinced that Paddy would not go the distance but, from the fifth round onwards, the big man took control and the result was never in doubt. When it was all over he was given a tremendous ovation. For his outstanding performance against McDermott, Paddy received the *Boxing News* Certificate of Merit.

On St Patrick's Day in 1949, Mrs Clara Copley, who had promoted fights for many years, died in Belfast at the age of eighty-three. That same year, on 24 September, the promising Belfast bantamweight Eddie McCullough, who, like Paddy Slavin, was managed by Frank McAloran, died in hospital, aged twenty-one.

In Paddy's first outing as All-Ireland Heavyweight Champion he was out-pointed by Don Cockell in London, and two consecutive defeats followed when he dropped decisions to Johnny Williams (rsc 3) and Lloyd Barnett from Jamaica (pts 8). The Ulster Hall crowd wasn't too happy with the latter result and they loudly booed the decision in favour of the giant West Indian boxer, who was fortunate to survive a torrid final round.

The Irish heavyweight had three more pay days in 1949. In the King's Hall on 24 June, on the same bill that Guido Ferracin, the European Bantamweight Champion, defeated Bunty Doran, there was a surprising and somewhat amusing ending to Paddy's fight with Egyptian Amad Ben Abdullah. In the fourth round, Abdullah started in whirlwind fashion, attacking Slavin with a two-handed barrage. Paddy forced his opponent into a corner and let go with a flourish of rights and lefts. This evidently sickened the Egyptian boxer, who looked as if he was short of ideas on how to get out of this tight spot. Suddenly, Abdullah stopped, lifted Paddy's hand to indicate that the Irishman was the winner and walked to his corner, leaving Slavin and everyone else in the famous venue more than a little bewildered.

In his penultimate contest of 1949, in the Hippodrome, Paddy lost on points over eight rounds to Canadian Heavyweight Champion, Don Mogard. In this, the main contest of the evening, Mogard opened up well, scoring with straight lefts. In the second, he was still on the offensive, coming in with rushes, but the Irish boy stopped him with straight punches. In the fourth, Slavin opened up with a terrific two-fisted attack, which shook the Canadian, while in the fifth Paddy's solid and accurate punching opened a cut over Mogard's left eye. After this, the local boy faded out of the picture and, despite rallying prior to the final bell, it was too little too late. Three months previously, the Canadian had withstood the sledgehammer blows of Rocky Marciano to become the first boxer to go the distance with "The Rock", who had won his first fifteen fights by knockout. Paddy's final contest of the year saw him boxing a draw with Welshman Dennis Powell.

On a George Connell promotion in the King's Hall on 22 February 1950, the top of the bill was a fifteen-round contest for the Northern Ireland Featherweight Championship between Eddie Magee and Jim McCann. McCann retained his title while, in a tough and bruising battle, Paddy touched gloves again with Dennis Powell, this time beating the Welsh Heavyweight Champion with whom he had drawn five months earlier.

Paddy lost his next three contests to the Dutchman Willie Schagen (pts 8), Piet Wilde from Belgium (pts 10) and the USA's Mel Brown (ko 1). However, his biggest loss of that year occurred when his first wife Annie died while giving birth to their second child. In his final contest of 1950, in London's Empress Hall, the Aughnacloy boxer knocked out Johnny McLeavey in the fourth round.

Paddy avenged a defeat by Willie Schagen when he met the Dutch Cruiserweight Champion on 26 March 1951 in the Ulster Hall. The fight was stopped at the end of the third round when Schagen sustained a damaged right eye. On April 30 in London, Slavin was out-pointed by Albert Finch, the former British Middleweight Champion. Then in Liverpool, Paddy did the out-pointing against Ansell Adams from Trinidad. The Irishman had a comfortable evening against the West Indian, who was giving away two stone.

During an evening of boxing in the Ulster Hall on 1 December 1951, twenty-one-year-old Tom Meli won the Northern Ireland middleweight crown when he beat Jackie Wilson, who was ten years his senior. As part of the same bill, Paddy beat Belfast rival Garnett Denny on points. Denny would shout long and hard in vain for a crack at Slavin's heavyweight title.

Paddy's boxing fortunes changed dramatically from 1952 onwards. His heart didn't seem to be in the game anymore. A friend of his confided that the big man had once said to him, "I'm just in the game to make a few quid – nothing else." Paddy did continue to entertain the fans but found victories hard to come by. He dropped decisions to Ansell Adams, Dennis Powell, Lou Strydom from South Africa, Don Cockell, Terry McDonald from Cudworth, Croydon's Mark Hart, Frank Bell from Barnoldswick, Joe Bygraves, Peter Bates from Shirebrook, Brian London, Cliff Purnell from Bath, Cardiff's Trevor Snell and George Cooper from Smethwick. He still had his moments of glory with wins over Lloyd Barnett, Glasgow's George Stern, the Londoner Joe Crickmar, Trinidad's Sammy Mercier and Johnny Williamson from Gloucester, as well as Bell and Purnell, whom he had conceded fights to.

The former seaman was in all probability contemplating dropping anchor on his career. On 18 February 1960 in the Theatre Royal, Dublin, he beat Cliff Purnell once again, winning on points over eight stanzas. Just over two months later, in the King's Hall, on the same bill that saw Johnny van Rensburg out-point Billy Kelly, Paddy took his All-Ireland heavyweight title out of mothballs for the first time in eleven years and put it on the line against twenty-two-year-old Dubliner, Pat Stapleton. Not unexpectedly, Slavin lost to the younger and stronger boxer who controlled the fight every step of the way. The referee stopped the contest in the sixth, after thirty-three-year-old Slavin sustained a badly gashed left eyebrow.

Paddy Slavin threw his first punch on 22 November 1947 and his last on 23 April 1960. He may not quite have climbed to the top of the boxing ladder but he did give thousands of boxing fans hours of pleasure with his gutsy performances. He died on 28 October 2004.

PROFESSIONAL CAREER
1947–1963: 55 traced contests: won 25, lost 28, drew 2.

Tom Meli

A gentleman and a formidable opponent

Tom Meli's grandparents, Alfredo and Mary, emigrated from Genoa in Italy to Belfast in the late 1800s. With true grit and a determination to succeed, they opened their first café, "The Ormonde", on the Crumlin Road. It was here that they brought up a large family of six boys and three girls. Thomas, the eldest child, married Mary McCluskey, a native of Cootehill in County Cavan, but the newlyweds continued to live and help out in the café. Thomas had aspirations of his own and, with a little help from mum and dad, opened the "Victory" café in York Street.

Thomas and Mary's son, Tom, came into the world on 28 March 1930. He attended St Patrick's School in Donegall Street during the day but, once lessons were over, he would spend many hours at the Brunswick Boxing Club in Sussex Street. Under the tutelage of Sammy Wallace, who had successfully trained John McNally in his quest for an Olympic medal in Helsinki, the young hopefuls at the club would be shown how to jab, block, hook, uppercut and feint. Tom was, at this stage, too young to participate, but he loved the exciting atmosphere and felt right at home. His grandmother played a big part in his becoming involved in the fight game. One day she asked him if he had set his heart on becoming a boxer. When he replied sheepishly that he had, she said, "Go for it, then, don't waste a minute. If you want to be a boxer you must start straight away." Tom didn't waste any time in joining the club and was amused whenever his grandmother used to ask him for a "progress report".

"How are you getting on?" she would ask. When he told her he was "doing fine", she would smile and say, "I am pleased."

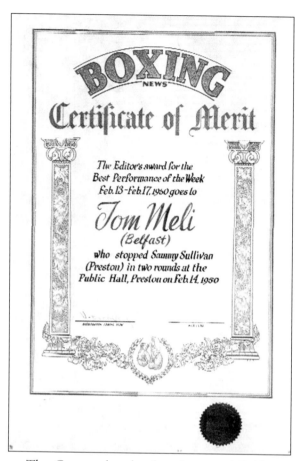

The German bombs that devastated Belfast in 1941 claimed the Meli family's home and business, but they were unharmed. The Brunswick Boxing Club also took the full count. Nevertheless, Tom's parents quickly opened a new café, the "Tivoli", on the Roseberry Road in east Belfast. Tom's final years of schooling were spent at St Anthony's on the Woodstock Road. On leaving, he got a job with the Baltic Timber Company at Belfast Harbour, where his workmates used to fill up a sack with sawdust and hang it in an old store for his use as a punchbag. Later, he became an apprentice electrician with Taggart and Company in Cromac Street.

At the age of fifteen he joined St George's Amateur Boxing Club, which is fondly remembered as the "Cradle of Champions". As a complete novice, Tom entered the competition, "A Search for Talent", organised by Bob Gardiner. He won no prizes but learned a lot from the experience. He went on to fight in the 1947-48 Ulster Senior Championships Middleweight Final but lost on points to Bobby Smith (Crown), who held on to his title the following year.

By participating in the Gardiner competition, Tom incurred the wrath of the boxing powers-that-be as he had unintentionally participated in a professional tournament while still an amateur. Fortunately, they were in a benevolent mood and let him off with a final warning.

Tom turned his back on what was a fairly successful amateur career when he heeded the advice of Stevie Boyle to join the professional ranks in 1948. He made his debut on 26 May against the experienced Belfast southpaw, John Weir, in the Ulster Hall. He soon realised the huge chasm between the two codes when he took a count of nine in the third round. However, he went on to record a points win against Weir with what was a fine and gutsy performance. He beat Weir again (pts 6) when they met later that year, as well as seeing off Jack Simpson (rsc 6) and Jackie Brown from Belfast (rtd 3).

It was most unlikely that Tom Meli participated in the 1948 New Year's Eve festivities, for he had an important meeting on 1 January with Garnett Denny, a local lad, who, since turning professional in 1947, had lost only once in fourteen fights. However, at the conclusion of the six rounds, the referee was undecided and opted for a draw.

After his fine performance against Denny, Tom lost to Belfast's Jim McGuinness (pts 6), but, on his first sojourn to England as a professional, he beat Corporal Jimmy Tipper from the Sherwood Foresters (pts 6) in Liverpool.

"Third time lucky" goes the saying, but this was a view not shared by John Weir when Tom completed a hat-trick of points victories inside a year over his Belfast adversary. Billy Watt from Liverpool simply didn't have enough voltage to shock Meli, and he lost (pts 8) in Blackpool and by a similar result four weeks later in Belfast.

Tom had another five fights in 1949, four of which took place in his home town and the other in Liverpool. In Belfast he beat Jim Josephs from Carrick (pts 8), Manchester's Tommy Turner (ko 2) and Les Benny from South Emsall (rtd 1). He boxed a draw with Jackie Brown, but in Liverpool he lost to Thornaby's Bruce Crawford (pts 8).

On 14 January 1950, he beat Lurgan's Gerry McCready (rsc 5) and this was followed by a magnificent win over Sammy Sullivan from Preston (rsc 2) on Sullivan's home turf. Tom received a beautifully inscribed *Boxing News* Certificate of Merit for his victory over Sullivan, whose father, "Battling" Sullivan had for many years ran a successful boxing booth in the North of England.

From 23 February to 30 October Tom had six fights, winning over Bangor's Jim Alsopp (pts 8) in Liverpool, Ryhope's Bert Ingram (ko 2) in Preston, and the Indian, Johnny Nuttall (pts 8), in Belfast. Nuttall was a very interesting character, indeed, as the Calcutta-born middleweight played test-cricket for Ceylon and was an excellent footballer, swimmer and athlete.

Tom boxed a draw with George Casson from North Shields, but lost for a second time to both Bruce Crawford (rsc 3) and the Gold Coast's Richard Armah (pts 8). Armah was a fighting journalist – as well as being a useful fighter, he was also a skilled writer.

Tom got off to a bad start in 1951, losing to Eric McQuade from

Tom Meli, ready for action

Downham (pts 8) and Belfast pug Tom Johnston (rtd 6). He overcame these setbacks to win over Glasgow's Alex Dobbins (pts 8) in Belfast, Poland's Gene Szczap (pts 8) in Preston, and Alf O'Neill from Newcastle (pts 8) in Belfast. In a final eliminator for the Northern Ireland middleweight title, he avenged a defeat inflicted on him eight months earlier by Tom Johnston, knocking out his old foe in the seventh round.

Tom Meli had been a professional since 1948 and, with twenty wins in twenty-nine contests, he became the Northern Ireland Middleweight Champion on 1 December 1951. This was as a result of an easy fourth round win over the holder Jackie Wilson, who had won the title from Freddie Webb. Wilson, who had trouble making the weight, took a real shellacking and was a poor facsimile of his old self.

In his first fight as middleweight champion, Tom accounted for Wolverhampton's George Roe (pts 8) in Birmingham, bringing his 1951 campaign to a satisfactory conclusion.

Tom's target for 1952 was a crack at the vacant Northern Ireland light-heavyweight title, which had been gathering dust for five years since Alex Woods retired. On the way to his goal he beat Bert Sanders from Kilburn (pts 8), lost to Leamington's Michael Stack (pts 8) and repeated a win over George Roe (pts 8) in Dublin. However, he lost to Doncaster's Jim Lindley (pts 8) in Belfast.

On 11 October 1952, Meli became a dual Northern Ireland Champion when he had a comfortable points win over Garnett Denny to win the light-heavyweight title. He relinquished this title, however, in 1954. Outside the ring Meli and Denny became the best of friends and, as well as pounding the roads together, would socialise on a regular basis.

Two days after Christmas in 1952, Tom had an unsuccessful return bout with Richard Armah, losing on points in Belfast. Tom's next six contests were on home ground. He clocked up points wins over Ron Grogan (Paddington), Johnny Douglas (Glasgow), Calvin Garraway (British Guiana) and Eric Metcalfe (Northwich). He drew with Wally Beckett from Carshalton but lost to Bedworth's Les Allen (pts 8). On 4 February 1954, he lost on points in Liverpool to Pat McAteer, who would go on to win the British and British Empire middleweight titles. Tom fought on, beating Peter Cain from Notting

Hill (rsc 7) in Belfast. Three months later, he lost to Jersey's Ron Duncombe (pts 8) on a Belfast card. On 18 November 1954, Tom Meli suffered the first knockout of his career at the hands of the Liverpudlian Billy Ellaway in front of Ellaway's home crowd.

The King's Hall on 22 January 1955 was a great night for Derry's Billy "Spider" Kelly. He won the British featherweight title from Stepney's Sammy "Smiler" McCarthy, adding this trophy to his Empire crown. Meli was not so lucky that night, as he was relieved of his Northern Ireland middleweight belt by George Lavery, who won on points over the twelve rounds.

While contemplating retiring from the boxing ring at that time, Tom's thoughts turned to a different kind of ring when he asked his girlfriend of one year, Patricia, for her hand in matrimony. The couple, for whom it had been the proverbial "love at first sight", became man and wife on 11 June 1955.

Tom's brother Bernie, meanwhile, was blazing a trail in the fight game. The former Immaculata boxer would be a Rome Olympian in 1960, and achieved the mantle of National Senior Light-Welterweight Champion in 1960, 1961 and 1962. Tom later revealed that Bernie had been offered financial inducements to turn professional, but he declined.

Tragedy befell the close-knit Meli family when Bernie's thirty-year-old son, Richard, was murdered in South Africa. He was stabbed with a screwdriver and then beaten to death after he disturbed burglars at the hotel where he worked in Witzoppies, north of Pretoria. Richard had previously been badly injured in a motorcycle accident and suffered lasting injuries which would have made it extremely difficult for him to defend himself during the attack. It was a despicable outrage, made all the more poignant as the family had gone to South Africa in search of a better and more peaceful life.

On 25 August 1955, seven years and forty-eight fights after making his debut against John Weir, Tom was knocked out in the first round by Liverpool's Vic Harrison. This was to be Meli's last fight.

Tom once told of the time he went to Paris to fight, only to discover when he got there that the bout was cancelled. With a bit of time on his hands, he rambled around this beautiful city, taking in the sights. He dropped into a bar run by Georges Carpentier, possibly the most famous fighter that France has ever produced. The two pugilists chatted, with boxing naturally coming top of the bill. The great man then accompanied the Belfast battler around some of the sights, supplying Tom with some well-cherished memories in the process.

Always the gentleman in life, Tom Meli died in hospital on 14 February 2003 after a short illness. He was seventy-three years of age.

PROFESSIONAL CAREER
1948–1955: 49 contests: won 29, lost 16, drew 4.

Bunty Adamson

The brightest star in County Down

There was a carnival atmosphere in Banbridge on Tuesday, 3 June 1930, the day before the Aga Khan's horse "Blenheim", ridden by Dick Dawson, won the Epsom Derby. Two special visitors, Lord and Lady Craigavon, were in town to inaugurate Banbridge Shopping Week. The vast crowd, which had gathered in front of the War Memorial to welcome the esteemed guests, had decorated the streets in their honour.

On the same day, in Rathriland Street, not too far from the noisy crowd, Martha and William Adamson became the proud parents of a baby son.

Robert, as he was to be named, was to be one of eight children in the Adamson household, which was quaintly called the "Wine Cutter".

At the age of six he attended Church School, where he remained for four years, before moving to Abercorn School. It is something of a mystery, however, how Robert managed to find the time to do any homework; from the age of eight, he was already a promising presence on the Banbridge amateur boxing scene. "Bunty", as he was now known to all and sundry, left school at the age of fourteen and gained employment with the local council. In the course of his working life, Bunty was also employed by Down Shoes, as well as having a stint as a bus driver.

As an amateur fighter, Bunty Adamson engaged in sixty-five contests, losing only four. The highlight of his career, wearing the vest of Banbridge Amateur Boxing Club, came in October 1948 at the Ulster Hall when he won the Ulster Junior welterweight title from George Lavery of St. George's.

Bunty made his professional debut at the same venue on 3 May 1950, taking out local boxer Jackie Hughes in two rounds. This victory was to be the beginning of an amazing run for the Banbridge boxer. Trained by Frank McDonnell and Sam Kerr, and managed by the great "Master" Albert U'Prichard (whose other protégés included Dessie Lennon, Jim Magennis, and the Feeney brothers – John, Michael, Jim and Bernie), Bunty became something of a "serial winner", clocking up thirty victories on the trot.

He faced tough Belfast man, Gerry Hassett, who like Bunty was also starting out on his professional career. Hassett had had three fights and three wins, but Bunty won on points over the six-round journey when the two met in the Ulster Hall.

Adamson was happy to celebrate his twentieth birthday under the hot arc lights of the Ulster Hall, earning a points win over Bangor's Jim Fitzgerald, who had a six-pound weight advantage. Other successes followed over Ronnie Jackson (Belfast) (twice on points), Fred Morton (Belfast) (rsc 6), Motherwell's Dave Baldry (rsc 3), Jim Scott from Edinburgh (ko 3) and Bessbrook's Jim Andrews (rtd 3). He scored another win over Scott when the Edinburgh boxer retired at the end of the sixth of a scheduled eight-rounder. Bunty went on to outfight Johnny Fox from St Helen's, winning with an eighth-round stoppage.

Another opponent, Rotherham's Stan Bagshaw, started off well but was no match for the Banbridge menace. When Bunty settled down in the first round, after absorbing some body shots, he took advantage of an opening to send home a strong right to the face, which put the Englishman on the canvas for a count of nine. In the second round, Bagshaw was mostly on the receiving end, and the third had barely started when Bunty dropped him for two counts of nine and one for eight. The referee then wisely stepped in to call a halt to the one-sided proceedings.

Contrary to the views of many that thirteen is an unlucky number, Bunty was considered very fortunate to get the decision in his thirteenth bout, which was also his first at the King's Hall in Belfast. The lanky Mancunian, Jimmy Brogden, proved a fair test for the Ulster boxer and Bunty found his opponent's defence hard to work out. The third round was a particularly good one for Brogden, who was doing most of the damage, his left leads drawing blood from Adamson's nose. Bunty fared better in the fourth when he scored with uppercuts and swings to force Brogden out of his stride. The tiring Manchester boxer could not hold off Adamson in the fifth and was driven all around the ring. Brogden was given no respite in the sixth and the Banbridge boy was getting through with greater ease than he had previously, and Jimmy was weary at the close of the round. The seventh was more of the same but it looked as if Adamson had punched himself out when Brogden came back in the eighth and took advantage of Bunty's wildness. However, Bunty had done enough to win five of the eight rounds.

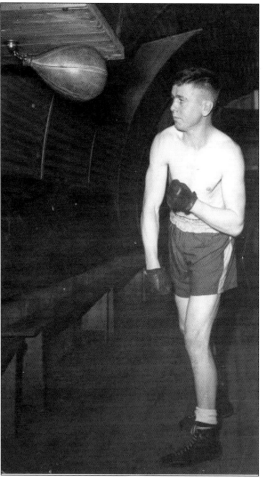

The "Star of the County Down" on the punch-bag

Two weeks later, Bunty disposed of Carlisle's Joe White in the third of an eight-rounder, cornering his opponent midway through the round and, after pumping in lefts and rights to the face, sending him down for the full count with a powerful left to the solar plexus.

On an Ulster Hall bill on 28 April 1951, which saw Tommy Armour retain his local welterweight title by defeating Billy O'Neill from Belfast, Adamson chalked up his fifteenth win by out-pointing Goldborne's Eric Billington. It looked to be all over in the second when Billington took three long counts, but he came back very gamely and had Bunty almost out on his feet. Billington took counts of eight in the fourth and fifth rounds and a seven count in the sixth, making Adamson a clear winner.

In an incident described as "unprecedented in the history of Belfast boxing", Harry Warner from Oldham was disqualified in the third round of his fight with Bunty. A packed Ulster Hall saw Adamson well on top at this stage of the fight during which Warner had visited the canvas a total of six times. He had been dropped for seven in the second, from a right to the temple, and all the fight went out of him. In the third round he went down again and referee Neilly Thompson promptly disqualified him for "not trying". Warner seemed dazed on his way back to the dressing-room where, when asked for his opinion of the result, he replied that he thought he had been "knocked out". Later, he returned to the ring and the MC announced that, on a doctor's examination, Warner had been "genuinely dazed" from the blow to the temple.

There was a transport strike in Belfast on 23 June but Bunty Adamson was still in action. This colourful bell-to-bell fighter with the awkward-looking stance had magnetic drawing power and another packed Ulster Hall witnessed him beating Glasgow's Billy Dickson on points over eight rounds. Dickson, who was a contender for the Scottish title, had an advantage of six pounds, but after sampling Bunty's quick and accurate punches he never looked as if he would trouble Bunty at any stage.

From September until the end of the year, Bunty would bring his undefeated tally to twenty-one with points wins over Len Ashworth from Burnley, Coventry's George Weston (twice) and Arthur Bell from British Guiana (rsc 2). Meanwhile, the British and British Empire welterweight titles had changed hands when Eddie Thomas lost to Wally Thom on points in London's Harringay Arena on 16 October 1951.

1951 was also the year that Randolph Turpin from Leamington Spa won the World middleweight title when he caused an upset of seismic proportions by beating Sugar Ray Robinson (pts 15) in London's Earl's Court on 10 July to become the first British boxer to win the 11st 6lbs title since Bob Fitzsimmons in 1891.

Bunty started 1952 in fine fashion by polishing off Peter Dawson from Huddersfield (rtd 5) and Crewe's Al Gamage (rtd 3). In a final eliminator for the Northern Ireland welterweight title, he halted Belfast's Joe McEntee in eight. McEntee's manager tossed in the towel when his boy rose groggily to his feet after being dropped for eight by a vicious right uppercut to the jaw.

Phil Mellish from Hyde proved a courageous little battler, shipping a lot of punishment over eight rounds, but Bunty moved and punched speedily, though he was inclined to slacken off at times. Time and time again, his piston-like lefts plunged into his opponent's face and made the opening for hard rights. Mellish survived four counts. He caught a lot of Bunty's punches on his arms and shoulders, and slipped others skilfully, but he could not cope with a hail of leather in the second round, during which he went down for two counts – for five from a right to the body, and for nine (the bell intervened) from a right to the jaw.

Mellish showed cleverness in clipping Bunty with two uppercuts and escaped the ropes. Adamson seemed to tire slightly but he came back with a vengeance in the fifth, punching viciously with both fists and sending Mellish down for seven with a right to the jaw. In the next round, a right to the body dropped Mellish for five. Bunty was the fourth local boxer that Mellish had dropped decisions to, the others being Jackie King, Sammy Hamilton and Jim Keery.

On a bill in the Ulster Hall where John Kelly had given a brilliant display in out-pointing Hogan Bassey, Bunty won on a disqualification against Israel Boyle from Nigeria. Boyle, who came to the ring having won twenty-nine out of forty-five fights, was expected to make it an uncomfortable evening for the undefeated Banbridge boxer. Boyle was a powerful puncher, and in the second round Bunty was pinned in his corner just as he rose from his stool. Boyle, punching furiously, drove in hard lefts and rights, but Adamson joined in with a determined burst and out-punched the Nigerian, who was glad to back away.

In the third, Boyle caught Adamson with a heavy left to the jaw and fired in punches as Bunty backed into his corner. Bunty covered up, swayed, and, to the dismay of his supporters, looked like going but he retaliated and smashed Boyle on the jaw with a beautifully-timed right hook. This fierce spell of in-fighting was interrupted when the referee stepped in and disqualified Boyle, whose brand of "fighting" would have made Harry Greb look like Mother Teresa. If the fight had been allowed to continue it could

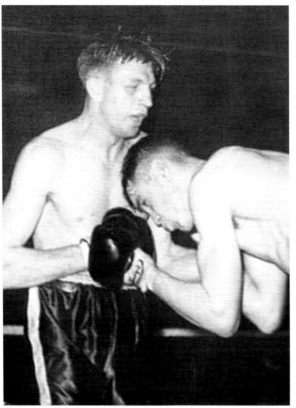

Taking on Giel de Roode

have gone either way and before Boyle left the ring his challenge to the Adamson camp for a return was accepted. However, a glance at Adamson's brilliant forty-three fight record shows that the return never materialised.

On 19 May 1952 in the Ulster Hall, Bunty emerged with flying colours by convincingly out-pointing Giel de Roode from Rotterdam. Belfast fight fans had not seen such courage, as was displayed by the Dutchman, for a long time. He took a tremendous pounding from Adamson yet kept moving forward and forced the Banbridge boy to fight for long spells with his back to the ropes. But this tactic was right up Bunty's street and no matter how de Roode pressed he could not stem the fury of Adamson's blistering punching.

By the second, Adamson had fully warmed to his task. He sent a stream of lefts into de Roode's face, punishing blows that carried every ounce of his weight, and thrown at such speed that de Roode's defence was incapable of dealing with them. Throughout the remaining rounds Bunty's left continued to bruise the Dutchman's face and de Roode never figured out a way to cope with it.

At close quarters, de Roode hit with venom without ever upsetting his opponent while Adamson jerked de Roode's head back with short, powerful uppercuts and slammed rib-bending rights to the body. In the fifth, de Roode clipped his rival on the jaw with a right and immediately gave an encore, but Bunty showed no signs of being hurt. He calmly slipped the Dutchman's right when it came again and then walloped hard to the body to put de Roode on the back foot. And so it went. Adamson was twice warned in the seventh for pulling his man on to the punch, but as soon as they were told to "box on" they charged with renewed vigour into the fray. Not for a single second did they let up, but someone had to give and, not surprisingly, considering the punishment he had absorbed, it was the Dutchman.

Two punch-packed minutes of the tenth and final round had elapsed when Adamson, sensing that at last the Dutchman was beginning to wilt, attacked with a fury that de Roode could not cope with. Heavy rights crashed into Giel's body and sent him reeling around the ring but, game to the last, he managed to hold out until the bell. The thunderous applause which greeted the end of the contest was as much a tribute to the gallant de Roode – sportingly first to congratulate the winner – as it was to the equally remarkable Adamson, and never were plaudits more worthily earned.

Bunty's home fans didn't have to travel too far to see their hero's next bout; at the Banbridge Showgrounds, he stopped Harry Warner from Goldborne in round seven as the result of a badly damaged eye. This was the second time that Bunty had beaten Warner, the first time being on a disqualification.

Adamson had by this time earned himself a shot at the Northern Ireland welterweight crown, which was in the keeping of Belfast's Mickey O'Neill. Before meeting O'Neill, he accounted for Wigan's Tony McTigue, whose corner threw in the towel at the end of the second after their boy had sustained a nasty gash at the corner of his left eye.

On 11 October 1952, on a George Connell promotion in the King's Hall, eleven thousand die-hard boxing fans flocked to see the Bunty Adamson-Mickey O'Neill showdown, an absorbing fight which neither man deserved to lose. The Banbridge star, who was favourite to win, was forced to fight every second of the way before he was awarded the decision against the Belfast man, a really tough in-fighter. Adamson used his left well, but the fierce body-punching of the stocky, former lightweight champion slowed him down a lot. O'Neill used the tactics expected of him – boring in, hooking viciously to the body, and he outclassed Bunty at close quarters. He also smashed him on the jaw with some powerful punches.

But Bunty came back gamely when O'Neill outfought him, and he used his straight left brilliantly to check the fierce onslaughts. Mickey's head was jerked back, and in the second round he was stopped in his tracks by a hard right to the jaw. In the seventh, O'Neill was hammered by a battery of rights, but they seemed to make no impression on the tough Belfast boxer. The fight was fought all-out the whole way and ended in a fierce punching spell in the twelfth round which saw Adamson get the decision from London referee, Tommy Little.

After the fight, Bunty was carried shoulder-high to his dressing-room by his jubilant supporters, but the bitterly disappointed O'Neill, who was convinced that he had done enough to win, challenged Adamson to a return, with or without the title at stake, and with the added incentive of a £500-per-man wager. The challenge was accepted.

Just as the turn of a card can make or break a gambler's fortune, so too can one punch make or break a fight. A perfect example of this is Billy Conn's first fight with Joe Louis when Billy, who was well ahead as the fight neared its end, was knocked out in the thirteenth round in New York on 19 June 1941. Nearer to home, on 19 November 1955, Billy Kelly seemed to be coasting towards the British Empire featherweight title in the King's Hall against Hogan Bassey when a bomb, in the form of a right hook, exploded on his chin in the eighth round, scrambling his senses and knocking him out of competition. Similarly, Bunty Adamson's thirty-first professional fight turned out to be a disastrous one for the Northern Ireland Welterweight Champion.

On 21 October 1952, at the Harringay Arena in London, Bunty was

Adamson versus O'Neill

matched in his first "away" fight with Bristol's Terry Ratcliffe. On the same bill Randy Turpin won the vacant British Empire middleweight title, adding it to his British and European crowns, by beating George Angelo from South Africa. The evening wasn't so kind to Bunty, however. Ratcliffe had a punch in his right hand as lethal as cyanide, and had won twenty-six of his thirty-three professional fights, sixteen inside the distance, but Bunty's British title aspirations were not expected to be jeopardised. In the sixth round he was well in front, having had the Bristol boxer in trouble time and time again. However, when Bunty was caught with a short right hook to the jaw, it was all over. Like Aldgate's Lew Lazar, who fell to Ratcliffe the following year after twenty-six consecutive victories to his name, Adamson's unbeaten record was in tatters.

This was a severe setback for the Banbridge boy, especially with British title eliminators on the horizon. But 1952 also brought happiness when Bunty married his sweetheart, Frances McAllister, a native of Carrickfergus. They were to have three fine sons. Frances once told a journalist, "I did not mind Bunty being a boxer, he was very good at it, and never got badly marked or disfigured."

Bunty shrugged off the Ratcliffe defeat when, in the space of three weeks, he beat Jimmy Stimpson from Tipton (rtd 4) and Langley's Dave Brandon (rtd 8).

Mickey O'Neill had waited patiently to even the score with Bunty and his chance came on 7 March 1953 in the King's Hall. It was a non-title fight, but there was the little matter of a £500 wager at stake. In another thriller, Bunty's immaculate straight lefts took him home clearly, but right to the end O'Neill was dangerous, as he showed in the last round. Adamson was well ahead by then but Mickey, fighting with tiger-like fury, put every ounce of energy into his punches. He moved after Bunty, trying desperately for a knockout win. One punch nearly paid off: a tremendous right tore open a jagged gash just above Bunty's left eyebrow, which Dr McHugh, the ringside medico, later had to knit together with two stitches. Spurred on by the frenzied cheering of his fans, Mickey tore into the attack again and Adamson, now startled by the stream of blood pouring down his cheek, went down for a count. It was thrilling stuff, but nobody could hear the count above the seething hubbub at ringside. Bunty wisely rested, kneeling on the canvas, looking anxiously towards his corner. But he steadied himself by the time he rose and kept out of trouble for the few remaining seconds of the bout. Aside from this incident, Bunty had never really been seriously troubled in the scrap.

After this great win, Bunty's vast army of supporters were shocked to the core when he was stopped in three rounds by Manchester's Peter King. The Mancunian had not lost a bout during his 1953 campaign and, after disposing of Bunty, would go on to knock out Gerry Hassett in one round and stop Mickey O'Neill in three, earning him the mantle "King – The Hammer of the Irish". He admitted after beating Adamson that he "wasn't scared of Bunty, just his reputation".

Another disappointment for the Banbridge lad came when he was out-pointed by Peter Smith from Huddersfield in the Ulster Hall on 5 August 1953. However, with his British welterweight title eliminator against Eddie Thomas just two weeks away, Bunty had a confidence-boosting win over Ted Ansell. In front of his Banbridge fans, he stopped the Jamaican in three rounds.

At the King's Hall on the evening of 25 September 1953, in an eliminator contest for Wally Thom's British welterweight title, Bunty climbed into the ring to face Eddie Thomas, the fighting miner from Merthyr Tydfil. Eddie was a former holder of the title, which he'd won from Sheffield's Henry Hall in November 1949. He had successfully defended his title against Cliff Curvis, and had won the vacant British Empire title by beating South African Pat Patrick in Johannesburg in January 1951. The fair-haired Welshman also beat Italian Michele Palermo for the European welterweight crown in Carmarthen. Despite having lost the European crown to Frenchman Charles Humez and his British and Empire titles to Thom, Eddie, who was also an outstanding rugby and soccer player, was the clear favourite to win. The occasion would be the first time a Northern Ireland boxer had contested a British welterweight title eliminator since Tommy Armour lost to Henry Hall in Sheffield in 1948.

Nevertheless, Bunty showed brilliant form over the first half of the bout, his left hand causing Thomas all sorts of problems. He produced the punch of the fight in the sixth – a powerful right to the jaw that made Thomas stumble and left him open for the following left, which knocked him against the ropes. It was an interesting rather than a great fight, with Thomas providing a storming last round as he hit out beautifully at Adamson. When referee Eugene Henderson, who had overseen a controversial pairing of Freddie Mills and Gus Lesnevich in Harringay in May 1945, announced a draw, the home crowd took it well, knowing that their boy would get another chance. While awaiting this chance, Bunty found time to avenge a defeat at the hands of Peter Smith almost four months previously.

Belfast fight fans were spoiled on the night of 27 February 1954. There were two great fights on the King's Hall bill: John Kelly was defending his European bantamweight title against Robert Cohen, and Bunty Adamson

Adamson and his entourage, post-fight

was renewing hostilities with Eddie Thomas in a British welterweight title eliminator. Kelly fans were to go home devastated after John was knocked out in the third. Adamson's followers, however, were in higher spirits after Bunty out-pointed Thomas to qualify for a final British welterweight title eliminator against Lew Lazar, who had won his eliminator against Terry Ratcliffe. Unfortunately, while preparing to fight Lazar, Adamson took a fight against Welshman Tim McLeary and was knocked out of the Ulster Hall ring and on to the press bench in the first round. He cracked the back of his head against the woodwork and was counted out, his head hanging down and his feet in the air. Bunty and his camp were adamant in their belief that it was an accident, that the ropes were slack and had parted when he was knocked against them. However, Bunty had definitely been hurt by a right hook before he took his tumble.

If the truth be told, some of Adamson's old spark had been missing since losing consecutively to Peter King (rtd 3) and Peter Smith (pts 8). Something was amiss. This was not the Bunty Adamson who had gone thirty fights without a hiccup. The mystery was solved when it was revealed that he had been suffering with a serious chest complaint for some considerable time. He had courageously kept this a secret, even from his closest sporting friends. Four days after the McLeary fight, on medical advice and to the dismay of his fans, Bunty announced his retirement.

He did attempt a comeback of sorts and lost to the Nigerian, Santos Martins (pts 8), and Charlie Currie from Coatbridge (pts 8), before hanging up his gloves for good. The "Star of the County Down" would twinkle no more. There was none of the dancing master in Bunty, he just got on with the job at hand. The tools at his disposal, according to Albert U'prichard, "were his excellent defence, his tremendous heart, and his hard, fast punch".

PROFESSIONAL CAREER
1950–1954: 43 contests: won 36, lost 6, drew 1.

Bob Gourley

Hard-punching novice lightweight

If you were to meet Bob Gourley you would gather from his appearance that here is a man whose profession had been that of a teacher or a lecturer, a writer or an artist. While Bob actually has two books to his credit (*Towards the Elimination of Human Error* and *The Elimination of Accidents*), you would be as wide off the mark as a haymaker from "Two-Ton" Tony Galento. Between 1948 and 1952, Bob was a tough, uncompromising, professional lightweight boxer, who beat twenty-two of his twenty-eight opponents, eleven inside the distance.

Weighing in at 13lbs, he was born in Dundonald on 3 January 1932, one of three sons and four daughters, to Mary and Jim Gourley. The Gourley

home was built over a stream and Bob's dad, a merchant seaman, used to go down into the cellar at night to catch the eels that populated the waters. He would then sell these to local pubs and fishmongers.

During the war, Bob and his sisters Mary and Nan were moved to the picturesque hamlet of Milltown, near Lurgan, and he fondly recalls the good times they had living in the country. Most satisfying of all for Bob at that time was being presented with a Bible for being the top student in Donaghcloney Public Elementary School.

When he returned to Belfast, Bob attended Boyd and Diamond Primary School on the Ravenhill Road, and with additional tuition from his self-educated dad, he continued to excel at schoolwork.

His success in the classroom didn't go unnoticed and he soon obtained the nickname "The Professor".

Bob passed the entrance examination for the Belfast Technical College but a lack of money meant that he could not attend. Instead, he obtained employment as a message boy with Siemen's Electric Bulb Company. Before long, he moved to Belfast Engine Works in the shipyard, becoming a blacksmith's helper. It was here that he met Bertie Todd, a fourth-year apprentice blacksmith who was also a professional boxer. Bertie invited Bob along to Frank McAloran's gym, the home to such greats as Paddy Slavin, Garnett Denny, Jim Townsley, George McCullough, Rickie McCullough, Rinty Monaghan and Eddie McCullough.

Bob trained hard, skipping, working on the punch-bag and sparring over many rounds several nights a week with George McCullough. But the best training of all, as he saw it, was when he worked in Hendron's Scrapyard at Pollock Dock. Here he broke cast metal with a sledgehammer, which developed his muscles, enabling him to punch harder. As a self-appointed chief slinger, he would attach large pieces of metal to the crane so that they could be lowered down to be broken into pieces, or burned if they were steel, for packing in the skips. For several hours each day Bob climbed a Mount Everest of scrap and hooked on the metal. This arduous work was a guaranteed way of developing strong leg muscles, transforming Bob into a more than useful scrapper.

Bob's first professional fight, which he lost to Belfast man Bert Wallace (pts 4), on 6 October 1948, was part of a show billed as "Discovery Night" in the Ulster Hall. At this time the big guns in British boxing were Bruce Woodcock (heavyweight), Freddie Mills (light-heavyweight), Dick Turpin (middleweight), Henry Hall (welterweight), Billy Thompson (lightweight), Ronnie Clayton (featherweight), Jackie Paterson (bantamweight) and Rinty Monaghan (flyweight). On the local scene, all the titles – with the exception of bantamweight (champion, Bunty Doran) and heavyweight (champion, Alex Woods) – were vacant. The top men in the lightweight division, where Bob would learn the ropes, included Jim Keery, Gerry Smyth, Tommy McMenamy, Al Gibson, Charlie Meikle and Rickie McCullough.

At the Ulster Hall on 28 September 1949, in which a minute's silence was observed by the crowd in memory of twenty-one-year-old Eddie McCullough, who had died from appendicitis, Bob had his first taste of success as a professional. He defeated fellow Belfast man John Elliott over the novice course of four rounds. Then, in the space of two weeks, he lost on points to two other Belfast fighters, Con McCullough and Ken McCready. Bob would meet McCready on three more occasions, winning two with knockouts and losing one on points.

In only his sixth fight, the hard-hitting Gourley was already making the sporting headlines when he stopped John "Silver" Thompson from Millbay in three rounds. One newspaper proclaimed: HARD-HITTING NOVICE

STEALS LIMELIGHT AT ULSTER HALL! Although lighter, Bob dominated "Silver", who took a lot of punishment and was forced to take a count of nine in the second. The courageous "Silver" made a gallant effort to get back into the fight but his sparkle had gone and the towel was thrown in during the next round. "Silver" met Gourley three more times, losing twice and obtaining a draw in the other contest.

A week later, Lurgan's Sam Malone felt the power of Bob Gourley's punching and was iced in the second round. Bob was now fighting with confidence and won seven of his next ten fights, gaining points victories over Monaghan fighters John Weir and Frank Hagan, John Haughey from Lurgan, Belfast's Billy Marley, John "Silver" Thompson and Carrick's Josh Josephs. However, he lost to Al Williams from Belfast when the referee stopped the fight because of a cut over Bob's right eye, caused by a clash of heads.

Phenomenal success followed in 1951 when Bob emerged as the winner from all eight of his contests. These were comprised of follow-up wins over John Weir (rtd 2) and John Haughey (points), another successful night against "Silver" Thompson (rtd 4), and victories over Jackie McKenna (Belfast) (points), Hugh Houston (Bangor) (ko 2), Jim Rooney (Belfast) (rtd 2), Billy Ferris (Belfast) (ko 2) and Bobby Booth (Randalstown), who was knocked out in the second stanza.

On 16 February 1952, Bob celebrated his first and only fight outside Belfast with a points win over Bangor's Harry Murvin in Derry's Guildhall. During the contest he had been violently ill as a result of eating bacon and eggs three hours before he was due in the ring. He found himself too weak to mix it with Murvin, so using his left while boxing on the retreat, he managed to scramble a points win. Another points win followed on 5 March over Belfast man Tommy Cochrane.

A month later, a gallant performance against Billy Corbett from Carrickfergus earned Bob more rave notices in the local papers. FOURTH ROUND SAW A DIFFERENT GOURLEY, declared one, while another proclaimed: CORBETT IN LEAD – THEN CAME K.O. For three of the scheduled six rounds, Bob took a beating and his guardian angel had to work overtime to bring him through. He was dropped in the second for eight by a right to the jaw and seemed to be heading for his first defeat in eleven contests.

But, in the fourth round, things began to happen. He got to work with his right and Corbett went down for nine. The Carrick man was dropped again for eight before Gourley, with brutal efficiency, finished the demolition job with a hard right hook to the temple. Bob considered that, out of all his opponents, "Billy Corbett had been the best."

With twenty-two wins from twenty-eight contests, things were looking rosy, but Bob now had other plans. He and his pretty girlfriend Beth, a legal secretary from east Belfast, married in Willowfield Church in 1954 and

Bob Gourley in his prime

decided to seek out a new life in Canada. Settling in Toronto, where Bob gained employment as a form carpenter, the couple had three children, David, Coleen and Susan.

There was one, albeit brief but amusing, interval in Toronto when Bob got the urge to don the gloves once again. Feeling that he was putting on weight, he joined a local boxing club and did a bit of training. His boxing shorts were full of holes but he liked them because, in the one hundred degrees temperature, they kept him cool. One of the other boxers in the gym started to take the mickey out of Bob by remarking that the shorts were "more holier than godly". Being the silent type, Gourley said nothing. Some time later the wise guy was looking for someone to spar with and Bob offered his services, admitting that he had done a "bit of boxing" back in Ireland. After taking two of Bob's specials to the side of the head, the Canadian, who was a professional in training for a fight, called it quits. As Bob put it, "He wouldn't come out to play for the second round."

Thinking little of the quality of some of the Canadian professionals, Bob decided that he could make some easy money and a fight was lined up for him. On the morning of the bout, however, the venue for the contest burned down. There would be no comeback for Bob; he was now, officially, retired. Eleven years later, he decided to return to Belfast where he took up his former employment at Hendron's Scrapyard.

Bob is adamant that he had one fight, not on his record, using the alias "Harry Gamble". With an impish grin, he recalls: "The MC announced me as 'Harry Gamble' and when I stayed put, Frank McAloran gave me a push and said, 'That's you.'" Bob won the fight but later asked McAloran the reason for the name change. Frank replied, "Because I couldn't get you a fight using the name Bob Gourley."

PROFESSIONAL CAREER
1948–1952: 28 contests: won 22, lost 5, drew 1.

John Kelly

His toughest opponent was his weight

There were times when John Kelly's life resembled something out of a classic Hollywood boxing movie. Whether it was his encounter with that wily Scot Peter Keenan or his confrontation with the French-Algerian Robert Cohen, Kelly never failed to thrill and entertain his many fans.

John was born on 17 January 1932 at 18 Outram Street on Belfast's

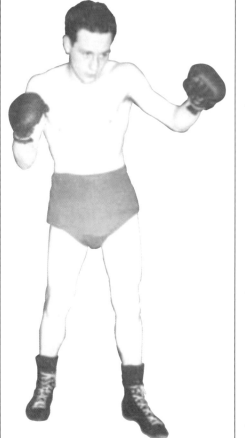

Ormeau Road. His parents were David, a caretaker who hailed from Enniskillen, and Marcella, who was originally from Dublin. John's older brother Pat was a talented featherweight, whose professional career spanned the years 1946 to 1954, and it was he who instigated Kelly's interest in the fight game. John was educated in St Colman's School in Eliza Street, later obtaining employment as a factory worker before landing himself highly-skilled jobs in Mackies and Rolls Royce.

As a fifteen-year-old, Pat Kelly was a regular visitor to St George's ABC (later renamed the Robinson Club) in Catherine Street North, often bringing eight-year-old John along to watch him train. John was intoxicated by the exciting, sweat-filled atmosphere as he watched top professionals go through their paces. Like a fish on the line, he was well and truly hooked. The "St George's Midget", as he was affectionately called, trained vigorously under the guidance of brother Pat, Jack Robinson and Peter McGuigan. His endeavours and dedication were duly rewarded when he won the Ulster Juvenile 6st title, the Ulster Youth 6st 7lbs title, the Ulster Youth 7st 7lbs title, the Ulster Junior flyweight title and the Ulster Senior bantamweight title. He would also box fourteen times for Ireland in many of Europe's leading cities, losing only three of his bouts.

At nineteen and now recognised as a top amateur, John was to have boxed J Kielty from Corinthians in a trial to see who would represent Ireland in the European Boxing Championships in Milan in May 1951. The Dublin boxer, however, withdrew due to a throat infection, leaving Kelly as the automatic choice. Kielty's infection did clear up but the standing committee of the Irish Amateur Boxing Association decided to pass him over.

The Irish team picked for the European Championships was: Flyweight, A Reddy (Sandymount); Bantamweight, J Kelly (St George's); Lightweight, D Connell (Avoca); Light-Welter, Terry Milligan (Short and Harland); and Heavyweight, G O'Colmain (North City). When the championships got under way, Reddy and O'Colmain were eliminated, and although Milligan and Connell went on to win bronze medals, it was the St George's boxer whose name was on everyone's lips after he lost narrowly to Italian Vincenzo Dall'Osso in the bantamweight final. On the way to the biggest night of his amateur career, John had beaten England's Tommy Nicholls, France's Jacques Dumesnil and Austria's Mazurkiewicz.

The contest against Dall'Osso was always gong to be an uphill struggle for the little Irish battler. In his semi-final clash with Mazurkiewicz he had sustained two injured eyebrows which meant that his carefully prepared script for the final would have to be tinkered with; in order to protect his suspect eyes in the final he had to be ultra-cautious. Although the Italian gave John little respite, he did not have things all his own way. Kelly, despite his defensive tactics, scored some good points and stayed the distance. The decision in favour of the tough Italian was not in doubt, but the Belfast boxer got a great reception for his plucky and skilful display.

It is worth mentioning that John was also a fine footballer, having played on the right wing for Cliftonville Strollers in the Junior League. When his boxing career concluded, he played in the same position for Shorts.

In his first outing since his Milan adventure, John wore his amateur vest for the final time when he stopped the National Coal Board Champion L McDermott from Birkenhead in the third round of an Ulster Hall tournament organised by Lisburn ABC.

Kelly's apprenticeship was over, and in the Ulster Hall on 8 December 1951, the Belfast southpaw, managed by Stevie Boyle, launched his ship as a professional. He made a winning and promising debut when he stopped Hull's Peter Morrison in the sixth.

In his second contest, however, on 12 January 1952, the former European silver medallist stumbled slightly against local boy Mickey King. For the first seven rounds John hardly got his hair ruffled but in the final stanza he took his foot off the pedal, and King caught him with a right to the chin which put Kelly down for a count of eight. John rose unsteadily but King, sensing an upset, connected with another right and, once again, John visited the

The "St George's Midget" (centre) as captured by a fellow club-member. His brother Pat is to the left of the picture

boards. With a commanding lead, Kelly weathered the storm until he could breathe a sigh of relief when the bell signalled that the contest was over.

Three weeks later, Birmingham's Billy Baker, deputising for Hyde's Ron Perry, must have regretted taking the job as he was completely outclassed by Kelly, and the one-sided affair was brought to a conclusion in the fourth. John made it four-in-a-row when he finally came up against Perry, knocking him out in the fourth of an eight-rounder. The first round was Perry's best: he had a dangerous right hand which found the Belfast boy three times. But John soon got his opponent's measure and, moving in close, scored with both hands to the body. John was the master in bursts of in-fighting where Perry was clearly outclassed. Taking a right to the body in the second, Kelly moved in close again and pasted Ron to the body. Perry's best punch was in his right hand, but it was losing its sting. Early in the third, Kelly prodded accurate right leads into Perry's face and checked his opponent with crisp, two-handed punching. Perry's head was jerked back by Kelly's right-handed punching in the fourth and he wilted under a battery of body blows. As Perry tried to bore in, his head was brought up by two snappy uppercuts and Kelly soon finished the job with a neat and meaty right hook to the body

As March of 1952 drew to a close Kelly was matched with Jim Dwyer and the Glasgow boy gave John all the trouble he wanted. It was only a grandstand finish in the eighth and final round that clinched victory for the St George's boy. Kelly, at a disadvantage in height and reach, found these handicaps difficult to surmount and he lost the first three rounds. Dwyer, also a southpaw, used a perfectly timed straight left to the face and rocked John lots of times with snappy left hooks to the chin. Bleeding from the nose and with a slight cut near his left eye Kelly looked to be in a spot of bother, but he forced the pace in the last three rounds and, with heavier punching, took the fourth, fifth and sixth stanzas. Dwyer sensed that the tide was turning against him and staged a desperate rally in the seventh, but he only shared the round. It all depended on the final round and Kelly punched with such venom that Dwyer was unable to use his right lead effectively, and could only land occasional punches. It was a difficult fight for John, but he showed tremendous pluck to get the decision. His runs on the Rocky Road and his sparring sessions with Jackie Briers, Billy Kelly and Bunty Doran, among others, was paying dividends in this tough business.

But the most notable victory of John Kelly's short professional career took place in Belfast on 26 April 1952 when he defeated the Nigerian and West African Bantamweight Champion Hogan Bassey on points over eight rounds. Bassey, who had won fifteen of his nineteen contests, would go to win the British and Empire featherweight titles when he knocked out Derry's Billy Kelly in November 1955. In June 1957, he added the vacant World featherweight title to his tally by beating (rsc 10) the European Featherweight Champion Cherif Hamia from Algeria in Paris.

Bassey, a heavily-muscled, dangerous and menacing looking fighter, was puzzled by John's southpaw stance in the first half of the contest. When he eventually did solve the Belfast boy's "wrong-way-round" posture he piled on the pressure in the last two rounds and threw tremendous hooks and swings. However, he had left it too late and Kelly was a worthy winner.

Kelly then accounted for Tommy Marsden from Halifax, winning on points over eight rounds. This was a good win since Marsden had so far been undefeated in his five fights in 1952. He had twice boxed Manchester's Neville Tetlow that year, drawing one and winning the other on a disqualification. Tetlow, at that time, was rated tenth in the British bantamweight ratings behind champion, Peter Keenan.

The majority of Kelly's contests would be fought in the Ulster Hall and it was here that the woefully unschooled, but game, Leeds boy Tony Kay was halted by Kelly in the third after being down a total of six times. Just over two months later, John, hooking effectively to the body with his right, dealt with the rough-and-tumble tactics of Bow's Alf Clarke and was clearly in the lead when his opponent retired with an injured shoulder after two rounds.

On 13 September, John came in as a substitute against Sheffield's Dennis Wild, who was also a substitute. Kelly had to work a little harder than in his previous two fights but, nevertheless, was a clear winner against an opponent who, at 8st 12lbs, was five pounds heavier than Kelly. Built more like a lightweight than a bantam, Wild was always dangerous. He continually ploughed in with his head lowered and, though an orthodox boxer, he usually led with his right. Occasionally, he did slow Kelly with hard body punches but the promising Belfast prospect's two-fisted punching was at times delightful to watch. By the third round Kelly had got Wild's measure and it looked as if the fight would soon end when he rocked the Englishman with

John trains under his brother's watchful eye

a barrage of punches, but Wild was tough and game. After this, Kelly dictated most of the scrap and when Wild did get aggressive, John showed good judgment and hit him as he came in. In the eighth and final round, Kelly was content to box Wild off with precision punching to coast home.

Jackie Fairclough from Preston was Kelly's next opponent. Fairclough was three years older than the Belfast boy and had not fought since 29 October 1951, when he lost to Tommy Proffitt in an eliminator for the Central Area bantamweight title. In the first round, Kelly fans were shocked when their boy sank to the canvas from a low blow thrown by the seventh-rated Fairclough. Although badly winded, cool-as-a-cumber Kelly survived the opening stanza and from the second round onwards he dominated the proceedings, peppering the Preston boxer's left eye with uncannily accurate right hands. By the fifth, Fairclough's eye was completely closed and, after some hesitation at the end of the round, his towel was thrown in.

Tuesday, 4 November 1952 was a sad day for boxing. After losing a contest in the Royal Albert Hall on points over ten rounds against Jake Tuli, the South African holder of the British Empire crown, the former French Flyweight Champion Honore Pratesi was taken to hospital where he died two days later. Tuli was deeply saddened by the tragedy but chose to fight on. Four weeks later, after defeating the Belgian Emile Delplanque in Nottingham, he donated his purse to the unfortunate boxer's widow, Colette.

Two days after Pratesi's death, Kelly showed perfect ring-craft and, punching with crispness and power, he easily out-pointed Neville Tetlow in the Ulster Hall. Kelly had never boxed better: deadly with both hands, he displayed perfect anticipation and timing which enabled him to do the right thing at precisely the right moment. At first he had to be wary since Tetlow, who had won eleven out of fifteen fights that year, was speedy and dangerous. Halfway through the first he knocked the Belfast boy onto the ropes with a sharp right to the jaw, and Kelly seemed to be troubled by Tetlow's long reach. But before the round ended he smashed Neville on the jaw with a perfectly timed right hook, the bell intervening when Tetlow was climbing off the canvas at eight. The Mancunian made a surprising recovery in the second and scored with some neat punches, but Kelly now began those two-fisted onslaughts which regularly forced his opponent backwards. From this round onwards, John was always the master, although before the sixth, the clever Tetlow was often dangerous, especially when he fired his punches to the jaw. Kelly could not be faulted; he was the perfect ring tactician and he carried the bigger punch. This would manifest when he decked his opponent for two in the third round.

John was nearly always first to the punch. He kept an eagle eye on Tetlow's dangerous right hand and usually avoided it by getting a punch in before Neville could score. One of his neatest punches was a short right to the body which regularly caught Tetlow under the heart. At slipping punches Kelly was proficient and when he was in a spot of bother he slipped away, scoring as he moved back. A scorching attack by Kelly completely sapped the Manchester boy's strength in the sixth and drained the power from his punches. He fell more from exhaustion than a blow for a brief count, but when he rose he was caught in a hail of leather, culminating in a left hook which toppled him for seven. Kelly took no chances, refusing to move in for the kill. Tetlow threw a flurry of punches at the beginning of the seventh, but they totally lacked sting and he was now relying on a harmless right. Kelly was little troubled in out-pointing him until the bell. As the boxers left the ring and the noise subsided, Keenan versus Kelly was the main topic of conversation.

Kelly's first year as a professional had been pretty impressive so far, and if he wanted to maintain his one hundred per cent record he would have two more hurdles to clear. This he did in comprehensive fashion against tough southpaw Len Shaw, from Sheffield, and the not so tough, but brave, Jimmy Jennings, from Clapton. Shaw had started off at a fast pace, moving in and

punching to the body, trying to throw Kelly out of his stride. John refused to be flustered and began to lead and counter with his deadly right, only using his left occasionally. His remarkable speed of movement and punch at times bewildered Shaw, making him retreat almost at a gallop. At close quarters, Shaw was rugged and Kelly could afford to take no chances, for he had sustained a cut over his left eye in the third round. The fourth was the best of the night with Kelly showing flashes of brilliance. Though the flow of blood from the injured eye had been checked considerably during the interval he let Shaw come only within hitting range, using the right admirably and pulling him up short with sharp right jabs. Soon Shaw's face was flushed and the region of his left eye swollen. Then, halfway through the round, a right jab opened a razor-slit gash under the Englishman's injured eye and Kelly peppered him with punches until the end of a one-sided stanza. Shaw's second threw in the towel at the interval.

The classy little Belfast bantamweight had a cameo role on George Connell's big Christmas bill in the Ulster Hall on 27 December, knocking out Jimmy Jennings, who was deputising for Dundee's Bobby Boland, in the first round. Jennings was, as the result would suggest, nowhere near Kelly's class. He had come out looking very aggressive but, after delivering some neat right-hand punches, Kelly dumped him for the full count with surprising ease with a right to the jaw.

Belfast fight fans knew that if Kelly steered a steady course and won his next few fights they were guaranteed a big night. The jewel in the crown of

Irish boxing didn't let them down for he reeled off four wins on the trot, accounting for Welshman Glyn David (disq 5), Nottingham's Johnny Haywood (rtd 5), Tommy Proffitt (rtd 5) and Ron Perry (ko 4). The sense that a Keenan versus Kelly dual title fight was imminent was realised when, twenty-four hours before Kelly relieved the old warrior Bunty Doran of his Northern Ireland and All-Ireland bantamweight belts, the British Boxing Board of Control announced that Keenan would have to defend his titles against Kelly.

In the Kelly versus Doran encounter, John would poke out his right jab to Bunty's face and hook calmly with both hands when the champion got in close. Kelly repeatedly slipped and evaded his onrushing opponent, who often found himself going headlong into the ropes. Every round was practically the same, with Kelly leading and jabbing at Doran, or spearing him off as he rushed in to land a hook or swing. The only time Kelly really looked as if he wished to let loose for a quick win was in the second when a combination of sharp punches toppled Doran for a count of eight. Over the rounds the punishment was mounting up and Bunty began to look weary. Finally, the end did come – at the conclusion of the eleventh – when Minty Rose threw in the towel as the little man went dejectedly to his corner, a champion no more. Kelly was presented with the Dalzell Shield after being voted Northern Ireland's Boxer of the Year, and it was announced to the packed hall that Bunty had fought for the last time.

Peter Keenan had lost only three times in thirty-eight outings. His setbacks had started with a challenge for South African Vic Toweel's World and Empire bantamweight titles in Johannesburg, which he lost on points over fifteen rounds. Then, in a defence of his European bantamweight crown against Belgium's Jean Sneyers in Glasgow, he was knocked out in round five. Keenan made it three losses in a row when he was stopped in the fifth by Italian Amleto Falcinelli in Paisley. He had won the British bantamweight belt when he knocked out Danny O'Sullivan from King's Cross in six rounds in May 1951 in Glasgow. On his way to lifting this prestigious title he had participated in two eliminators, beating Bunty Doran (pts 10) and Tommy Proffitt (ko 2). He had successfully defended his British title on two occasions, beating Bobby Boland (rsc 12) and Frankie Williams from Birkenhead (rsc 7). Keenan had won his European title on 5 September 1951 by beating Spain's Luis Romero on points over fifteen rounds in Paisley, but would, as already mentioned, lose it to Sneyers.

It was thought that Keenan may have shot his bolt after losing three-in-a-row but Peter had other ideas and, in Coronation Year, he was once more crowned King of Europe when he beat the Frenchman Maurice Sandeyron on points over fifteen rounds at Firhill Park in Glasgow on 17 June. Prior to regaining his continental title he had beaten Liverpool's Stan Rowan.

On the afternoon of 3 October 1953 thousands of Scottish soccer fans had watched their team beat Northern Ireland 3-1 at Windsor Park. Many of

Robert Cohen (centre) celebrates after beating Kelly

those fans would be present in the King's Hall later that evening to watch their British and European Bantamweight Champion, Peter Keenan, try to bring off a Scottish double. There may have been a crowd of 58,248 at the football earlier that day but, compared to the noise made by John Kelly fans in the King's Hall, Windsor must have been as noisy as an octogenarian's birthday party. The vast arena pulsated and throbbed to the exultant cheers and roars of 18,000 wildly excited spectators. As they watched the local boy gave a brilliant display of jabbing and moving, the Belfast crowd bantered Keenan and his supporters with regular cries of "Who's John Kelly? Who's John Kelly?" The previous February, when Keenan visited Belfast, an *Irish News* reporter had asked the Scot would he consider fighting John Kelly. Keenan, albeit with tongue in cheek, had replied, "Who's John Kelly?" Although the Keenan camp was confident of victory, Peter's manager, Tommy Gilmour, said before the fight, "I have a strong abhorrence of southpaw fighters. To put it bluntly, if I had my way I would wrap the majority of them into a bundle and toss it into the deep blue sea." Perhaps Gilmour had had a premonition about the outcome.

After a quiet first round, Kelly soon settled down and, growing in confidence with every second that passed, he began to outbox the Scot, zipping his right lead into Keenan's face with almost monotonous regularity and using the ring brilliantly to make his opponent miss. Kelly was particularly good against the ropes, turning smartly out of the way as the curly-haired Keenan came in, only to be left floundering on the ropes.

Keenan was particularly wild in the earlier rounds when, for spells, he went right-hand crazy, but Kelly easily evaded his wild swings and countered smartly. Kelly didn't use his left hand very much but, when he did, his neat hooks and crosses connected very solidly. Keenan was much more effective when he began to use a good straight left and he made up leeway in the second half of the contest, though there was no disputing that Kelly was winning clearly. Peter's best punches were short rights to the body, which must have been weakening, but Kelly stood up to them well. Keenan tried to pull the fight out of the fire in the last few rounds – he missed and swung himself out onto the ring apron in the thirteenth – but Kelly was always ready and calmly riddled the Scot with punches as he came in. Keenan found renewed strength in these rounds, but even when he tried for a knockout in the last round, he was unable to catch his very elusive opponent. When referee Jack Hart raised Kelly's hand in victory, the crowd as one rose and sang "When Irish Eyes Are Smiling", and there were many among the tartan supporters who joined in tribute to the new champion.

After the fight, Keenan, with his left eye completely closed and his face badly bruised, praised his tormentor saying, "What a grand fighter he is. I didn't underestimate him but I definitely didn't expect him to be so brilliant. I've no complaints. Johnny won OK but I'd like a return." Peter also cleared up the "Who's John Kelly?" remark which he had made eight months previously, stating that he "didn't mean it as a smart alec slur on Johnny. Fight fans can pick up things wrong, especially if anything is said about their favourite. It was only a joke." Mr J Onslow Fane, of the BBBC, had barely put the Lonsdale Belt around Kelly's slim waist when the new champ, now rated number four by *The Ring* in the line-up for the world title held by Australian Jimmy Carruthers, was ordered by the European Boxing Union to defend his title against French-Algerian Robert Cohen. The fight was originally scheduled for the end of January 1954, and George Connell outdid his rival Bob Gardiner by clinching the right to promote it. However, two weeks before the big event, Cohen sustained an injury to his back, resulting in a new date – 27 February 1954 – being pencilled in.

Inconvenienced though he was by the change of plans, John returned to the scene of his greatest triumph for a date with Belgian Jean Kidy, and he gave another outstanding display to win on points over ten rounds. Kidy had won three of his last four fights, his loss coming in a challenge for the vacant Belgian bantamweight title when he lost on points to Pierre Cossemyns.

Belfast fans did not believe that Robert Cohen, a powerfully-built bantam who had only lost once in thirty-three fights, had a chance against Kelly. They were not aware, however, of the pain and agony endured by John in his efforts to make the weight in the run-up to the Cohen fight. With the exception of the Keenan bout, when he was three ounces inside the limit, all of John's contests as a professional had been in overweight bouts which gave him a bit of breathing space. Although he worked like a Trojan to make the bantamweight limit and remain strong, he was a like a corner shop trying to compete with a supermarket. Casting his mind back to the night of his encounter with the French-Algerian, Kelly admitted, "I knew I was beat before I got into the ring."

Cohen's last fight had been against Jake Tuli in Manchester, which he won on points over ten rounds. Afterwards Tuli's manager, Jim Wicks, called Cohen "the best bantamweight I have ever seen – and I have seen most of them in my lifetime. He will be world champion – make no mistake." Wicks's prophecy would be spot-on; on 18 September 1954, before a crowd of 69,692 in Bangkok, Cohen would win the world title (not recognised in

America) when he beat Chamrern Songkitrat on points.

This then was the awesome task that confronted Kelly as he climbed into the ring in the King's Hall on 27 February 1954. The bookmakers had Cohen at 4/5, with Kelly at evens. From the opening bell, John was on the defensive as Cohen, ignoring the champion's jabs, backed his opponent into the ropes and dished out rib-roasters. It was in the second round that John's real nightmare started and the hearts of his supporters sank to the pits of their stomachs. As John came off the ropes he was caught by a right hook that clearly dazed him, and another right hook put the champion down for three. Belfast's favourite son was in big trouble. John was clearly flustered and when he got up he was wide open; Cohen floored him again with a vicious left and right to the chin. The Italian referee, Antonio Gilardi, counted up to six as the horrified crowd watched the European crown slip from their hero's head. This was not the same fighter who had beaten a world class fighter called Peter Keenan. When Kelly arose he backed away, perhaps hoping that the hurricane in which he was enveloped would ease off even for a second. But he was caught again by another right hook and he went down for two; before the round ended another punch thundered home putting him down for nine. Then Cohen let loose with another cracking right just as the bell rang, and it landed flush on John's jaw a fraction of a second later as Kelly dropped his arms. This was the punch that manager Stevie Boyle blamed for finishing the fight. John was out to the wide and had to be dragged to his corner.

The brave and battered little champion came out wearily for the third to meet the bantamweight version of Jack Dempsey. What happened next was not unlike Dempsey's slaughter of Jess Willard in Toledo, Ohio, on 4 July 1919. After punishing Kelly to the body with a barrage of hooks, Cohen switched to the face and caught John with another left hook and it was all over. There is no doubt that Cohen was the chief architect in the defeat of Kelly but he had a little help from John's continuing struggle with his weight.

To regain his confidence it was imperative that Kelly had a win over a top-class opponent, and the man chosen was the Belgian Bantamweight Champion Pierre Cossemyns, who was undefeated in twenty-five contests. In the King's Hall on 10 April 1954, it looked like Kelly might have exorcised his demons after building up a commanding lead in the first seven rounds. However, he seemed to tire significantly in the eighth and the curse of trying to defy nature by persistently boiling himself down to an unnatural weight came back to haunt him yet again. One minute into the ninth, Cossemyns let go with a left hook which caught Kelly on the point of the chin. He was in serious trouble and, as he tried valiantly to fight back, he was tagged twice more and sagged against the ropes until he was sitting on the bottom strand, staring with a dazed look towards his corner. He struggled to regain his footing as referee Andy Smyth shouted "eight" but he was in no position to defend himself and was counted out.

Kelly could still claim that he had never been beaten by a British bantamweight at this stage, but that too would change when he was knocked out for the third time in a row when he defended his British title against Keenan on 21 September 1954 in Paisley Ice Rink. Since losing his titles to Kelly, Keenan was unbeaten in four fights and was a clear favourite to regain his title.

Keenan had learned his lesson from the first fight and never once was John permitted to use his superior boxing skills. From the first bell Keenan rushed into the attack, chasing the champion all over the ring with swings and hooks to the head and body, and it was not until the fifth that the Belfast man was able to do anything in the way of retaliation. Then, in the sixth, Keenan caught Kelly with a beautiful right hook to the jaw, dropping him for a count of nine. When he got to his feet, John's nose was bleeding profusely and he looked very distressed. Keenan went berserk, rushing Kelly to the ropes and punishing him with punches from all angles. Eventually the brave little champion wilted under the bombardment. He made a gallant effort to rise and was getting to his feet when he was counted out. After the fight, Kelly said, "There is no question that the better man won. I have finished fighting as a bantamweight."

When John returned to the King's Hall as a featherweight to fight Glasgow-born Laurie McShane he was given a tremendous ovation. There was no doubt that the former champ was still box-office and his fans went home happy when McShane, after taking heavy punishment in the third round, remained seated in the fourth.

Three months later, an Ulster Hall that was so packed that many people were unable to get in, bore witness to Kelly's defeat of Belgium's Aime Devisch, who had come in as a substitute. But a giant-sized monkey wrench was thrown into John's comeback plans when he was knocked out in the first round of an Ulster Hall show on 13 August 1955 by Bournemouth's Teddy Peckham.

John took a year out in 1956 and, on 25 May 1957, he fought for the last time when he knocked out Swindon's Teddy Barker in eight rounds, the contest taking place at Grosvenor Park.

With his boxing days over, the former British and European Bantamweight Champion trained St George's amateurs and took out a manager's licence which enabled him to look after the interests of Jim Jordan, a former Irish internationalist and silver medal winner at the 1958 Commonwealth Games. He also resumed his soccer career by playing on the right wing for Shorts second string. He is today a valuable member of the Northern Ireland Ex-Boxers' Association.

PROFESSIONAL CAREER
1951–1957: 28 contests: won 24, lost 4.

Billy "Spider" Kelly

Inherited the boxing DNA of his father

One of the most daring robberies of all time occurred in the King's Hall, Belfast, on 4 February 1956 before 9,000 disbelieving witnesses. The victim was Billy "Spider" Kelly, the son of one of the greatest ring craftsmen ever to climb between the ropes, Jimmy "Spider" Kelly. The immediate outcome of the robbery was a riot by those gathered under the King's Hall's rafters, and the whole incident was to provide fans with one of the most continually debated subjects in the history of the local fight scene.

Billy Kelly was born on 21 April 1932 in Derry's Long Tower Street. His father had won twenty-nine of his thirty-seven fights at the time of his son's birth, including his conquest of Belfast's Jim Sharpe for the vacant Irish Flyweight Championship, the first of five titles he would garner before his

career was over. Billy went to Long Tower Primary School and later got a job as a message boy in Foyle Hatcheries before working for Robert Keys, a timber merchant. His first taste of the boxing game was when he joined Ashfield Hall, which was run by Davy Moore and Billy McDaid. Other clubs he was associated with were City of Derry Boxing Club and St John Bosco. Two of his finest wins wearing the amateur vest were against Gerry Hassett of St Matthew's, who was the Ulster and All-Ireland Juvenile Champion, and Paddy McAuley from St John Bosco, whom he beat in the final of the Miller Cup on 26 March 1948.

On 2 August 1950, Lee Savold, an American of Scandinavian descent, recognised by the BBBC and EBU as World Heavyweight Champion, was attracting huge crowds of holiday-makers when he visited Butlin's holiday camp in Mosney, County Meath. Savold had stopped Doncaster's Bruce Woodcock in four rounds at White City on 6 June 1950 to get his title. On the same August day, Billy was in Morcambe, where he shared accommodation with other boxers, including Derry compatriot Harry Rodgers. Billy was working as a swimming pool attendant and in the town's Savoy Restaurant but, later that evening, he would be making his professional boxing debut at featherweight against Preston's Peter Walmsley. In a four round contest, he beat Walmsley on points, repeating the dose two weeks later.

When Billy "Spider" Kelly returned home he was inactive for six months but shook off the cobwebs to resume his career on 21 February 1951 when he knocked out Pat McCusker from Belfast in two rounds in the Ulster Hall. From March to December he had seventeen contests, fifteen of which he won: he beat Maurice Gordon (Dublin) (rtd 3), Bob O'Hara (Portadown) (pts 8), Jackie Malloy (Liverpool) (rtd 6), John Griffin (Belfast) (rtd 4), Jim O'Brien (Belfast) (ko 8), Pepi Smith (Jamaica) (ko 3), Len Shaw (Sheffield) (pts 8), Bobby Dodoo (Gold Coast) (pts 8), Harry Croker (Leeds) (pts 8), Pat McCoy (Galway) (pts 8), Jock Bonas (Hickleton Main) (pts 8) and Joe King (Belfast) (rsc 8) in contests which took place in Belfast. Other victories were gained against Nelson Blackburn (Glasgow) (pts 6) in Glasgow, Jackie Malloy (Liverpool) (ko 1) in Glasgow and Arthur Jarrett (Jamaica) (pts 8) in Derry. Billy's two defeats were at the hands of Don McTaggart (Dundee) (pts 6) in Ayr and Hugh Mackie (British Guiana) (rsc 3) in Derry.

1952 saw Billy chalk up twelve consecutive wins before losing to Scottish Featherweight Champion Tommy Miller from West Lothian (pts 8) in the King's Hall. Miller was placed third in the British featherweight ratings behind champion Ronnie Clayton from Blackpool. This defeat was only Billy's third in thirty-three contests, but he would avenge it six months later. His wins in Belfast that year were against Roy Bennett (Salford) (pts 8), Charlie Simpkins (Bridlington) (pts 8), Brian Jelley (Bury) (rsc 4), Dan Collie (Nigeria) (pts 8), Bobby Dodoo (pts 8), Gene Caffrey (Glasgow) (pts 8), Bernard Fairbanks (Hanley) (rsc 4), Jack Walton (Leeds) (ko 3), Jackie Horseman (West Hartlepool) (pts 8) and George Lamont (Glasgow) (pts 8). He also beat both Harry Croker (pts 8) and Teddy Odus (pts 8) in Derry, and drew with Airdrie's Jim Travers in Belfast. Billy brought 1952, a year in which he became the first holder of the Dalzell Memorial Shield (awarded to Northern Ireland's "Boxer of the Year") to a close with a win (rtd 5) over Eddie Moran from Leeds in Belfast.

Billy had ten ring engagements in 1953, but the most important engagement of all was when he put the wedding ring on the finger of his girlfriend, Pamela McGilloway, in St Columba's Church. Pamela and Billy would have six children – four girls and two boys – as well as eighteen grandchildren and twelve great-grandchildren.

Bob. Gardiner.
PRESENTS

British & Empire Featherweight Championship

Sammy   Billy
MᶜCarthy v Kelly

THE KING'S HALL, BELFAST

On 17 January 1953 Billy stopped the Gold Coast's Rufus Cobbson in five rounds in Belfast, maintaining his outstanding form by beating Sheffield's Denny Dawson (pts 8), Tommy Miller (pts 8) and Tommy Higgins from Hanley (rtd 6). He also avenged an earlier defeat by Hugh Mackie with a victory (pts 8) over the British Guianan in Derry.

On 29 July 1953 in the Guildhall, a capacity crowd rose to their feet when Billy won the Northern Ireland featherweight belt from Belfast's John Griffen, who had garnered the vacant title five weeks earlier by beating fellow Belfast fighter Pat Kelly in four rounds. Billy's dad was in his corner, and was obviously reminded of the night seventeen years earlier when he beat Frank McAloran in the fourteenth for the same title. Griffen's best efforts came in the third and eighth rounds when he got through with some solid, left-

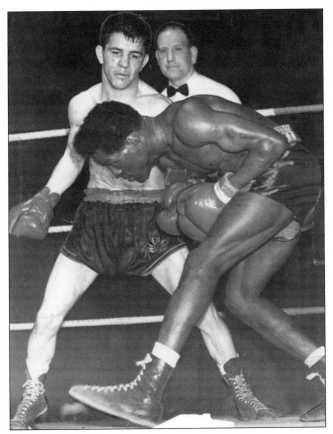

Billy loses to Ankrah in the King's Hall; he would avenge this defeat six months later

handed body blows. In the last two rounds, Kelly gave an absolutely brilliant boxing exhibition, highlighting his growing maturity. It was the second time that Billy had beaten Griffen.

Billy had a non-title date with British Featherweight Champion Ronnie Clayton in Belfast on 3 October, and when the Derry lad climbed into the Ulster Hall ring on 29 August to meet Jamaican Al Young, the champ was there to see how Kelly performed. "Spider" beat southpaw Young on points over eight rounds but afterwards Clayton told waiting reporters, "To tell you the truth, I was unimpressed."

Before the fight Clayton was introduced from the ring and the British, former British Empire and European Featherweight Champion took his bow like a showman, posing for a photo with his arm around Kelly. Then, to the cheers of the audience, he held aloft his two Lord Lonsdale challenge belts, which he had won outright by defeating Tiger Al Phillips, Johnny Molloy, Jim Kenny, Dai Davies and Freddie King. When Kelly and Clayton finally met in October in the King's Hall, Ronnie won in the ninth when Billy retired with a cut eye.

Billy drew the curtain on 1953 with wins (pts 10) over Eddie McCormick from Islington in Belfast and the Nigerian, Hogan "Kid" Bassey (pts 10), in Harringay Arena on a Jack Solomons promotion. The Bassey fight was Billy's first outing in London and the crowd loved his elusiveness, skill, class and courage. Two months previously in London Bassey had beaten (pts 10) Sammy McCarthy from Stepney, who was the number one contender for Clayton's crown. Billy's win over Bassey, obtained despite the handicap of a cut eye, which he sustained halfway through the fight, was a massive fillip for his confidence. He moved up a rung on the ratings ladder to become the number two challenger for the British featherweight title.

Two months later, again in Harringay, Billy beat Italian Featherweight Champion Altidoro Polidori in the second when the referee stopped the bout because of a severe cut over the Italian's left eyebrow. On 10 April in the King's Hall, it was a bad night for the Kelly name when John lost (ko 9) to Pierre Cossemyns, the Belgian Bantamweight Champion, and Billy lost to

A dejected looking Kelly after his European title fight with Famechon

Roy Ankrah, the holder of the Empire featherweight crown. On 11 June, Billy returned to winning ways with a ten rounds points victory over Frenchman Jacques Legendre in the King's Hall. It was a close decision but referee Billy Duncan had no hesitation in awarding the fight to Kelly, who on occasion had had to call upon his vast repertoire of skills to keep out of trouble.

On a Bob Gardiner promotion in Windsor Park, Madrid's Juan Cardenas scored an own goal when he was disqualified in the sixth for punching low. He had been warned in the fifth for elbowing and, in the next round, left Kelly rolling on the canvas with a right to the groin. Billy had no sooner got to his feet when he was dropped again by another low punch. Referee Jack Hinds senior was left with no alternative but to disqualify Cardenas as Billy squirmed in agony, almost rolling out of the ring.

On 2 October 1954, Billy celebrated his fiftieth professional fight by donning the British Empire featherweight crown when he beat the "Black Flash" Roy Ankrah with a magnificent fifteen rounds points win in the King's Hall. Back in Derry thousands cheered the new champion, just as they had when Billy's dad won the same title in November 1938. It was only six months since the Ankrah had beaten Billy and the cynics had said that the Derry man would not be able to deal with the "Flash's" fists, which were reminiscent of a crazed octopus with gloves on its tentacles. Pundits added that Billy was as good as beaten and if the fight went more than ten rounds

Famechon versus Kelly

he would be unable to last the blistering pace set by Ankrah. "He wasn't a stayer," they scoffed but Billy proved them wrong; battered and bruised though he was, he out-boxed and outlasted the dynamo from Nigeria. After the fight Ankrah told Jim McCafferty, Billy's advisor, that he "doubted if there was another featherweight in the world as elusive in the ring as Billy Kelly".

The new champion's next outing was against Juan Alvarez, who was Spanish-born but residing in Brussels. Alvarez had on two occasions gone the distance with Ankrah and had beaten Hogan Bassey over ten rounds in Newcastle. At the weigh-in Billy was four ounces over the limit (the fight was made at 9st 2lbs) but he managed to off-load the surplus and ran out an easy points winner over ten rounds.

The name Billy "Spider" Kelly had a magnetic ring to it and he had a following which other champion boxers at that time must have envied. As well as being "Derry's favourite son", Billy was a master tactician in the ring, exhibiting a style which was pure poetry. His propensity for ducking and weaving, which his supporters loved but referees detested, more often than not left his opponent floundering and punching smoke-filled air. If there was a weakness in Billy's make-up it was the fragile skin tissue around the eyes, especially his left eye, and he unfortunately lacked a punch that would quench instantaneously an opponent's hopes.

On 22 January 1955, sixteen thousand fight fans, the vast majority of

Hogan "Kid"
Bassey

whom were Kelly supporters, packed the King's Hall to see their idol give an uncanny exhibition of boxing brilliance to win the British featherweight title by beating Sammy "Smiler" McCarthy from Stepney. McCarthy had won the title from Ronnie Clayton, who retired in round eight in the White City in June 1954. Again, Billy emulated his dad who had held the same title. The betting before the fight was 11/10 Kelly, 4/6 McCarthy but these odds were made to look ridiculous as Billy took round after round. His crisp, straight left found its mark time and time again on McCarthy's very accessible face. When "Smiler" did attack, Billy bobbed and weaved tantalisingly out of reach. To McCarthy, "Spider" Kelly must have been like a mirage – in range, but impossible to tag. When the final bell sounded the cheers pealed forth like thunder, and when the Lonsdale Belt was put around his son's slim waist, Jimmy Kelly looked as pleased as punch. The crowd were in a frenzy of excitement and even Billy joined in the singing of "When Irish Eyes are Smiling". Needless to say there was great jubilation in Derry, and when the train carrying Billy arrived at the Great Northern Railway station, he received a hero's welcome. The celebrations continued long into the night and the night after that. On the same bill, George Lavery won the Northern Ireland middleweight title when he beat Tom Meli on points.

A week later, the Frenchman Ray Famechon, who was one of three brothers to have won national titles, was due to defend his European featherweight belt (which he had won from Ronnie Clayton) against Italy's Sergio Milan. The cries from Billy's huge army of supporters to "Bring on Famechon!" were perhaps a little premature. However, Ray retained his belt with a points win over fifteen rounds in Milan, and the way was now open for Kelly to challenge the European champion. Before doing so, Billy had a date with tough Teddy Peckham from Bournemouth, the Southern Area Featherweight Champion, in Streatham Ice Rink on 15 March. Peckham had won his area title eleven days previously by knocking out Camberwell's Charlie Tucker in the first round in Bournemouth. "Spider" Kelly's chin was a bit more difficult to hit than Tucker's and Billy won on points over ten rounds.

When Billy stepped into the ring in Dublin's Donnybrook Bus Garage on Friday, 27 May 1955 to fight for the European featherweight title (on a card promoted by Jack Solomons), he was rated the number nine challenger for New York-born Sandy Saddler's World featherweight crown. Famechon was number three. Billy failed to halt the French invader and, at the end, Dutch referee Banend Bergstroem held aloft Famechon's hand to indicate that he was still in possession of his European title. A 6,000-strong whistling chorus answered the verdict and some unsavoury incidents followed. Billy's advisor Jim McCafferty said, "It's a bitter disappointment; we thought we had got the decision and could scarcely believe it when the referee gave his verdict. Kelly should be champion tonight." Chief second John McBride went one better: "I'm just too shocked to say anything about the verdict. We were quite confident that Billy had won decisively."

Four months later, the British and Empire Featherweight Champion got a shock when his left eye was badly cut in an Ulster Hall contest against Italian Flaviano Ciancarelli. Jackie Briers, Billy's chief second, did a great job in stemming the flow and the champ won on points over ten rounds.

On 19 November 1955 on a George Connell promotion in the King's Hall, Billy entered the ring prepared to defend his British Empire featherweight title against Hogan "Kid" Bassey, who had knocked out Joe Quinn less than six weeks previously in Belfast. Quinn, who was fighting in front of a home crowd, had been terminated by a peach of a left hook in the first round. The Quinn contest wasn't the first time that Bassey had fought in Belfast; on 26 April 1952 he had lost to John Kelly there. As a seventeen-year-old, Bassey had won the Nigerian flyweight belt by beating Dick Turpin; when he moved up a weight, he added the Nigerian bantamweight title to his credit. Billy had already beaten Bassey on 8 December 1953 and it was felt that his superior boxing ability would see him overcome this formidable hurdle.

Veteran boxing fans who were present in the King's Hall that night have little recollection of the fight itself; what is indelibly imprinted in their minds is the eighth round: the Nigerian had a nasty cut over his left eye which the referee, Glasgow's Peter Muir, had already scrutinised. Bassey was in trouble as Kelly was in front and coasting. Although there was a long way to go, it looked a foregone conclusion that Billy would retain his title, but no one was prepared for the sensational turn of events which climaxed this wonderful duel of wits. Kelly appeared to lose concentration for a moment and his flawless defence, which at times seemed to mesmerise Bassey, developed a puncture. As Billy moved in towards Bassey, left hand held low, he presented the Nigerian with his one and only chance of the evening and Bassey seized it brilliantly. A right hook that was three parts dynamite flashed through the air and the fist crashed home on Kelly's jaw. No matador had ever dispatched a bull with such efficiency. Billy was out to the wide and 15,000 of his loyal fans were shocked and numbed – some were even in tears – into disbelieving silence. The impact on the crowd was akin to a child being told that Santa Claus had died. This was the first time that Kelly had been knocked out in fifty-six fights.

Hogan Bassey made a bit of history that night, becoming the first Nigerian to win the Empire title. He was also to become the first Nigerian to win a world title when he beat the European Champion, French-Algerian

Cherif Hamia, in Paris on 24 June 1957. He would later be awarded an MBE.

Two days after Christmas, Billy beat Frenchman Louis Poncy on points over ten rounds in Belfast, thus bringing an eventful and emotional 1955 to a conclusion.

Then, on 4 February 1956, came the great robbery.

Tommy Little had once said, "One of the prime assets of a first-class boxer is to be a master of footwork." Tommy, a BBBC "A" Star referee who had been the third man in many famous and intriguing tussles (including those between Randy Turpin and Don Cockell, Eric Boon and Robert Villemain, Johnny Williams and Jack Gardner, Joey Giardello and Terry Downes, and Joe Brown and Dave Charnley to name but a few) would have done well to have remembered his own words when he was umpiring the clash between Billy "Spider" Kelly and Cambuslang's Charlie Hill on that fateful February evening. Throughout the bout, Little had the best seat in the house and would have seen that Kelly was as slippery as an eel covered in cooking oil. Billy's speed, hitting, jabbing, countering, ducking, hooking and feinting were also a joy to behold, and it was difficult to comprehend why, at the end of the fight, Tommy Little had lifted Charlie Hill's hand in victory. Hill had fought courageously and proved to be a difficult opponent, but he most definitely was not the winner by any stretch of the imagination.

When the bell signalled the end of the contest and Hill was handed Kelly's title, the crowd gasped in astonishment. There were five seconds of complete silence before the storm broke. There were scenes of wild confusion and uproar as the referee, surrounded by stewards and policemen, became the centre of an angry sea of disapproval. Kelly supporters threw bottles from the balcony and others plucked missiles from anywhere they could. But the worst was yet to come. The rioters were now utterly out of control and, for almost thirty minutes, they converged on ringside, hurling the tip-up seats through the ropes, injuring spectators, officials and members of the press. One reporter was hit on the head with a bottle, and a cameraman was knocked down and kicked into unconsciousness. His valuable camera was hurled into the hysterical crowd and never recovered. Tommy Little escaped shaken but unscathed to his dressing-room, leaving behind a frightening scene of pandemonium in the arena. The MC, James Allen, climbed into the ring and, taking the microphone, tried to appeal to the sporting instincts of the disgruntled members of the audience, but more flying chairs and missiles came from all directions and the courageous Mr Allen fled the ring like a greyhound coming out of the trap. The uproar lasted another fifteen minutes before the police, drawing their batons, restored order with a charge up one of the aisles. After this, things slowly but surely returned to normal but it was some time before the ring was cleared and the ringside seats reorganised. A veteran Scottish newspaperman described the scenes as unbelievable. "I have seen ugly scenes in Glasgow's

Kelvin Hall," he said, "but they never had the same venom and ferocity as this."

Billy Kelly said that when the riot broke out he attempted to get to the middle of the ring to appeal for calm but was kept in his corner because of the danger from flying bottles. He went on to say, "It was a demonstration by thousands of people against the decision of one man. I have previously seen protests in the King's Hall – the stomping of feet, booing and slow hand-clapping – but never anything like that." He continued, "The thing I want now is to get a couple of stones more weight and meet referee Tommy Little in a contest in the ring ... I am not discouraged, just disgusted."

From the opening bell of the bout, Kelly took control, doing his utmost to land a right hand punch. In round two, he had Hill on the deck for a count of eight with a sharp right hook and, a few rounds later, a two-handed attack sent the Scot staggering around the ring. Billy was never noted for his punching power but his ducking and weaving – which had on more than one occasion landed him in hot water with referees – alongside his great balance and wonderful skill provided a beautiful exhibition of boxing that night. In the last three rounds, Hill had a mountain to climb and he was absolutely and utterly exhausted. His manager Tommy Gilmour admitted that, from the fourteenth round, "Charlie was continuing on courage alone." When the final bell sounded, there was joy for the man from Scotland and the rest is history.

When Billy faced Salvator Vangi from France in Manchester's Belle Vue on 27 February the only title he had left to defend was the famous Kelly name. However, as expected, he had a comfortable (pts 10) if unspectacular win. He later lost to both Charlie Tucker (rtd 7) in Belfast and Percy Lewis from Trinidad (pts 8) in London. The Lewis fight, which Billy took at short notice, was his first outing as a lightweight; as the result would indicate it didn't go too well and Billy finished with a cut on his right eyelid and another under his left eye. Although a section of the crowd booed the decision, Billy said that he was "not quarrelling with the verdict". Three fights later, on 9 December 1957, Lewis won the British Empire featherweight title when he stopped Charlie Hill in ten rounds in Nottingham. Billy ended 1956 with a victory (pts 10) over Liverpool's Syd Greb in Belfast.

The following year, Billy had five contests, winning one, losing three, and drawing one: he lost to Trinidad's Boswell St Louis (rsc 7) in Belfast and Willie Toweel from South Africa, the Empire Lightweight Champion (pts 10) in Glasgow. Toweel came from a famous fighting family and his brother Vic, as well as winning national bantamweight and featherweight titles, also captured both the British Empire and the World bantamweight crowns. Two years before his meeting with Kelly in the Kelvin Hall in Glasgow, Toweel had boxed a draw with World Bantamweight Champion Robert Cohen in Johannesburg. Even though he lost, this was a fine performance by Billy against the Empire champion. The verdict in favour of Toweel was greeted

A riot followed Charlie Hill's victory over Kelly

with howls of derision and afterwards the South African called Billy "the cleverest boxer he had ever fought".

Billy was knocked out three weeks later in round eight by Birmingham's Johnny Mann, the Midlands Area Champion, in Manchester's Belle Vue. Kelly appeared to be coasting to a comfortable points win when Mann got in with a telling punch to the head, which cut Kelly's left eye. The Brummie followed up by landing a second blow that put Billy down. The Derry man was struggling to his feet when he was counted out. On a George Connell promotion in the Ulster Hall four weeks later, Billy boxed a draw with France's Fernand Nollet. He finished 1957 with a points victory over tough, local boy Jimmy Brown in a thrilling fight in the King's Hall. Kelly excelled against Brown and the latter's manager Mike Callaghan said after the fight, "Kelly is a great boxer, a wonderful artist."

"Spider" got the chance to re-establish himself as a serious title contender when he was matched with Bermondsey's George Martin in an eliminator for the British lightweight title. The crown was held by Dave Charnley from Dartford, who had won it when he beat Mile End's Joe Lucy on 9 April 1957. If Billy won this encounter, his next opponent in all likelihood would be Ron Hinson from Dagenham, who had already beaten Martin. On 8 March 1958 in the King's Hall, Billy gave a superb exhibition of boxing and toyed with the twenty-four-year-old lightweight pretender. Referee Eugene Henderson from Edinburgh didn't have any mathematical problems at all when the gong ended the contest.

Four weeks later, in a final eliminator for the lightweight belt in the King's Hall, Billy did indeed face Hinson but lost a bitterly disputed decision over twelve rounds. So incensed was the crowd that for a period it looked like the bedlam which erupted after the Charlie Hill title fight might be repeated. Sanity thankfully prevailed.

Billy's next opponent was France's Guy Gracia, who had stopped Willie Toweel on his last outing and was known as the "scourge of British lightweights" after victories over Joe Lucy, Sammy McCarthy, Willie Lloyd, John McNally and Dave Charnley. The Derry battler's old nemesis, the cut eye, deprived him yet again of certain victory in Glasgow's Kelvin Hall. He received the cut in the ninth and the referee, after careful inspection, had no hesitation in halting the proceedings.

Billy's last fight of 1958 was a losing one against Louis van Hoeck, the Belgian Lightweight Champion. In the second round, Billy sustained a cut above his right eye but it was the serious damage to his left eye in the sixth that forced him to call it a night when he was well on top of the limited Belgian.

It must have been heart-breaking for a boxer, gifted with such natural ability, to keep losing fights as a result of eye damage, especially when ahead by the proverbial mile. Billy decided that it was time to approach the Musgrave Park Hospital in Belfast for an operation on the eyes to remove the heavy scar-tissue.

In a return fight with Gracia, on 18 April 1959 in Belfast, a draw was the outcome. Two months later, in Glasgow's Firhill Park, Billy was disqualified by referee Frank Wilson (the same referee who had decided that Ron Hinson had beaten Kelly in a final eliminator for the British lightweight title in Belfast exactly a year previously) for persistent ducking below the waistline of his opponent, British and Empire Lightweight Champion, Dave Charnley. Unlike Wilson, who received a police escort from the ring, Billy was cheered by the 7,000-strong crowd as he made his way to the dressing-room.

"Spider" Kelly was definitely a hard man to keep down and he was back in title contention once more when he out-pointed Barney Beale from Lambeth in a British lightweight title eliminator in Wembley. Although Billy won, the fight was a real snorefest and the crowd voiced their disapproval time and time again.

Kelly got his own back on Hinson in a final eliminator for the British lightweight belt when he beat the Dagenham boxer (pts 8) in the King's Hall on 5 December 1959. Although he won a close contest he was not too happy with his performance and said in his dressing-room afterwards, "I only took the fight a fortnight ago, and that's not enough time. It's not fair to the fans and it's not fair to myself. I thought I won. I was definitely the stronger over the last couple of rounds." The reason why Billy was not too upbeat was because there had been some booing from the audience at the decision. At least the booing proved that Belfast fight fans were scrupulously fair.

Billy's first fight of 1960 took place in the Dublin's Theatre Royal on 18 February. Despite his eye operation, he was beaten by Cardiff's Teddy Best, the Welsh Lightweight Champion, when his right eye was ripped open in the fourth. This setback aside, Billy retained his rating as number one challenger for Charnley's title. He was hoping to celebrate his twenty-eighth birthday with a win over Johnny van Rensberg in the King's Hall but the South African turned out to be a real party-pooper, beating Billy on points over ten rounds.

In London's Streatham Ice Rink on 30 August, Kelly's hard-luck saga continued when he lost to Peter Heath from Coventry with, need it be said, a cut eye in the fifth round.

Two months later, in his first appearance in Cork, Kelly drew a capacity crowd to Mike Callaghan's promotion in the City Hall, and he was a decisive points winner over West Africa's Sammy Etioloja. In a final eliminator for the British lightweight title he was out-pointed by the Welshman Darkie Hughes, and in February 1961, he lost (pts 8) to Nottingham's Brian Jones in Birmingham.

Billy was coming to the end of his illustrious, often controversial, career. In his penultimate contest he was knocked out in the second round by the Liverpudlian Dave Coventry in Liverpool Stadium. This was only the third time in eighty-two fights that a knockout punch had penetrated the "Spider's" defensive skills.

On 3 March 1962 in the King's Hall, on the same bill that Freddie Gilroy won a Lonsdale belt outright by beating Billy Rafferty (ko 12), Billy "Spider" Kelly boxed for the last time when he drew with Jim "Spike" McCormack, the Northern Ireland Lightweight Champion, over eight rounds. Billy may not have been a potent puncher but he could make an experienced opponent look like a novice, and was capable of dissolving when cornered and reincarnating himself at the other side of the ring. He had left fight aficionados everywhere with a great legacy of indescribably dramatic memories from his encounters with Charlie Hill, Hogan Bassey, Sammy McCarthy, Roy Ankrah and Ray Famechon, among others. Like his father before him, Billy never failed to be anything less than a class act.

PROFESSIONAL CAREER
1950–1962: 83 contests: won 56, lost 23, drew 4.

Paddy Graham

The red-headed battler

On Thursday, 5 May 1932, the main headlines in the local papers were STARVATION IN CO. DOWN! and DEARER BUS FARES! In the Royal Cinema in Belfast's Arthur Square, a "weepie" boxing film by the name of *The Champ*, starring Wallace Beery and Jackie Cooper, was drawing large crowds, and on stage at the Grand Opera House a play called *It's A Girl!* was also proving to be a popular hit. Meanwhile, about twenty-eight miles from Belfast, in the village of Killough, there were shouts of "It's a boy!" as a new baby was born to the former Catherine Hanna, a native of Belfast, and Richard Graham, a carter from Minerstown in Rossglass. The child, Patrick, was to be the first of three children for the couple.

When Paddy settled in Belfast with his mother and father he went to St Colman's School on Eliza Street. His father was an avid boxing fan and took a particular interest in the careers of "The Irish Thunderbolt" Terry McStravick from the New Lodge, and the former Light-Heavyweight Champion of the World, Archie Moore. Paddy's uncle, John Murphy, was Secretary of that famous old boxing club St George's, while another uncle, Barney, who was with the Horse Soldiers in India, boxed for the army. It seemed almost inevitable that Paddy would soon be donning the mitts, and he had his first fight for St George's on HMS *Caroline*, which is even today still berthed in Alexandra Docks. Paddy recalled that his first bout "was against a chap called Peter Duffy (St John Bosco) who beat me on points".

St George's had been in existence since

A champion-to-be

1929 and was the oldest boxing club in Ireland. Located right in the heart of Belfast's Markets district it had given its fair share of champions to both the professional and amateur codes. Jack Robinson from Magherafelt, who founded the club, had one great boast: "The club has never closed." During the Belfast Blitz, "Old Jack", as he was affectionately known, slept in the premises, which remained open to anyone who wanted to don the gloves. Under the tutelage of this master craftsman, who taught Paddy to skip properly and use the spring-ball, young Graham was in good hands. Jack had been introduced to the fight game at the age of nineteen. He had a good run of success until sunstroke and failing sight intervened. Undeterred, Jack decided to teach the sport, spawning in the process some of Ireland's greatest exponents of the fistic art, including Jack O'Brien, Pat O'Connor, Martin Thornton, Freddie Price, Paddy Sullivan, Pat Marrinan and Con McCann, whom he coached to reach the finals of the £500 Morcambe Belt Competition. In one year, Jack trained three boys who all won titles: Tommy Connolly, Billy Smyth and Jackie Quinn. He also assisted Tommy Farr and Jackie Paterson, and his son Spike was another successful boxer. Jack was in Paterson's corner when he knocked out Rinty Monaghan in five rounds at the Oval on 23 July 1938. In short, if Paddy Graham wanted a good grounding in the boxing trade, St George's was most definitely the place to get it. By crossing its hallowed threshold, Paddy would be joining the ranks of the club's other outstanding contemporary fighters, such as Jim McStravick, Jim McCann, Akkie Kelly, Dave Dowling and Joe Mitchell.

In 1945, in the Ulster Juvenile 5st final, young Graham lost on points to the aforementioned Peter Duffy; in 1946's final, he had another loss on points to George O'Neill from St Georges; but in 1947, he won the Ulster Juvenile 5½st title by beating John McNally of St Mary's. In 1950's Ulster Junior Flyweight Final, Paddy lost on points to White City's John McNally, but redeemed himself with two significant 1952 victories, securing both the Ulster Junior bantamweight title (by beating Crown's Hugh Magill) and the

The undefeated Welterweight Champion of Northern Ireland

Ulster Senior featherweight title (by beating Short and Harlands' Bobby McAvoy). In 1953, in the Ulster Senior Featherweight Final, he lost on points to Jimmy Brown of White City. The decision by the judges in the latter contest to award the fight to Brown didn't go down too well in the Ulster Hall. The contest was stopped when Brown inflicted a nasty gash on Paddy's left eye at the end of the first round. But the rules of the IABA stated that, in such circumstances, the decision would go to the boxer deemed to be winning on points at the time of the stoppage. It looked as if Paddy was a certainty to get the decision as he appeared to be well in front. It was not to be, however, and Brown, best remembered for his eighth-round knockout of Bobby Neill in a final eliminator for the British featherweight title, was awarded the fight.

In all, Paddy Graham had about one hundred and thirty amateur contests, including two international vests against Germany and the ABA. When he turned professional he had his first fight in the King's Hall on Boxing Day in 1953, stopping Stewartstown's Tommy Bleeks with a cut eye in the first round of a scheduled six-rounder. On the same bill Roy Baird beat Mickey O'Neill (rtd 7), who had accompanied Paddy on his training runs on many an occasion, in a Northern Ireland welterweight title final eliminator for the right to challenge Bunty Adamson. That same evening saw Gerry Hassett beat London's Alf Danahar (disq 7), and Glasgow's Charlie Hill knock out Banbridge's Michael Feeney in the first.

Now managed by John McCabe, Paddy had his first fight of the New Year on 9 January, when he stopped local boy Gerry O'Neill in the seventh. Lisburn's Leo McCutcheon was next to experience the strength and fury of the tough redhead from the Markets when he succumbed in the second. Paddy's first cross-channel opponent was Welshman Emrys Jones, from Oswestry, whom he met in the Ulster Hall. Jones had lost only once in his previous six outings and had been nominated for a crack at the Welsh lightweight title. Paddy, however, built up a clear lead in the early rounds and achieved a notable victory.

The Ulster Hall was again the setting for a brilliant Graham display of power-punching. Polmont's Billy Ferguson, who was billed as an Inter-Services Champion, tasted the resin four times. Although "Fergie" had guts

Paddy drew with Tommy Molloy in Liverpool

in abundance, he tottered around the ring like a baby taking his first uncertain steps and wisely retired in the second.

On Halloween Eve in the Ulster Hall, Paddy was probably hoping to provide his fans with a fireworks display, but it was five rounds before Glasgow's Tommy Cavan fizzled out, giving Paddy his sixth straight win. Four weeks later, again in the Ulster Hall, in the first mid-week show of the season, Paddy didn't have things his own way against a rugged Glaswegian, John Ward. In the first round, a cuffing left ripped a gash along Paddy's right eyebrow and a wild right put him down for eight in the second. Ward was cautioned several times for ducking low and on two occasions the referee ordered him to his feet when he thought that Ward had gone down without being hit. This was a fine performance by Paddy, who stopped his opponent in the fourth.

On 1 January 1955 in the Ulster Hall, Paddy did a neat and compact job in knocking out Motherwell's Dick Knox in the second. Knox was being tipped to go far and there was plenty of evidence to justify this claim: he had won eight of his last ten contests. From the moment they squared up it was a most entertaining fight. Knox had a fast, left hand and he hit out snappily with both mitts every time Paddy moved in on him. In the second stanza, Graham, whose face was now a delicate shade of pink, where he had taken those lefts, got the chance he had been looking for and, to give Paddy full credit, he didn't require another. A short right hand exploded on Knox's jaw and the Scot did a rapid fold-up. At seven, he managed to hoist himself off the canvas, but he stood dazed and stupefied and could, technically, have been counted out as he was not in a position to defend himself. It took only the slightest of taps to plant him on the floor again; this time he managed to make a gallant, but fruitless, effort to rise at nine but collapsed again, and was counted out as he lay flat on his face.

On 15 January, Paddy shared the Ulster Hall ring with Johnny Delmore from Leeds. There was plenty of interest in this confrontation, the reason being that Paddy's next outing was to be against Peter Sharpe in a final eliminator for the Northern Ireland lightweight title. The current holder was tough guy Gerry Smyth, who had beaten Ricky McCullough in September 1953 for the prize. Sharpe had met Delmore on two occasions: on 4 December 1954, he had out-pointed the Leeds man over eight rounds in Belfast; prior to that, on 29 November 1952, Delmore had knocked the Belfast stylist out in seven rounds. Graham looked like doing the business in the third when he opened up after coasting the first two, obviously hesitant about mixing matters with an opponent who carried a really decisive dig in his right hand. Delmore was on the floor when the bell ended the third but, hard as he tried in the next round, Paddy could not keep his durable opponent on the deck. However, he did drop him three times without counts. For the last four rounds, science was thrown out the window as both fighters slugged it out, but Paddy was a worthy winner of an interesting contest.

Next was the mouth-watering meal that only a master chef like George Connell could cook up: Graham versus Sharpe in a final eliminator for the Northern Ireland Lightweight Championship. In a contest that was closer than Siamese twins, Sharpe was supreme in the first three rounds. He countered Graham's flurrying rushes beautifully with a short right to the body and a good right cross, and in the third, he dumped Paddy on the seat of his pants for an eight count with a wicked left hook. But Graham kept swarming in and ruffling Sharpe during the fourth, which was definitely Paddy's round. He kept up the pressure and, although his punches may not have been as solid as Sharpe's left jab and short right-handers, he was making the fight by his sheer all-out aggression. His fast flurries of rights to the face must have been as annoying as a bluebottle buzzing around Sharpe's nose on a hot summer's day. Peter was perhaps a little too negative, for he kept moving backwards and countering with his hands held high, and when Graham attacked him on the ropes he crouched and covered up. In the earlier rounds Sharpe had looked good when he fought his way out of corners, lashing out at Graham with his right and catching wild punches on his arms, but he became more and more negative as the fight progressed. He did come more into it in the eighth when he pistoned a solid jab which brought the blood gushing from Graham's nose, and jabbed away during the ninth. But Paddy summoned up all his energy in a last round which he took by forcefulness and determination. It was a very close affair but referee Billy Duncan deemed that Graham had done enough to snatch the verdict.

On 26 March 1955, "Quare Times", ridden by Pat Taaffe, won the Grand National at odds of 9/1. But later that evening, on a George Connell promotion in the King's Hall, Paddy Graham fans didn't have a "quare time", for their man lost to champion Gerry Smyth on points over twelve rounds in a clash for the Northern Ireland lightweight crown. This was the first smudge

Willie Toweel

on Graham's slate but he did well against the vastly experienced Smyth, who was nine years older. From the outset, Paddy did his best to knock Gerry, who was having weight trouble, out of his stride but as the fight progressed, he was punished to the head and body. He never lost his smiling confidence and remained lightning fast with accurate lefts to the face, preparing to mix it at the slightest opportunity. However, Smyth's versatility, leads, hooks and uppercuts steadily piled up a winning margin and, by the end of the ninth, only a knockout could have brought victory to Paddy. Another champion to retain his title that night was featherweight Joe Quinn, who defeated John McNally on points.

After losing to Smyth, Paddy was in brilliant form in the Ulster Hall against Manchester's Bob Raglan. The referee stopped the contest midway through the third when Raglan was taking the mother and father of a hiding and the Englishman was on the canvas five times. He just hadn't the skill or the punch to match Graham and was in constant trouble from the time Paddy dropped him for a count of eight with a right hook to the chin in the second.

On 4 June, the Ulster Hall crowd weren't too happy when Paddy stopped Cyril Evans from Welwyn Garden City, who retired at the end of the second round. The two previous bouts on the bill had not lasted three rounds between them and the disgruntled fans started booing and catcalling. On 4 July, Paddy sojourned to Newcastle to meet the Mancunian Stan Skinkiss and lost his second fight (pts 8) in fourteen outings. At Belle Vue in Manchester on 2 September, Paddy stopped Birkenhead's Leo Molloy in the seventh. Graham put his opponent down for nine with a hard right to the jaw in the first, and had him down five times in the fifth for respective counts of nine, nine, eight, eight and four. In the seventh, Molloy was down again for nine; it was then that the referee intervened because of the Englishman's cut eye – or perhaps it was because his throat was parched from counting.

On 8 October 1955, the Northern Ireland soccer team beat Scotland 2-1 at Windsor Park. But on a George Connell promotion in the King's Hall that same evening, Scots boxers dominated their Irish opponents. Paddy Graham lost on a cut-eye stoppage to Glasgow's Bobby Kilpatrick, Dublin's Eddie O'Connor lost to Dalmarnock's Dick Currie (pts 8), Garnett Denny was stopped in the fourth by Greenock's Hugh Ferns, and John McNally was stopped in the seventh round by Glasgow's Matt Fulton. It wasn't only the Scots, however, who inflicted defeats on the locals: Joe Quinn was stopped in the first by Nigeria's Hogan Bassey, and George Lavery succumbed in the sixth to the "Killer from the Gold Coast", Vincent O'Kine.

In the Ulster Hall on 29 October, Paddy lost on points to the Gold Coast's Peter Cobblah. He just could not get going at all against southpaw Cobblah and he failed to work out his opponent's unorthodox stance. When he stayed out and boxed he looked superior but he courted disaster when he elected to rush in and slug it out with his vicious little adversary. When he did that, Cobblah opened up with streams of hooks and swings, and had he closed his gloves properly when he was delivering the punches, Paddy would have been in trouble. As it was, Graham was caught by a few teeth-jarring wallops, but the hardest was a left hook in the third when he was pinned against the ropes and was unable to ride back with the punch. Badly shaken, Paddy was tumbled for a count of nine. However, from the fifth, Paddy shaped up a little better and hurt Cobblah with an occasional sharp right, but the Gold Coast fighter got the verdict.

On the under-card of a bill in Newcastle, which was topped by Sammy "Smiler" McCarthy, Paddy met Chesterfield's Billy Cobb, whom he out-pointed.

Paddy's father and brother Tony used to come to his fights, but his mother had never seen her son box. On the one occasion that she did, he was in top form, dismantling Southport's Andy Monahan in the third round at the Ulster Hall. Catherine, however, was not too keen on gloved conflict and asked her son, "What did you hit him like that for?" She never went to another fight.

Paddy brought 1955 to a close by stopping Glasgow's Bobby Kilpatrick in the first round with a damaged eye. Although it was a brief encounter, it was thrilling while it lasted with both boxers having been down in the round. Paddy thus avenged a previous defeat inflicted on him by Kilpatrick on 8 October.

It was a great night for the Irish on 27 February 1956 in the King's Hall at Belle Vue in Manchester. Billy Kelly beat France's Salvator Vangi (pts 10), Joe Quinn beat Nigeria's Jimmy Zale (ko 1), and Paddy Graham beat London's Ron Hinson (rtd 4). Irish eyes weren't smiling on Paddy, however, on St Patrick's Day in Belfast's King's Hall, as he lost on points over eight rounds to Gordon Goodman from Christchurch. On the same bill Spike McCormack out-pointed Bournemouth's Dave Goodwin, Matt Fulton from Glasgow knocked out Joe Quinn in the eighth, and Jim Fisher beat Liverpool's Terry McHale.

On 21 April, Paddy renewed what would be a long-term ring relationship with Peter Sharpe in a final eliminator for the Northern Ireland Lightweight Championship. Many fans thought that Peter would be too crafty and skilful for Paddy, but Graham was a bit like the tax man: he never gave up, and his aggression and forcefulness saw him get the nod from the referee.

A few days before Paddy was due to meet Manchester's Derek Clark in the Ulster Hall, the Board of Control, in their wisdom, ruled out the match, having decided that Clark had as much chance of winning as that great detractor of the sport, Edith Summerskill, had of fighting Ma Copley in the King's Hall. The Board relented, however, and the fight went ahead, which, on reflection, was not a very bright idea. In the second round, Clark was down for two counts of nine and as the bell went he was on his knees. In the third, the Manchester pugilist took a lot of punishment and well-placed rights deposited him on the canvas for another count of nine. The brave Clark climbed shakily to his feet but the referee stopped the one-sided proceedings.

On 26 May in the Ulster Hall, Paddy had an eight-rounds points win over Austrian Kurt Ernst, a tough, craggy journeyman who was boxing out of Exeter. The Austrian had a crab-like style, good use of his straight left, and brought over occasional right-handers to the chin, which provided Paddy with some anxious moments. Only Paddy's sporadic streams of left jabs was keeping him in the picture for, when he shot his right, Ernst had a habit of cracking him on the chin with a fast counter, and he was also punching well to the body in close. Paddy came more into the fight in the fourth and got his left hand working with each round. By the sixth, he was constantly jabbing Kurt's head back. The Irish lad proved that he was every bit as tough as the Austrian in really tough exchanges. In the seventh, Kurt began to tire and took a lot of punishment; but in the final round, he managed to put all his remaining energy into a last-stand slugfest. As the crowd roared, both fighters were wearily pumping their arms at each other's body with heads lowered on each other's shoulder, as if propping themselves up to relieve their tired legs. It may not have been classic fighting but it was entertaining stuff.

On 30 June in Belfast, Paddy gave a great performance to outpoint Stan Skinkiss, giving him ample revenge for the points verdict he had dropped to Skinkiss in Newcastle-on-Tyne the previous July. A second dose of revenge came on 29 September when he out-pointed Peter Cobblah in Belfast. He also achieved a very notable victory when he beat South African Alby Tissong on points over ten rounds in Belfast. In 1955, Tissong had won the South African title (non-European) and had gone the distance with Italy's Duilio Loi, the European Lightweight Champion. Loi would go on to win the World Junior welterweight title.

On 15 December 1956 in the King's Hall, Paddy put up the performance of his life when he beat Boswell St Louis from Trinidad. St Louis, a cold, calculating dynamo of a fighter, who jabbed, hooked and looped punches from every conceivable angle, was one of the best lightweights seen on these shores for some time. Many a boxer would have been sickened and disheartened by the ceaseless attacks from the leather whips that Boswell called his arms, but not Paddy Graham. He looked tired in the seventh and eighth, and it looked as if his strength was ebbing. Perhaps it was but his fighting heart was still intact and he hurled everything he had into a magnificent rally. His straight lefts plunged out and his looping right crashed on Boswell's jaw. Both men hammered out the last round shoulder to shoulder, rope to rope. Paddy was so tired he could barely lift his arms but he pinned St Louis against the ropes and pumped both fists at him in slow motion. Boswell, who married a girl from Cookstown, died from a massive stroke at the age of fifty-eight.

Paddy had now moved up to welterweight and was rated number four for Peter Waterman's title. In 1957 he lost to Cardiff's Darkie Hughes (pts 10) in Belfast but gained revenge later in the year by beating him in London (ko 3). Another encounter with Boswell St Louis in Belfast resulted in a win on points for the Trinidadian, but Paddy would secure additional victories of his own that year against Islington's Ernie Fossey (pts 10), Belgium's Jean Paternotte (pts 10) and Preston's Jackie Butler (ko 4). Paddy was also named as "Ulster Boxer of the Year" for 1957, but perhaps his most memorable moment over these twelve months was when he married Adeline, a union that led to three daughters and six grandchildren.

On 19 April 1958 in the King's Hall, Paddy, who was now being looked after by millionaire scrap merchant Jimmy Lumb, beat Dundee's Jimmy Croll over eight murderously tough rounds. Croll was groggy and in bad trouble as Paddy battered him against the ropes towards the end of the second. Just when it seemed that Paddy, lashing out angrily with both hands, would win by the knockout, the bell came to the Scot's rescue. Graham won clearly but Croll, who was just about the toughest customer you could have met in the ring, soaked up punishment without apparent effect and had Paddy's face sore and bleeding at the finish. This was a very impressive performance by Paddy since Croll had stopped Cork's Mick Leahy in four rounds on 13 January and, exactly one month later, had gone ten rounds in Cagliari with Fortunato Manca. He had also inside the distance wins to his credit over Teddy Barrow, Albert Carroll, Les Morgan, Ken Regan, Leo Maloney, Denis Read and Paul King.

On 18 July, Paddy travelled to Rome to fight Teddy Wright from Detroit. Prior to meeting Paddy, Wright had won his last nine contests. He made it a perfect ten when he stopped Paddy in the second. On 4 October in the King's Hall, Paddy lost to tough Nigerian Sandy Manuel who, on his last outing, had beaten Mick Leahy. In April of that year, Manuel had also gone the distance with Teddy Wright in Rome. In the second round, Paddy was down for counts of eight and seven from two trip-hammer punches which very few fighters would have survived. It was a rugged, needle-charged affair and

Paddy couldn't get his favourite long, plunging left on the target at all.

On 17 January 1959 in Birmingham, the Cork-born steel erector Mick Leahy beat Paddy on points. Leahy would go on to win the British middleweight title when he stopped George Aldridge in the first in Nottingham on 28 May 1963.

Paddy should definitely have got a crack at the British welterweight belt when he boxed a draw over eight rounds with champion Tommy Molloy from Liverpool. When the referee raised the arms of both fighters the crowd erupted into a storm of booing. They were not only in apparent disagreement with the decision, but were also registering their disappointment at the poor showing of their home-grown champion, who was fighting in his own backyard for the very first time. Even allowing for his inactivity since he had beaten Jimmy Newman for the vacant title, Molloy looked a very ordinary champion indeed. Paddy was the one showing aggression and, unlike Molloy, was willing to have a go, but he never did get a crack at the title.

On 18 April, Paddy Graham and Peter Sharpe met to contest the vacant Northern Ireland welterweight crown, with Sharpe lifting the honours with a points win over twelve intriguing rounds. When referee Jim McCreanor lifted Peter's arms in victory, Paddy showed great sportsmanship by rushing over to congratulate his old foe. Sharpe was right on top of his form and he was punching crisply and using a wide variety of blows. His long left popped into Paddy's face solidly and, though Graham kept forcing the fight, he was inclined to paw with his left and his blows lacked snap. It was an interesting fight and there was always the chance that Paddy would use his iron strength to turn the tables but Sharpe, who had improved since moving up a weight, was always confident and clinched the title.

On 2 June, Paddy travelled to Wembley Pool in London but lost on points over eight rounds to Swansea's Len Barrow. Next up was a meeting in Liverpool with Hull's Brian Husband, and what a performance it was from the Markets man! He knocked out Husband, who had won his last eight fights, in the seventh, providing himself with a good confidence booster.

One of the best men Paddy ever met was South African Willie Toweel, the former Empire Lightweight Champion. At the King's Hall on 3 October 1959, in what was Willie's first bout as a welterweight, Paddy was forced to retire at the end of the fourth with a badly cut left eye. This was Toweel's first contest since losing his British Empire lightweight title (ko 10) to Dave Charnley on 12 May. Hard as Paddy tried to get in with a damaging punch, he could never get past the pumping fists of the cultured Toweel, who must have been one of the most accomplished boxers ever to have stepped into the King's Hall ring.

Graham brought 1959 to a close with a third meeting against his old adversary, the "Human Windmill", Boswell St Louis in Nottingham. Boswell, who took the fight at twenty-four hours' notice, was too busy for Paddy, who finished with his face scarlet and his right eye cut and nearly closed.

On 11 January 1960 in Manchester, Paddy was stopped in the fifth by the rising Welsh star, Brian Curvis. The referee had gone to Paddy's corner at the end of the fourth to inspect an ugly eye injury but Jimmy Lumb pleaded that his boy was fit to continue. Although the eye had not substantially worsened during the fifth, Lumb wisely decided to retire his gutsy fighter. It was a brave effort by Paddy. Curvis would go on to win both the British Empire and British welterweight titles, and challenge Emile Griffith, unsuccessfully, for the world title.

It was ten months before Paddy was in action again, making the trip to London to be stopped in four rounds by Johnny Kramer from Canning Town. On 27 March, 1961, Paddy knocked out Northampton's Cliff Brown in the sixth and, on 10 November, he journeyed to Kilkenny, where he had a points victory over Newry's Pat Price.

At thirty years of age and in the twilight of his career, Paddy Graham was offered another shot at local glory and he didn't slip up: he beat Peter Sharpe to win the Northern Ireland welterweight belt. He had three more fights in 1962, losing to Billy Tarrant from Bermondsey (pts 8) in London, Bristol's Tex Woodward (pts 4) in Birmingham and Sammy Cowan (rtd 2) in Belfast. The contest against Cowan proved to be Paddy's last, closing the book as it did on the ring career of a perfect gentleman.

PROFESSIONAL CAREER
1953–1962: 53 contests: won 33, lost 19, drew 1.

Jimmy Carson Senior

Underestimated by Halimi

Like a concerned mother, worried that little Jimmy might run foul of the school bully or the local roughnecks, the boxing pundits, in their so-called wisdom, pleaded, "Don't take this fight, Jimmy!" The object of their well-intentioned concern was Jimmy Carson, a slim, twenty-five-year-old, hard-punching bantamweight from the Falls Road in Belfast, who was ranked number two in the British ratings behind Scottish champion, Peter Keenan. Carson had been offered what every fighter dreams of, but seldom gets – a chance to share the ring with a world champion.

It was to be an overweight fight, made at 8st 8lbs with no title at stake, and was scheduled to take place on Tuesday, 4 June 1957 in London's Harringay Arena. The top of the bill that night was Dave Charnley versus Johnny Gonsalves and, just for the record, Charnley won in the eighth. However, the champ against whom Jimmy was matched was the French-Algerian Alphonse Halimi, who had garnered the World bantamweight title on 1 April that year in Paris. After only nineteen fights, Halimi had beaten Italian deaf mute Mario D'Agata, and was still unbeaten. Not only did the little Italian's title go up in smoke that night, he almost followed suit when the lighting above the ring exploded and burst into flames. Sharp and smouldering debris fell on D'Agata and the contest was halted for fifteen minutes while medics attended to his injuries. The fight resumed with Halimi winning on points.

At that time, the National Boxing Association (NBA), which in 1962 would become the World Boxing Association (WBA), recognised Mexican Raton Macias as World Champion, but there was no argument as to who was the undisputed champion when Halimi beat Macias on points in November 1957 in Los Angeles.

Newspaper pundits were not alone in thinking that the Belfast lad was on a hiding to nothing. Bookmakers too were advising people looking to have a flutter on Jimmy to catch themselves on. Even the most elastic imagination could not stretch far enough to envision Jimmy beating Halimi.

The reason for the understandable apprehension in fight circles was that, exactly four weeks earlier, in Rand Stadium, Johannesburg, a South African fighter, Jimmy Elliott, had died after being knocked out in six rounds by Birkenhead's Pat McAteer, who was defending his British Empire middleweight titles. Until that tragic moment there had been no knockdowns but, when floored, Jimmy banged his head. He struggled up at eight but lurched forward, face down. Jimmy Elliott never regained consciousness. Three weeks later, another boxer, Manchester's Jackie Tiller, was in a coma for ten weeks after losing to Retford's Eric Brett in Doncaster. He also never recovered.

So, Jimmy Carson, a rank outsider, who was just there to give the champ a nice workout, stood in his corner, looking across a sea of canvas at his handsome, illustrious opponent. The MC stood in the centre of the ring, microphone in hand and, in cultured tones, announced, "My lords, ladies and gentlemen . . ." Jimmy's big night had arrived.

Carson was born in 44 Cullingtree Road, Belfast on 30 April 1934, although record books mistakenly give his date of birth as 25 February 1932. His parents were Margaret and Arthur Carson, a carter. He was one of nine children, with four sisters and four brothers. His years at St Comgall's School slipped by and Jimmy, like most adolescents, had no plans for the future. The future, however, had big plans for him.

His first fight was not in the grand surroundings of the King's Hall, or even the Ulster Hall; it was on waste ground not far from Belfast city centre when he was eleven years of age. Jimmy and another young lad were doing their utmost to change each other's features when an angry voice boomed, "Stop it! Catch yourselves on." The voice belonged to Harry Fulton, who had founded the famous Kent Street-based Star Amateur Boxing Club in 1938 with his half-brother Alan "Akkie" Kelly. "If the both of you are so interested in fighting, join a boxing club."

Jimmy heeded Fulton's advice and, if Olympic gold medals were handed out for dedication, he could have filled a wheelie-bin with them. Every hour, every minute, every second outside of school was spent in the Star, where he would remain until his career was over. He was taught every move in the boxing cannon and at the age of thirteen he captured his first schoolboy title.

Jimmy left school and found employment as a riveter in the shipyard, but the majority of his working life would be in the construction industry, first as a plasterer, then as a self-employed builder, erecting and repairing homes all over the city.

A youthful Jimmy Carson, a "Star" performer

In 1962, his first season outside the juvenile division was marked by his winning the Ulster Junior and Senior flyweight titles and, as his career flourished, he was widely recognised as one of the amateur sport's brightest new faces, getting more impressive with each fight. Jimmy beat John Smillie, then rated as the number two amateur in the British Isles, and who, when he turned professional, had an unsuccessful tilt (rsc 6) in Firhill Park, Glasgow, at Peter Keenan's British and British Empire bantamweight titles. Carson also won the East of Scotland title and, three months later, he travelled to Nottingham, where he grasped the British National Coal Board title.

Jimmy got his chance at international level against England in London on 9 February 1953 when he replaced Dublin flyweight Andrew Reddy, who had difficulty in making the weight. Carson had an excellent points win over the highly-rated Eddie Walker from Stepney Institute in an evening when Ireland lost 6-4. In another international, against Austria, Jimmy had another notable points win, this time over the hard-hitting H Huber, helping Ireland to a 6-4 victory.

Away from his hectic training schedule, Jimmy liked nothing better than to go fishing and hunting at the weekend, also going to the occasional dance. At one such dance he met his future wife Lily O'Neill from Carrick Hill. Lily told me that she was "horrified" when he told her he was a boxer, but love prevailed and the couple married, bearing four sons: Barry, Henry, Martin and Jimmy junior.

When Jimmy swapped his vest for purses, he was managed by Frank McAloran and soon became a firm favourite with local fans. He was an exciting little scrapper who punched hard, fast and often. He made his professional debut on 25 September 1954 in Belfast, stopping Fishburn's Billy Gibson in the third. Just over two weeks later, he halted Mancunian Bob Skinkiss in two rounds, again in Belfast.

In February 1955 he beat Eric Lord from Bacup (ko 1), following this with victories over Camberwell's Dave Robbins (pts 8), Dubliner Mickey Roche (pts 8) and Tommy Gillen from Hayes (ko 1), all in his native city. However, on his first venture as a professional across the water he lost on points to the useful Alan Sillett from Acton in Birmingham.

In 1956, Jimmy had a fifty per cent success rate. He beat the Gold Coast's Ogli Tettey (rsc 6) in Belfast, lost to George Dormer from East Ham (pts 8) in London, lost to Fauldhouse's John Smillie (pts 8) in West Hartlepool, but avenged a defeat ten months previously by Dormer when he beat the East Ham boxer (pts 8) in Belfast.

But 1957 was a turning point in the career of Jimmy Carson. On 19 January he turned the tables on John Smillie (pts 8) in Belfast, and this win sent him hurtling up the ratings to sit snugly at number two. Below Jimmy at that particular point in his career were George Bowes, Dick Currie, Freddie Gilroy, Eric Brett, Billy Rafferty, Derry Treanor, Johnny Morrissey, Kenny Langford and Jimmy Cardew. This list of fighters gives some indication of how difficult the bantamweight division was at this time.

When Jimmy learned from Frank McAloran that he had been offered a shot at Alphonse Halimi, the Bantamweight Champion of the World, he was over the moon. It was like manna from heaven or winning the pools, and he was to get the largest purse of his career so far. When the bell sounded for this supposedly one-sided encounter to begin, Jimmy was embarking on his thirteenth professional fight. Would it be unlucky number thirteen for the Belfast boy? Jimmy gave a marvellous exhibition of counter-punching, and never in any stanza looked like being overawed by Halimi's status.

Round after round followed the same pattern, with Halimi relentlessly stalking Jimmy but without being able to convert his aggression into anything meaningful. The crowd, however, were still convinced that something sensational was about to happen. After all, this was the world champion fighting a lad who had never even topped a bill. And something sensational did happen. From a flurry of blows by Carson in the seventh, a trickle of crimson liquid emerged from a cut over the champ's left eye. Two more punches landed on the cut and the blood flowed freely. The world champion was in serious trouble.

Halimi came out for the eighth looking, to say the least, very concerned, and he stepped up a few gears. Jimmy didn't back off and, amazingly, staggered the champ with a solid punch to the chin. The crowd was roaring for the gallant, little Belfast man and Jimmy's pre-fight detractors were starting to go red in the face. Worse was yet to come for Halimi as the blood seeped from over his right eye and Carson piled on the pressure. One minute into the ninth, the boxing world was turned upside down when referee Jack

Jimmy and Spike McCormack, two up-and-coming hopefuls

Hart stopped the fight. Both Halimi's eyes were in a bad way but Jimmy was relatively unmarked, and he looked more like a world champion than Alphonse. The French-Algerian was full of praise for Jimmy, calling his opponent a "very good fighter", adding that he thought it was Jimmy's head which had caused the damage.

On 27 July 1957, with the scalp of the world champion proudly dangling from his belt, Jimmy travelled to Cagliari in Italy to fight Piero Rollo, the Italian Bantamweight Champion, who would go on to win the European title from Mario D'Agata. Jimmy dominated the first eight rounds but in the ninth, the Italian suddenly cut loose and Carson was floored three times. He was in serious trouble and the referee had no other option but to stop the fight.

In light of Jimmy's famous win over Halimi and his magnificent showing against Rollo, it was expected that Frank McAloran would strike while the iron was hot. Surely, Jimmy was in line for a crack at the champion Peter Keenan? Frank, however, held out for bigger purses, resulting in Jimmy not having another fight for eleven months, a long time for an ambitious young fighter to be inactive. Coming out of this hibernation, he lost to Johnny Morrissey from Newarthill (pts 8) and Eric Brett (rtd 2) on respective Glasgow cards.

Jimmy had another fifteen months of inactivity, during which time McAloran had departed the scene, and John McGuinness came on board as manager. The new partnership got off to a good start with Jimmy beating the Jamaican, Con Mount Bassie, on 5 December 1959 in Belfast.

Now boxing at featherweight, Jimmy's career ebbed and flowed, winning some and losing some. In March 1960, he beat Hugh O'Neill from Walsworth (disq 2) in Belfast, put up a creditable performance in Gothenburg, where he boxed a draw with Tibador Balogh, and beat Glasgow's George Judge (pts 8) at Wembley Pool. Then, disaster struck: he was knocked out in the third round in Liverpool by British Featherweight

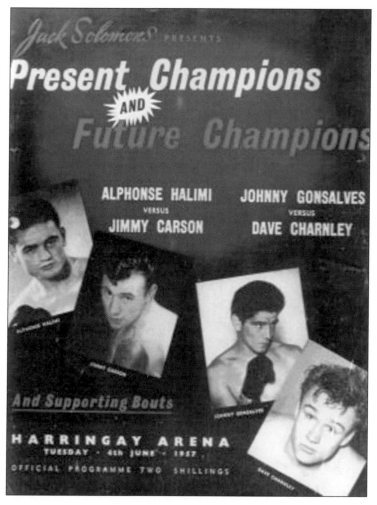

Champion Bobby Neill of Edinburgh, who had won the title from Cambuslang's Charlie Hill. Undeterred by this major setback, Jimmy was back in action within a few months, stopping Belfast man Terry McManus in four rounds.

On 10 September 1960, three years and three months after his best-ever career performance, Jimmy got another crack at Halimi. The French-Algerian had lost his world title seven months earlier when he was knocked out by Mexican Joe Becerra in the eighth round in Los Angeles. Jimmy's return with the former champion took place in Algiers and the posters billed it as a "revanche" (revenge) fight for the defeat inflicted on Halimi in 1957. Halimi certainly got his "revanche", ironically stopping Jimmy with a cut eye in the ninth.

On 4 February 1961, Jimmy travelled to Brussels to fight Pierre Cossemyns but was knocked out in the second round. Five months later, Cossemyns would lift the European bantamweight title when he stopped Freddie Gilroy in nine rounds. Jimmy had three more fights that year, losing

Alphonse Halimi

to Billy Davis of Bow (pts 8) in London and Mick Greaves (rtd 2) in Greaves's home town of Leicester, but emerging victorious over Halifax's Phil McGrath (pts 8) in Cork.

Jimmy Carson had now been in the "punch-for-pay" business since 1954 and was at the sunset of his career. He had three fights in 1962, losing to Ghana's Dennis Adjei (ko 2) in London, Derry's Paddy Kelly (pts 6) in the King's Hall (on the same bill that Freddie Gilroy successfully defended his British and British Empire titles against Glaswegian Billy Rafferty), and on his second visit to Brussels, he lost (ko 5) to Belgium's Jean Renard.

Jimmy had mixed it with some tough fighters and, on 29 January 1963 in London, he faced nineteen-year-old knockout specialist Lennie "The Lion" Williams from Masteg. Since turning professional in 1961, Williams had packed in an amazing thirty contests, winning twenty-three by the short route. He now made it twenty-four by knocking Carson out in the second. The Falls Road man had announced his retirement on previous occasions; this time it was official.

Jimmy Carson died on 2 February 1991, aged fifty-seven. The high esteem in which he was held was manifest by the massive attendance at the church and funeral. Even today, when having a conversation about boxing with any "old-timers", if Jimmy's name is mentioned, the inevitable reply will be: "Oh yes, Jimmy Carson. He beat the world champion, Halimi."

PROFESSIONAL CAREER
1954–1963: 31 contests: won 15, lost 15, drew 1.

Charlie Cosgrove

The chef who could dish it out

Charlie Cosgrove was a chef by trade, conjuring up many a mouth-watering meal. He was also a tough professional boxer and, at his fighting best, he dished out left hooks, jabs and uppercuts of such power and ferocity that opponents like Paddy Bergin, Joe Toner, Sam Thompson, Eddie Baker and Jack Armstrong were despatched quicker than you could finish off a fish supper.

Charlie had no intention of remaining in the "pain game" any longer than was necessary and endeavoured to make his presence felt as quickly as possible. Despite serving up some tasty displays of fine boxing and hard punching, in what turned out to be a short professional career, he didn't quite attain his goal of having a Lord Lonsdale belt placed around his slim waist.

He did, however, come pretty close to challenging for British welterweight honours.

Charlie was born on 7 March 1935 in Mawhinney's Court, Brown Square, Peter's Hill in Belfast. His parents were Sam Cosgrove, a riveter in the Belfast shipyard, and Rebecca. He was one of three brothers, Sammy "Cisco", a former professional boxer at featherweight, and Robert.

Charlie went to Hemsworth Square PES, off Agnes Street on the Shankill Road, and he spent his childhood in The Hammer district, where any disputes between youngsters were settled with fists. But Charlie, who along with Sammy, was a member of the White City Boxing Club, was pretty useful with his fists and school bullies were never a problem. In 1949, he won the 8st Ulster Juvenile title and, when he had filled out a little more, he lifted the Ulster Juvenile lightweight title the following season.

On leaving school, Charlie obtained employment in Edenderry Mill on the Crumlin Road, but mill work was not to his liking and he left after three days. He wasn't idle for too long, securing a position in Henry Taylor's, an engineering company in Brown Square. But lady luck smiled on young Cosgrove when he was offered an apprenticeship as a commis chef in the Orpheus Restaurant in York Street. So competent did he become that, when he went to Southport at the age of seventeen to stay with his brother Robert, his culinary expertise obtained for him a position at the Prince of Wales Hotel. He remained there for two years before returning home to seek fresh employment and to resume his amateur boxing career. He worked for a while at Murray's tobacco factory in Sandy Row, but for twenty-five years he was a chef in Gallagher's cigarette factory in York Street.

Charlie felt that he had been harshly treated by the Irish amateur boxing selectors when, on the strength of a fine win over Andy Keogh from Arbour Hill, it looked like the White City boxer had deservedly earned a place on one of the Irish sides to oppose an American Golden Gloves contingent in Dublin on 9 May 1955, and in the Ulster Hall just over a week later. The Central Council decided that Charlie would take the place of Bernie Ingle, who was not available, in the Dublin match. Charlie was absolutely delighted and immediately stepped up his training for what would be his first international bout, an outing that could lead to the European championships. Then came the bombshell that Charlie would not, after all, take Ingle's place. Instead, Joe Foley from Dunshaughlin was picked to box in Dublin. But what really annoyed Cosgrove was the fact that Keogh, whom Charlie had already beaten, was to box for the Irish selection in the Ulster Hall. In Dublin, Ireland beat the Golden Gloves 6-4, and in the Ulster Hall the Americans gained revenge with a 7-3 win. Joe Foley won in Dublin and Andy Keogh lost in Belfast. But Charlie Cosgrove wasn't interested in any of the two results, so disgusted was he at the way in which he had been treated. He decided to join the paid ranks.

Under the tutelage of Sammy Wallace, who also trained John McNally, Jimmy Brown and Davy Bell, and managed by the former Northern Ireland Flyweight Champion, Jackie Briers, Charlie knew that if he was to get anywhere in the tough and merciless business of professional boxing he would have to put his heart and soul into training. This he did religiously, for early every morning, he could be found running up the Shankill Road, across the Ballygomartin Road to Glencairn, up the Crumlin Road towards Ligoniel, and returning home with an appetite as sharp as a biting arctic wind. He would then freshen up, breakfast, and head for work, coming home in the evening to cover the same eight-mile route once again, no matter what the weather conditions were like. And what a start the Belfast chef had to his professional career. Using every ingredient on his pugilistic menu he stopped Dublin's Paddy Bergin in the second round on the latter's home turf on 22 July 1955.

On 13 August in the Ulster Hall, Belfast fight fans were stunned into complete silence when John Kelly, their local idol, was knocked out in the first round by Teddy Peckham from Bournemouth. But the smiles soon returned to their faces as they watched twenty-year-old Charlie Cosgrove put on a brilliant display to stop Teddy Peckham's club mate Eddie Baker in the dying seconds of their six-round bout. Although it was a cut eye which ended the contest, Charlie was always the master and, at times, his powerful right-hand punching was a joy to watch. His stable-mate Jimmy Brown also won, stopping Manchester's Jackie Tiller in the third stanza.

Charlie notched up his third win when he beat rugged Doncaster boxer Don Cope, who was unable to cope with Cosgrove's repertoire of punches.

Jack Armstrong, a twenty-six-year-old from the Gold Coast had, on 24 February 1953, drawn with Clapham's Peter Waterman, a former ABA Light-Welterweight Champion and British Olympic representative. As this was only Waterman's fourth contest – he had won his first three inside the distance – not too much notice was taken of the Gold Coast boxer's performance. However, Waterman would win his next twenty-eight contests, twenty-five inside the distance, and go on to win the British welterweight title by stopping Wally Thom in five rounds on 5 June 1956; he would also lift the European welterweight title with a win (rsc 14) over Italy's Emilio Marconi in London in January 1958. Taking these facts into consideration, it might be concluded that, after earning a draw with such a brilliant ring craftsman as Waterman, Armstrong might have done well in the professional game. Nothing could be further from the truth. After the Waterman contest, he beat Harlow's Johnny Fish and drew with Jimmy Croll from Dundee, but lost nine in a row between April 1953 and December 1954. Before meeting Cosgrove in the Ulster Hall on 10 September 1955, he did chalk up four wins, defeating Terry Bellamy (ko 2), Reg Fisher (rsc 6), Vic Smith (pts 6) and Fisher again (pts 6). Nevertheless, he was no match for Cosgrove and was caught with a constant stream of straight lefts and sharp right crosses to the ribs. He retired a weary fighter at the end of the sixth with a badly-gashed mouth. Armstrong ended the night in hospital because, after losing his gum-shield, he had been caught on the mouth, resulting in his teeth coming through his tongue.

The penultimate fight of Charlie's 1955 campaign saw him matched with tough Nigerian Santos Martins in a contest which should never have taken place. The Belfast lad was suffering badly from the 'flu and had great difficulty in breathing, a condition not helped by the presence of the gum-shield. Charlie retired in the sixth in great distress.

When Charlie was fit again he beat the former Scottish Welterweight Champion, Roy McGregor, who was disqualified in the third round for

Mr and Mrs Cosgrove

biting. The disqualification was unpopular since the crowd didn't seem to understand why the Scot had been dismissed. At the time, Cosgrove was boxing confidently and hurting his rugged opponent with a swinging uppercut to the body. This was the first time that Charlie's girlfriend, June, whom he had met two years previously, had been to see him fight. When she found out that Charlie's opponent had bitten him she was not too pleased, asking her boyfriend, "Why didn't you bite him back?" On the same bill, Charlie's brother Sammy defeated Benny Vaughan.

At the start of 1956 the boxers holding the local titles were: Joe Quinn (featherweight), Gerry Smyth (lightweight), Roy Baird (welterweight), George Lavery (middleweight), Tom Meli (light-heavyweight) and Paddy Slavin (heavyweight). Charlie started that year with wins over Jamaican Bobby Gill (pts 8) and Belfast's Sam Thompson (rtd 4). In his third contest of 1956, Charlie's opponent, Belfast man Joe Toner, came in as a substitute for Edinburgh's Eddie Philips but the classy Cosgrove was much too good for his fellow townsman, punishing him continuously with straight lefts and right crosses, which had his nose and mouth bleeding profusely. The end, to the relief of everyone, came in the third after a cracking right dropped Toner for a nine count. When Joe gamely got unsteadily to his feet, Cosgrove waded in and slammed him with both fists against the ropes until Toner's knees buckled and, once again, he went down for nine. For the second time, the brave Belfast boy got to his feet but the referee mercifully ended the one-sided contest.

On a George Connell promotion in the Ulster Hall on 24 March, Charlie was to have boxed Nigerian Joe Rufus in the chief supporting bout and Sammy Hamilton was due to box Jeff Dudu, also from Nigeria, in the principal contest of the evening. When Hamilton pulled out because of an injured hand, Connell asked Charlie to fill the breach. This he did in style, beating Dudu on points over eight rounds.

Manchester's Jimmy Brogden had, in the course of his thirty-seven fight career, won more than fifty per cent of his bouts, including a first round knockout of Belfast's Sammy Cowan and a fifth round stoppage of Lisburn man Jim Keery. He had also gone the distance with Banbridge's classy Bunty Adamson, who, at that point, was undefeated in twelve contests and would remain undefeated in thirty before losing to Terry Ratcliffe. But when Brogden met Cosgrove in the Ulster Hall on Saturday, 28 April 1956, he was completely outclassed. So often and accurately did Charlie catch Jimmy with jabs, hooks, body-punches and upper-cuts that he broke a knuckle in his right hand. He did tire a little, and Brogden began to land the occasional punch, but overall the Mancunian did well to stay the course.

On that same day, World Heavyweight Champion Rocky Marciano announced his retirement from the ring, stating that he was doing so for the "sake of his family". His final defence of the title, which he had won on 23 September 1952 and defended six times, was against Archie Moore, whom the "Rock" knocked out in the ninth.

For his next job, Charlie travelled to Glasgow, where he won with plenty to spare against Danny Harvey. On the same bill, Chic Brogan, who was managed by Mike Callaghan, was out-pointed by fellow Glaswegian Malcolm Grant in a fight for the Scottish bantamweight title.

Charlie's manager Jackie Briers was visibly upset when his boxer won on a disqualification in the dying moments of an eight-round contest against Derby's Ken Ashwood in the Ulster Hall on 13 October. "I thought the fight should have been allowed to go on," Briers complained. "After all, there wasn't even a round to go. The pity is that the verdict would take the gilt off Charlie's win." Referee Andy McDowell's reason for penalising the raw, rugged Ashwood was for "persistent holding". Perhaps, as there was only seconds to go in the contest, he should have exercised more discretion. There had been controversy between Briers and McDowell as early as the fourth round. Jackie had shouted to the referee to interrupt the round so that a trailing end of one of Ashwood's bandages could be adjusted. McDowell angrily warned him "not to interfere" and didn't do anything about the bandage until the end of the round. Briers was, needless to say, quite angry, claiming that the trailing bandage was a "danger to Charlie's eyes". The contest itself didn't see one of Charlie's better performances and he took unnecessary punishment. The cumbersome Ashwood shook him a number of times and, in the closing rounds, Charlie's face was bruised and swollen.

In Charlie's last fight of 1956 he travelled to West Ham Baths, where for the second time in a month he won on a disqualification, his opponent being Ron Richardson from Canning Town. Richardson's record included wins over Al Sharpe and Gerry McStravick, but he was being more than matched by Cosgrove's snappy counter-punching when he rushed in and accidentally caught the Belfast boxer in the groin. The bell rang at almost the same moment that the incident had occurred, but the referee, Tommy Little, had no hesitation in awarding the fight to Cosgrove. Charlie, who had caught Richardson with some solid punches, had been making his London debut.

On 23 February 1957 in the Ulster Hall, Charlie out-pointed Nigeria's Bob Roberts. For the first four rounds the muscular Roberts gave Charlie plenty of trouble, catching him with swings and hooks, but when Charlie settled down he ran out a comfortable winner.

As mentioned earlier, Charlie came tantalisingly close to fighting for the British welterweight crown. He was pencilled in to fight Liverpool's Tommy Molloy for the title that had been vacated by Peter Waterman, but the proposed date wasn't suitable for him as it clashed with the preparations being made for his wedding to June. She had always been concerned when Charlie was fighting, but there was no way she was going to let her marriage plans be jeopardised by her husband-to-be boxing a short time before their big day. Charlie smiled when he recalled June saying, "If you think that I'm going to walk down the aisle with you sporting a black eye . . ." Charlie's fight with Molloy did not, of course, materialise but the wedding did and the happy couple went on to have two girls and a boy. The contest against Bob Roberts turned out to be Charlie Cosgrove's last fight.

Today, Charlie is a Born Again Christian and sings in the church choir. The boxer-cum-chef might have had a comparatively short career, but whether he was in action in the kitchen or the ring, there was one thing that was guaranteed – the customers always went home happy.

PROFESSIONAL CAREER
1955–1957: 15 contests: won 14, lost 1, drew 0.

Sammy Cowan

Trilogy of thrillers with Hamilton

When the Ulster Hall in Bedford Street, Belfast, first opened its doors in May 1862 it was one of the largest music halls in the British Isles. Later it earned a deserved reputation as one of the key venues for boxing in the country. Indeed, even the "Boston strong boy" John L Sullivan honoured the establishment with his presence during a tour of Britain and Ireland between 1887 and 1888. Many other glovemen from yesteryear, and from closer to home than Sullivan, also graced the ring in the Ulster Hall, and their triumphs and defeats have been recorded elsewhere in this book. But there is one fighter in particular, whose appearances, especially in a trilogy of battles with fellow Belfast man Jim Hamilton, have left more than a lasting impression. And his name is Sammy Cowan.

Sammy was born on Friday, 24 September 1937, at Boyne Square in Sandy Row to labourer father, James, and mother, Mary. One of four children (he had three sisters), he attended Linfield Primary School. When he was fourteen, he obtained employment in a printing works, an industry which in those days was quite difficult to get into, before moving into the building trade. Together with a few snooker buddies, he formed a skiffle group called The Black Shirts, with whom he played guitar. While posing no threat to Lonnie Donegan, the group were regularly offered spots on shows and concerts as support to the headline acts. They also displayed their musical talents on the *Show of Shows*, an annual gala charity

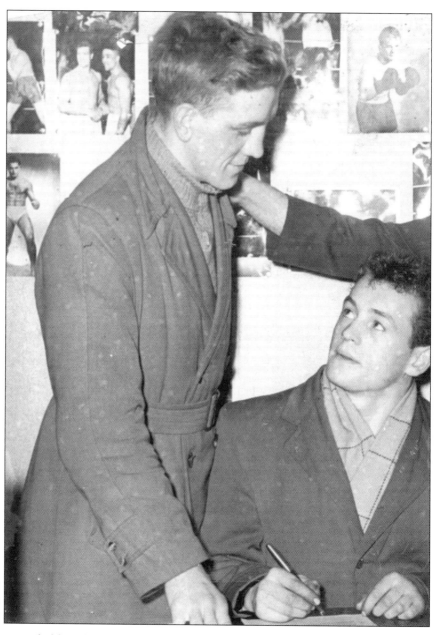

Sammy signs to fight Jim Hamilton

event held in the Ulster Hall in aid of handicapped children. Sammy was also an outstanding vocalist – so outstanding in fact that an old adversary of his, Peter Sharpe, once remarked, "If I had a voice like Sammy Cowan, I wouldn't be boxing."

In due course, the snooker hall where Sammy and his pals used to hang out became the Glenburn Boxing Club and one of its early members was seventeen-year-old Sammy himself. Two of his uncles had also boxed in the past (under the names Al Summers and Buffer Burns), and Sammy fondly recalled how "Al" (real name Sammy Henry) used to drive a Ford 8 behind

him to make sure that he completed at least seven or eight miles of roadwork as he pounded along the leafy Malone Road to Shaw's Bridge before returning home via the Lagan towpath. One dark morning, while driving behind Sammy on his run, Uncle "Al" was booked by the police for having faulty lighting on his vehicle and had to appear in court. Alongside working out for his boxing, Sammy would walk all the way to Greencastle every day, where he

Dougie Swaffield and Sammy Cowan

worked on a building site; after eight hours of hard graft, he would walk all the way home again.

He made his professional debut in the Ulster Hall on 27 November 1954, where, boxing under the name of Summers, he was too hot for local boy Harry Johnston, stopping his opponent in two rounds. On 8 December, Sammy, who was being managed by former boxer Dougie Swaffield and trained by Norman McCormick drew with Jim Hughes from Belfast. Then, a week before Christmas, the Glenburn southpaw, now using his proper surname, boxed another draw, this time against Bangor's Arty White.

Sammy obtained his second win in four starts when, on 1 January 1955, he had a points win over local boxer Bobbie O'Neill. Exactly a month later, in the Ulster Hall, he beat Arty White in a return bout. Sammy had learned a lot from their first encounter and his jabs and hooks piled up the points to give him a confidence-boosting victory.

In the space of seven days, Sammy knocked out Belfast boxers Brian Finnegan and Eddie Bamber and, four weeks later, he did the same to Lisburn's Jim Taggart in the first round. But he then lost three fights on the trot when he was stopped by Albert U'prichard protégé Jim Feeney from Banbridge (rtd 3), Belfast's Jim O'Brien (ko 3) and Lisburn's Billy Graham (ko 7). Sammy did come back and stopped Derry's Pat Milligan in the first round.

He made his first English appearance on 29 November 1955, but he was knocked out in the second round by Birmingham's Andy Baird. The bad run continued when, on Christmas Eve, he was stopped in four rounds by Belfast's Jim Fisher.

On 7 January 1956, in the Ulster Hall, when Sammy Cowan met Jim Hamilton for the first time, one sports journalist estimated that Cowan was down on the canvas nineteen times compared to Hamilton's being down fifteen times. Both men put on such an exhilarating display of boxing, however, that it seemed as if every person present threw "nubbins" (coins) into the ring.

As for the fight itself, it was gruelling and relentless. Like a great mystery thriller, no one in the hall had an inkling how it would end, with the tide flowing first one way and then the other. Hamilton was very fortunate not to have lost in the fifth. He had just been battered into the ropes when referee Andy McDowell went over to him as if to stop the bout, but Hamilton pushed him aside and belted Cowan to the floor in a fierce counter-attack. That is how it continued throughout. Both men were so utterly exhausted that they could barely lift their arms. Hamilton won in the sixth when Sammy rose with incredible courage from the canvas yet again and attempted to put up his fists, only for the referee to stop the fight.

This contest delivered the sort of excruciating excitement that transcends sport and speaks to our primal instincts. After the fight, Sammy was taken to the Royal Victoria Hospital, where he was detained overnight suffering from concussion.

In their second shootout in the Ulster Hall three weeks later, referee Neilly Thompson caused uproar when he disqualified Cowan in the fourth round. Sammy seemed to be well on his way to victory when he sent Hamilton out of the ring with a stiff right to the body. In the process, he lost his balance and went tumbling after him. Both men scrambled back into the ring and, most unexpectedly, the referee disqualified Cowan when he threw a punch without getting permission to box on. At that, the crowd began to stomp and boo and it was quite a while before their annoyance subsided. Hamilton had been taking heavy punishment and he was dropped three times in the first round. He was also down in the third and fourth rounds. It looked odds-on that Cowan's right hand would finish the job inside the distance, even though he too was in a bit of trouble when he took a vicious left to the body in the third.

The third Hamilton-Cowan clash didn't need "selling" but the papers tried to make out that there was a feud between these two brave battlers. This was nonsense. As Sammy later stated, while there may have been rivalry in the ring, in "Civvy Street", the men were friends. When they met again on 18 February, Cowan avenged his two previous defeats when, somehow, he managed to muster every ounce of strength to hurl a dynamite-laden left hook that knocked Hamilton on his back, arms outspread, legs quivering, cold as ice, for the full count in the sixth round. Right before this "bomb" was detonated, Sammy had looked every inch a beaten fighter. He did

Cowan and manager Dougie Swaffield sign a bet with Peter Sharpe and his manager, Tommy Vance

temporarily shake the grim-faced Jim, even downing him for a couple of no-counts, but Cowan's strength had been sapped by the power of his own punches, which had shaken Hamilton to his foundations and dropped him for seven counts (several of them outside the ring) in the first four rounds.

In a couple of rounds Sammy took no less than ten counts and his right eye, which had been injured in the first, was now completely obscured by the purple bruise surrounding it. Sammy's arms dropped like melting candles, and he stumbled forward on legs which were more like stone pillars. His manager, who had a substantial wager on the outcome, had lost his smile of the earlier rounds and was now nervously gnawing the ends of a towel draped around his neck. In the ring, the boxers were desperately weary. As their stamina left them they pushed rather than punched each other, resulting in them both tumbling together, arms tangled, to the canvas.

By the sixth, Cowan's supporters were worried, reluctantly agreeing that this looked like the last hurrah for brave Sammy. Suddenly, like a bolt of lightning from the sky, Cowan's left hook caught Hamilton on the point of the jaw and he was knocked colder than a freshly caught fish. The first aid men jumped into the ring to administer assistance to the prostate fighter on whose face his seconds were splashing water. Sammy, still dazed, stood smiling as Dougie Swaffield danced a little jig of joy. The fans cheered both boys and the "nubbins" rained into the ring.

No one would have been in the least surprised if Cowan had taken some time out after his three clashes with Hamilton but, on 16 April, he filled in for welterweight Charlie Cosgrove against Jimmy Brogden in the Ulster Hall. Unfortunately, he was knocked out in the first round for his trouble, highlighting perhaps the ten pounds he was giving away to the Manchester boxer. Shaking off this setback, he out-pointed Greenock's Tony McCrorey on a visit to Glasgow and, three weeks later in the Ulster Hall, he made it a double over McCrorey with another points win.

Burnley's Derek Clark had the scalps of local boxers Johnny Blane, Spike McCormick and Jim Fisher hanging from his belt, and he added Sammy's to his collection by knocking him out in the Ulster Hall on 16 June. It was later revealed that Sammy had boxed for five rounds with a broken bone in his left hand. Nevertheless, Clark repeated the task with a second-round knockout on 15 September.

Sammy had won three of his eight 1956 contests, but he increased that to five when he knocked out Belfast fighter Al Thomas in two rounds and Manchester's Neville Tetlow in three. In the latter bout, which again took place in the Ulster Hall, Cowan took a six count in the first round when Tetlow knocked him out of the ring. Sammy landed on the timekeeper's table but returned to the battleground and in the next round it was Tetlow's turn to take a count. In the third, a swinging right to the temple put Tetlow on the boards for a count of seven. When he got up he was still groggy and Cowan put him away for the full count.

Sammy's 1957 campaign got off to a fine start in the Ulster Hall when he knocked out Lisburn's Leo McCutcheon in the sixth. He followed this up by stopping Bryn Phillips from Fishguard in seven.

In a top of the bill contest in West Ham on 28 March, Sammy stopped Dagenham's Ron Hinson in four rounds, the referee calling an end to proceedings when Hinson sustained a nasty cut over his left eye. After a three month lay-off, Cowan travelled to Dudley, where he knocked out Birmingham's Andy Baird in the eighth round. The June heat in the Hippodrome in Dudley was suffocating but it didn't deter Sammy, who was in fine form. From the first bell, he had tried his best to have an early night but the Birmingham boy used the ring well to keep out of harm's way. Baird was not very enterprising; he boxed well on the retreat but rarely tried anything adventurous. At close range, Baird got in to the ribs but Cowan's right jab and following left were always a source of danger. In the final round, Andy was just not quick enough to get out of the way of a sizzling right hand, which landed flush on his chin, and he went down for the full count. Andy, by the way, was the brother of Roy Baird, the former Northern Ireland Welterweight Champion.

On 5 October, the Asian 'flu played havoc with a George Connell promotion in the King's Hall but it didn't prevent the Sammy Cowan-Peter Sharpe £100 "Challenge Fight" going ahead. Sharpe, who was having his sixty-second fight, forty-two of which he had won, stopped Sammy in round six.

Sammy's first opponent of 1958 was Ghana's Peter Cobblah, who had won four of his last six contests by the short route, including knocking out Spike McCormick in the first round. What was more ominous for Sammy was that Cobblah had knocked out Derek Clark in seven rounds. And so it transpired that the Ghana fighter got the better of Sammy by stopping him in the second during a Middlesbrough bout.

Cowan was now only fighting three or four times a year and lost his final two fights of 1958 when he was stopped by another Ghanaian Esso Lamptey (ko 3), and by Peter Sharpe (rsc 6). His personal life that year produced much happier memories when, on 22 November, he married Jean Fitzsimmons from Belfast. The couple would go on to have two boys and a girl.

Sammy resumed boxing on 17 January 1959, stopping Jamaican Jimmy Sansu in the fourth round. Both boys had an unenviable job: Cowan was faced by a crouching and "slippery-as-an-eel" Sansu, while the Jamaican had to deal with Sammy's "wrong-way-round" stance. Sansu's trouble started in the third when Sammy started to counter-punch and sent his opponent's gum-shield flying with a right hook which swung Jimmy's head around as if it was on a swivel. It was in this round that Sammy's right-hooking brought up a weal under Jimmy's right eye and drew blood from his nose and mouth.

Sansu's gum-shield was again punched from his mouth in the fourth during a wild spell in which Cowan had his left eye cut and Jimmy went down for a count of seven. As he sank to his knees Cowan failed to check a right hook to Sansu's head and was bundled out of the way by referee Billy Duncan. When Jimmy returned to his corner at the end of the round his mouth was bleeding freely and it was no surprise when he retired.

Next time out Sammy had a convincing points win over Peter Sharpe's brother, Joe, and just over a month later he drew with Pat Loughran of Belfast in Newry Town Hall. It would be eight months before Sammy fought again, and when he did the crowd in the Ulster Hall didn't give the local boy the credit he so richly deserved after out-pointing Ken Hignett from Liverpool. In an awkward, scrambling fight between two southpaws – by no means an ideal pairing – Hignett's right-hand jabbing had been undoubtedly the stiffer but Cowan used his longer reach to good advantage from the end of the fourth. In the fifth, he scored well when Ken lunged in. Cowan won the last two rounds but it was an untidy affair. Sammy put Hignett down for a count of four in the seventh but the Liverpudlian was able to keep out of trouble by spoiling and holding. Cowan went wading in, obviously confident he could put Hignett away in the last round. He launched some wild swings, many of which missed, but when he did land, Hignett was sent reeling back on the ropes. One swing dropped him for nine but Sammy was impatient and, instead of biding his time, he went tearing in, letting Hignett off the hook. When it was all over, referee Andy McDowell's decision in favour of Sammy wasn't too well received, and the booing and cat-calling continued even after the boxers had returned to their dressing-rooms. Nevertheless, there could be no doubting that Sammy was a worthy winner.

Three weeks after losing to Cowan, Hignett won the Central Area lightweight title when he knocked out Alf Cottam in six rounds, so he must have been in confident mood when he met Sammy for the second time on 18 February 1960 in the Theatre Royal, Dublin. But the Liverpool boy was no match for Sammy and was knocked out in the first.

On 5 April in Leeds Town Hall, Sammy met Nottingham's Brian Jones, who was fourth in line for a crack at Dave Charnley's British lightweight title. A cursory glance at Jones's record showed that out of his last sixteen fights he had won eleven of them on points, which indicated that he didn't carry a dig. Jones had to work hard for his win but Sammy, as always, never gave up trying. The fight from the start was one of vicious punching, although not all of them landed. Jones, with a short, hammer-like right as his chief weapon, scored solidly to Cowan's body but the Belfast boy retaliated with some good counter-punches which were wasted by landing too high up on Jones's head. As the fight neared its end, Cowan threw everything in a last desperate attempt to land a pay-off punch but the compact, workmanlike Jones kept well out of trouble and just about deserved his victory over a tough opponent.

On a bill in Fivemiletown, Sammy doubled his wins over Joe Sharpe with a fourth round stoppage. However, on a Cardiff card, in which Belfast's George O'Neill lost to Welshman Phil Jones and Dubliner Eddie O'Connor lost to Welshman Terry Crimmins, Sammy also lost to a Welsh man by being disqualified in the fifth against Darkie Hughes. It was announced that Sammy had been disqualified for "not trying". He brought his 1960 campaign to a close when he knocked out Richie Edwardson from Bootle in the first round.

In his first contest of 1961, and fighting at welterweight, Sammy out-pointed Dubliner Tommy Corrigan over six rounds in Belfast. In Dublin's Tolka Park on 28 July, he knocked out Cork's Sean Leahy in the first. This contest only lasted one minute and twenty seconds and, during that short period, Sammy only threw three punches – all of them right hooks to the head. The third punch knocked Leahy cold and he lay a full five minutes before being carried out on a stretcher. He was taken to hospital for observation.

Cowan had only one more fight in 1961, and it was one which produced the most significant win of his career. That win was against West Ham's Johnny Kramer, who since turning professional in 1959, had won twenty-two of his twenty-six contests, with sixteen inside the distance. Kramer was also number five in the British ratings for Brian Curvis' British welterweight title.

From the opening gong it was obvious that Cowan meant business, and it was in the first round that he did the damage that would end the contest by inflicting a nasty cut over Kramer's left eye. Johnny's corner managed to stem the flow of blood for a while and in rounds two and three the West Ham youngster showed the form which had made him such an outstanding prospect. He picked his punches with calculated calm and it seemed as if Sammy may have shot his bolt in a bid for a quick win. In the fourth round, however, the tough Belfast welterweight found a new lease of life and another powerful swing reopened Kramer's cut. This time the referee decided it was too bad for him to continue.

After his win over fifth-rated Kramer, Sammy had a wonderful opportunity to catapult himself into title contention when he met Liverpool's Jimmy McGrail on 7 February 1962 in Blackpool. Prior to meeting Sammy, McGrail had won twenty of his twenty-two fights, sixteen inside the distance. His list of victims included Freddie Tiedt, Jimmy Croll, Peter Sharpe, George Palin and Nat Jacobs. Twelve months previously, he had lost on points to Mick Leahy in an eliminator for the British welterweight title.

Sammy would rather have fought very poorly and won; instead he fought brilliantly but was caught with a short, fierce right to the jaw in the seventh and was counted out. In the first round, Sammy had caught McGrail with a right to the chin and Jimmy had taken a five count. Although he wasn't hurt he treated the Belfast boy with the utmost caution. In the same round, Sammy got through twice more with looping rights but, from the third round onwards, he was slowed down by McGrail's crisp body-punching. A cut above Jimmy's left eye stung the Liverpool boxer into action in the fourth, and with right hooks he had Sammy down for counts of eight and nine. Cowan took another count when the bell ended the round. All of this, of course, was a mere preamble before the predestined knockout midway through the seventh.

No one could accuse Sammy of taking easy fights and they didn't come any more difficult than his next opponent. Nottingham-born Wally Swift was an extremely gifted left-hand counter-puncher who had won the British welterweight crown in February 1960 by beating Tommy Molloy of Birkenhead on points over fifteen rounds. Although Dougie Swaffield had been shouting long and hard, especially after his boy's win over Kramer, for Sammy to be included in any British title eliminators that may have arisen, his hopes were dashed when Cowan, after losing to McGrail, was quickly knocked out by Swift in the first round in Birmingham.

It was a good night for the Sharpe brothers on St Patrick's Night 1962 on a Jim Aiken promotion in St Mary's Hall in Belfast. After losing his Northern Ireland welterweight belt to Paddy Graham two weeks previously, Peter knocked out Cork's Sean Leahy in five rounds, while his younger brother Joe stopped Sammy Cowan in six rounds as the result of Sammy sustaining a damaged right eye.

The unpredictable Sammy came back with yet another first-class performance when, as part of the Gilroy-Caldwell bill in the King's Hall on 20 October 1962, he stopped the Northern Ireland Welterweight Champion, Paddy Graham. The St George's boxer was saved by the bell when a stunning right hook put him down at the end of the second round. Paddy called the referee over, motioned to a cut left eye and called it a day. This was Graham's last fight as a professional.

At the end of 1962, the twenty-five-year-old Sandy Row man went to live in London, where he would remain for thirty years or so. Whilst there, Sammy obtained many jobs, as well as playing guitar in bars in the Holloway district. Country and western music was his particular speciality. Of course, he had not retired from the fight game and used to train in the Lonsdale Gym in Warren Street. Before he eventually did call it a day, at the age of twenty-seven, he had four more contests, one of which was against Joe Sharpe on a Larry McMahon promotion in Carrickfergus, when he made it a hat trick of wins by halting Joe in the fifth.

Two months later, in the Troxy Cinema in Belfast, Sammy was disqualified in the fifth for allegedly butting George Palin from Crewe. It had been a tough, highly-charged fight in which Palin had been warned twice for butting and once for ducking below the waistline.

On 22 October 1963 in Derry's Guildhall, Sammy was stopped in the second round by hard-hitting Cyril Panther from Ghana. In his final contest of a career that had been anything but dull, Cowan lost to Doncaster's Fred Powney when he was stopped in the third at the Wyvern Sporting Club in Manchester.

Sammy, who carries no souvenirs of his ring wars and looks in pretty good condition, is today employed as a gardener. He lives with his charming second wife Frances in their beautiful home in the shadow of Scrabo Tower in Newtownards. And while you might be hard pushed to find anyone around nowadays who can remember local skiffle group The Black Shirts, you are certain to have better luck with the name of their guitarist, the hard-working and hard-punching Sammy Cowan.

PROFESSIONAL CAREER
1954–1964: 52 contests: won 27, lost 22, drew 3.

Freddie Gilroy

A magnificent amateur and a world-class professional

O ne of my most striking memories of Freddie Gilroy did not directly involve the great man himself. On the morning of Tuesday, 25 October 1960, I met up with my friend, Seamus Bryans, to board the ship that would carry us on our way to London where Freddie – the British, British Empire and European Bantamweight Champion – was fighting that night in Wembley's Empire Pool in a bid to wrest the vacant world bantamweight title from Alphonse Halimi. Surrounded by hundreds of the local lad's fans on the ship – among them, Rinty Monaghan, who kept everyone amused with his banter and jokes – all was going fine until Seamus asked to have a look at my ticket for the fight. On checking my wallet I broke out in a cold sweat, for the ticket was not there. I desperately thrust my hands deep into every pocket in a futile effort to locate it when I remembered, albeit a trifle too late, that I had left it underneath the television set at home for safekeeping, and, in the excitement of the morning, had stupidly forgotten to take it with me. With not enough money to buy another one, all hope of seeing my idol in action was fading until Seamus said that he would provide me with the entrance fee. It was a bad start to the day, and it would prove to be an even more disastrous evening, when Freddie Gilroy's luck was also to desert him.

Born on 7 March 1936 in Belfast's Short Strand area to Maeve and Frederick Gilroy, Freddie tried his hand at most sports as a kid, but was especially drawn to boxing. Under the tutelage of Jimmy McAree in the St John Bosco ABC, the legendary club which was once visited by Father Joseph Flanagan (portrayed by

Spencer Tracy in the screen classic *Boy's Town*), Freddie took to the fight game like crocodiles take to terrified wildebeest trying to cross the Mara River.

From schoolboy titles he progressed to take four Down and Connor championships. With his superb ring-craft and punching ability he won the Ulster flyweight and All-Ireland junior flyweight titles in 1955, before snatching the Ulster and All-Ireland Senior bantamweight belts the following year, producing a first-round knockout over Sarsfield's Corporal H Naughton in the process.

Prior to winning Ulster and National titles in 1956, Freddie impressed with a magnificent win in the Ulster Hall when, representing Ulster in a 5-5 draw against the British army, he knocked out Private J Jones with a beautiful left hook in the second round. Before the squaddie was put to sleep he had already taken an eight count from an identical punch. By this stage, Gilroy was rightly setting himself apart as something special, making a name for himself as a knockout specialist.

In Dublin, just over a week later, Ireland retained the Kuttner Shield by beating Scotland six bouts to four in a match that saw Freddie outpoint Derry Treanor; in West Germany less than two weeks after that, Gilroy was victorious once again when he defeated Ernst Kappelmann. On that occasion Ireland lost 6-3.

At the Corinthians' Annual Tournament in The Stadium, Dublin, on 24 February 1956, Freddie doubled his wins over Monaghan-born, Scottish amateur champion Derry Treanor. In a thrilling contest Treanor had the Ulster champion down for a count of eight in the first round, but Gilroy proved that he could take a punch as well as give one, and rallied magnificently for a close win. The fine wins over Treanor were a good indicator as to the calibre of Gilroy: when the Scot turned professional he was to have wins over Terry Spinks (who would go on to win the British featherweight title by stopping Bobby Neill in September 1960) and the reigning British and British Empire Champion Peter Keenan, whom he stopped in two rounds in August 1958. Perhaps the best performance of Treanor's career was when he went fourteen rounds in a featherweight championship fight against champion Howard Winstone in April 1962. He was halted with a cut eye.

Another notable performance was served up by Freddie in the Ulster Hall in March 1956 when, representing a strong local selection, he clearly out-pointed Scottish Midland Champion Davy Ford. Gilroy punished his opponent mercilessly and at will with solid straight rights and left hooks. Practically the only time Ford tried to abandon his crab-like tactics to box properly was in the fifth, and then he was dumped on his pants for a nine count by a lovely one-two.

In April 1956, Freddie was selected to box in America, where he had the opportunity to show his undoubted talents to a wider audience. Before a crowd of 11,000 boxing fans in Chicago on 11 May, in the 19th Golden

Road work on Cavehill in preparation for the showdown with Halimi

Gloves Tournament, he out-pointed Don Erdington. At one stage Ireland led 5-1, but the match ended all square at 5-5. Ireland's other winners were Johnny Caldwell, Martin Smith, Tommy Byrne and Harry Perry.

The Irish team then travelled to Montreal, where they had a magnificent 7-3 win over a combined team of Quebec and Montreal champions. About 5,000 people watched the match and Gilroy scored freely with his left to beat Montreal's Gabriel Mancini.

When the Irish Olympic boxing team was named in the first week of October 1956, eyebrows were raised when it was announced that Gilroy had not been selected. However, it seems that it was all a misunderstanding over Freddie's weight. When his manager intervened, the problem was resolved but funds were still collected at every opportunity to make sure that Freddie was sent to Melbourne; an Irish squad without Freddie Gilroy would have been like an army going into battle without its heavy artillery.

Against Wales in Dublin, on 5 October, Gilroy was at his very best, knocking out the unfortunate P Jones from Cardiff inside eighty seconds with a Gilroy specialty, a left hook to the body. Jones needed some time to recover before he could leave the ring. Four days later, in a match against Scotland in Paisley Ice Rink, Ireland trounced Scotland 7-3, with Gilroy defeating Johnny Morrissey.

On 30 October, Ireland drew 5-5 with a German team from Hamburg. The match, staged at the New Cinema, Banbridge, in County Down, saw southpaw Gilroy at his devastating best, punishing his hapless opponent Albert Nissan with contemptuous ease. Freddie put Nissan down for nine towards the end of the first round with a left to the "breadbasket" and the German was taking a hammering when the round ended. During the interval he very wisely called it a day.

In 1956, the Melbourne Olympics were overshadowed somewhat by world events, such as the brutal Russian invasion of Hungary, and some participants withdrew or threatened to withdraw. However, when the boxing got under way, one person who probably wished that he *had* withdrawn was the Russian favourite for the bantamweight gold medal, Boris Stefano, who was up against Freddie Gilroy. In the third, Freddie feinted with his right and, as the Russian moved away from the expected blow, the Irishman let go with his lethal left hook; for Mr Stefano, it was all over. The Irish contingent in the stadium went wild, as did quite a few Hungarians. The Russians, as their medal haul of thirty-seven gold, twenty-nine silver and thirty-two bronze for these Games testified, were arguably the best athletes on the planet, and their boxers were professional in everything but name, so Freddie's victory rightfully made headlines all over the world.

In the quarter-finals, Freddie out-pointed Italy's M Sutra but lost to the eventual gold medal winner, Germany's W Behrendt, in the semi-finals. As well as being a memorable Olympics for Gilroy, Melbourne also saw Johnny Caldwell and Tony Byrne winning bronze medals, and Dublin boxer Freddie Tiedt winning silver.

On their return home, Gilroy, Caldwell and Martin Smith were given a rousing welcome. Speaking of his semi-final loss, Freddie said, "I was certain that I had won, for the fight against the Italian had been far more difficult, yet I got a clear verdict in it." On his victory over the Russian, he declared, "I came 12,000 miles to deliver that knockout punch, but it was worth it."

There were strong rumours that Freddie was on the brink of turning professional; before doing so he had a date in the Ulster Hall with the British army's "Sapper" Alex Ambrose. Freddie easily won on points, but Ulster were trounced 9-1 by the military team.

Gilroy's professional career took off on Saturday, 11 February 1957, in the Ulster Hall, where, using boxing's most potent weapon – the deadly left hook – he knocked out Derek McReynolds from Old Colwyn in two minutes and ten seconds, including the count.

The next sacrificial lamb to face Gilroy was Dundee's Danny McNamee. The Scot took tremendous punishment in the second before being counted out. McNamee, who had come in as a substitute, was caught with a succession of vicious left hooks and, when he went down, his head hit the canvas with a loud thud and it was all over.

In Freddie's third contest, against Manchester's Jackie Tiller, he was more cool, calm and collected, giving a terrific display of power punching to win on points. He scored repeatedly with his deadly left to the head and ribs, and let loose with a beauty to drop Tiller for eight in the fifth; but he was in no hurry and was happy to go the full course.

Gilroy versus Rollo

Next up was Glaswegian, Jimmy Cresswell. The second round was one minute, thirty seconds old when Gilroy looped his left arm in a short, vicious arc. The glove, which must have contained TNT, connected with Cresswell's jaw as he came off the ropes. For a split second he swayed, and his eyes rolled like cherries on a gaming machine, then he collapsed and lay rigid on his back. Referee Billy Duncan counted over him, but could just as easily have gone for a tea-break: the unfortunate Scot would still have been lying there on his return.

Freddie claimed his fourth knockout in five fights when he disposed of

Liverpool bantamweight Terry McHale. Nothing much happened in the opening round, but at the start of the second Gilroy moved up a gear and trapped McHale against the ropes. There was no escape. Gilroy whipped in his right lead first and, as the Scouser's right was prodded out, his body was left unguarded. Freddie's left hook travelled no more than a few inches; as McHale's knees buckled and his breath came rasping through his rubber dentures, that same deadly fist flashed in an arc to his temple. He slumped sideways to the canvas, lay on his side until "seven" before instinctively trying to rise. He only managed to lever himself into a crouch and, like someone under the influence, swayed dizzily across the ring and collapsed in a heap to be counted out.

Freddie's next two contests were in Glasgow: at Firhill Park, he knocked out hometown boxer Archie Downie in the second of an eight-round contest; about four weeks later at the same venue, he defeated Spaniard Jose Alvareze in the fifth.

Gilroy's reputation as a powerful hitter was spreading like wildfire, making it difficult for promoter George Connell to get opponents for him. He commented, "I have tried my best to get Freddie opponents for Grosvenor [Park], but once you mention his name, cross-channel bantams either shy away like frightened horses or they ask for ridiculous purses, which is the easiest way of saying no." Connell continued, "If any reasonably good bantam would like to fight Freddie, then I would like to hear from him."

In his final contest of 1957, at the King's Hall, Freddie finished the year as he began with an inside-the-distance win, his victim being local boxer George O'Neill. In the first two rounds it seemed more than likely that Gilroy would knock out O'Neill, as his long, solid right lead had been jolting his opponent's head back and reddening his face. However, George's pluck and experience kept him in contention and he would score to the body in close-quarter spells, using a neat countering right hand very well.

Gilroy never stopped attacking, and he hurt his deadly left hand early on. Nevertheless, it was still potent enough to down O'Neill in the seventh. George also sustained an ugly injury above his left orb and was in a bad state when the referee halted the proceedings. This was a fine win over a man who, in his last contest, had gone eight rounds with Scot Dick Currie, who was number three in the British ratings for a crack at Peter Keenan's bantamweight title.

Freddie would now step up in class and, in the King's Hall on 8 March 1959, he faced the Belgian Bantamweight Champion, Pierre Cossemyns, who in January had gone ten rounds with World Champion Hogan "Kid" Bassey. Gilroy's performance was absolutely amazing and he knocked Cossemyns out in the fourth.

Freddie moved a step closer to a tilt at Peter Keenan's British and British Empire bantamweight titles when he out-pointed local boxer George Bowes over ten rounds in West Hartlepool. Bowes was rarely able to land a telling punch in the latter half of the fight and Freddie finished a good points winner. He lived up to his deserved reputation as a devastating puncher when he dropped Bowes in the third, making it the first time that Bowes had taken a count in his professional career; it was also his first defeat in twelve outings.

However, in a final eliminator for Keenan's titles, the Belfast southpaw had a sterner task when he met Johnny Morrissey, whom he had previously encountered – and beaten – in their Simon Pure days. In the early rounds the fight was disappointing and Freddie found it difficult to get through the Scot's defence. After the first three rounds, however, the Belfast warrior showed signs of getting on top and, in the sixth, he drew crimson from Morrissey's nose.

The fireworks started in the seventh after a tussle in which there was not much between the fighters. After scoring freely with lefts and rights, Gilroy walked into a fierce right and went down for a count of nine. Morrissey failed to nail his man before the bell and came out in the eighth determined to follow up his advantage, but Freddie caught him with a powerful left hook, dumping him, also for nine.

Johnny got up but was no sooner on his feet than he was pounded down again for another count, this time for eight. Gilroy went after him, tossing rights and lefts in an attempt to get it all over in a hurry. He hammered the tall Scot to the canvas again for a five count; Morrissey was saved by the bell. Johnny complained to the corner of a damaged jaw and his seconds signalled to the referee that he was unable to continue. The ref announced to the 11,000-strong crowd that Morrissey had retired.

Freddie had now taken care of two title contenders in their own back yards. In his final contest of 1958, he squared up to the Spanish Featherweight Champion, Jose Luis Martinez. Would this bout prove to be unlucky thirteen for Gilroy? While not one of Freddie's better performances, the referee still raised the Belfast man's hand in victory at the finish. There was some protesting, but Freddie had won handily enough.

Freddie was finally rewarded with a crack at thirty-one-year-old Peter Keenan's titles. Gilroy, who was a huge admirer of Keenan, recalls meeting the curly-haired Scot at the weigh-in. As he was shaking his opponent's hand, Keenan said, "Let's have a good fight, Freddie. If you win, I'm packing it up. It's been a great life, boxing. This is your chance."

Gilroy wasn't going to let that chance slip. When he stepped into the King's Hall ring on the evening of Saturday, 10 January 1959, he looked more like a choirboy than a professional fighter; but if Freddie was to win, there was every chance that he would get a shot at the world champ Alphonse Halimi.

When the preliminaries were over and the bell sounded for the start, the 16,000 crowd roared themselves hoarse, urging Freddie to do the business. When a Belfast fight crowd gets behind you, it's like having an extra hand. Gilroy went after his prey like a hound chasing a fox. It was obvious, even at this early stage of the proceedings, what Keenan's game plan was – to survive at all costs. Peter had been around for a long time and had fought, and beaten, Europe's best, but he must have known in his brave Scottish heart that, barring a miracle, he would be saying goodbye to his titles, as well as to a professional boxing career that had been characterised by dignity and humility.

As early as the third round he was on the deck from a right hook to the jaw but, amazingly, he got up without taking a breather. No sooner was he on his feet than Freddie was on him like a vulture on a carcass. He did survive a torrid round, and performed a little better at the beginning of the fourth, but nothing to set alarm bells ringing in the Gilroy corner.

In the fifth, Freddie caught the champ with a beautiful right uppercut under the heart, following it with a left hook to the stomach that sent Keenan reeling against the ropes. Peter was so tired that he actually dropped his guard. Round six saw Freddie taking it a bit easier, but he was still the boss. Keenan obtained a well-earned moment of respite when Gilroy asked the referee to clean the champ's gloves, on which resin dust had accumulated.

Freddie had another quiet round in the seventh, but from then on, it was all systems go. A right hook to the head sent Peter reeling against the hempen strands and a left hook put the Scot down for five. He got up once again, showing supreme courage, only to run into punches that came at him from all angles. Peter Keenan's reign was drawing to a close and he was surviving on sheer guts alone.

In the tenth, the torment continued for Keenan. He was hit by every punch in Gilroy's vast repertoire and was on the brink of a knockout from a left uppercut to the body. The contest was, to say the least, pretty one-sided. In the eleventh, Keenan must have thought that he had died and gone to hell, for where else could such punishment be dished out? As his hard-earned crown slipped from his sweating head he went down for a count of three, but this was more from a slip than a punch, and when he slipped yet again, the referee pulled him to his feet. One of the hardest punches Freddie Gilroy had ever thrown – a heavy right hook under the heart – put Peter down for nine. The referee had done so much counting over this magnificently brave Scot that his mouth must have been as dry as the Sahara. Another merciless bombardment from his baby-faced tormentor resulted in Keenan taking a five count. When he touched down from a left hook to the temple, the bell sounded to give him a minute's respite.

Peter looked a pathetic sight and, as the referee helped him on to his stool, he asked the Scot if he wanted to pack it in; Keenan refused. However, the referee was having none of it, and brought the curtain down not only on the fight but also on Peter Keenan's career. Just before Teddy Waltham, General Secretary of the British Boxing Board of Control, placed the shining Lonsdale belt around Freddie's slim waist, Peter announced his retirement from the ring. The crowd sang "When Irish Eyes Are Smiling" in honour of the new

Slugging it out with Pina

champ and, when they switched to "Glasgow Belongs To Me", the tears ran down Keenan's face.

Freddie recalled that "My dressing room swarmed with well-wishers, and my back was sore from hearty back-slaps – even more than my face and chest was by blows in the ring. Then I went into Keenan's dressing room. He was sitting – talking and laughing. I was surprised to find him so cheerful. Hadn't he just lost his titles to me?" Peter told Freddie that he had "come to the end of the road", adding that "I'm all in one piece… For you, the struggle is just starting. Good luck, Freddie, and never lose confidence in yourself."

Gilroy next faced Frenchman Jacques Collomb, who had plenty of losses on his CV. Still, Freddie did what he had to do, and he did it competently, stopping his opponent in six rounds in the King's Hall.

In April, another Frenchman, Charlie Sylla, fell victim to a Gilroy onslaught and was counted out while still standing in round two. Sylla was dropped in his own corner, but somehow got to his feet to face another bombardment. He was dumped once more for a count of four. It was obvious that, in his distress, he had not the presence of mind to take a longer count, even though his seconds were pleading with him to do so. He was a sitting target for Gilroy, and his head was punched from side to side like a buoy on a turbulent ocean. Sylla took another count, this time for eight, and, once again, rose bravely to his feet. He tried feebly to put up some kind of resistance but his punches were like candyfloss; the referee counted him out when he was longer able to defend himself.

Gilroy, who was now rated third in the world rankings, had wins over Al Asunction from the Philippines and Italian Mario D'Agata, a deaf mute who was the former European and World Bantamweight Champion. This was a step up in class for Gilroy, who was now undefeated in eighteen contests. The D'Agata fight would be the acid test for the Belfast boy and if he came out on top, a crack at the European crown, followed by a tilt at the world title was inevitable. In a thrilling fight at the Empire Pool, Wembley, in September 1959, Freddie passed his toughest test to date with honours, winning on points over ten tough rounds.

He thoroughly deserved his win over D'Agata: from the third round, he fought with a nasty cut on his left eyelid against a man who brought all the experience of a long and distinguished ring career into play. Yet Gilroy never gave up trying and towards the end of the fight was giving out punishment freely with both hands, although he was inclined to risk further damage to his left eye by boring in with his head down.

D'Agata, whose seconds gave him instructions in sign language, and who was signalled the beginning and end of each round by four flashing lights at the corners of the ring that blinked simultaneously with the bell, paid tribute with his gesticulations to Gilroy afterwards. He was obviously not too dissatisfied with Mr Jack Hart's decision. D'Agata went around the ring with hands raised to earn the cheers of the crowd.

It was in every way a satisfactory performance by Gilroy. In D'Agata, he faced a boxer who ducked, weaved and slipped out of many an awkward situation and who rarely neglected to score when Gilroy presented an open target. Several times both men continued to fight after the bell, perhaps due to D'Agata not noticing that the flashing lights were on. The early stages of the fight were marked by much close-quarter work, the two men frequently falling into clinches and aiming for the body. Gilroy seemed to have got the measure of his opponent, particularly in the second round, and he caught him with a quick right to the chin as they came off the ropes that had the Italian distinctly worried.

Shortly afterwards, D'Agata motioned that Gilroy had caught him with his head, but the referee took no notice and the fight was allowed to continue. Only a few seconds after the third round had opened, Gilroy came out of a clinch with blood streaming from the cut on his eyelid, provoking the Italian into further effort. D'Agata caught the dogged little Irishman with several good punches, one of which – a right to the body – had Gilroy in trouble. Freddie seemed relieved when the bell went for the end of the round, but he

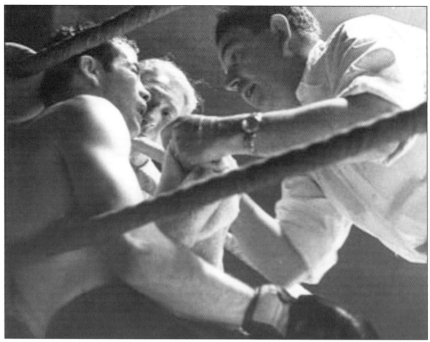

Freddie receiving attention from his seconds during the Pina bout

came back in the next session refreshed and staggered his man with a right to the head that compelled him to hang on.

Near the end of the round D'Agata put Gilroy through the ropes with a magnificent body punch and nearly fell on top of him. The Belfast lad got up at six and managed to evade any further trouble.

The subsequent rounds saw both men dealing out punishment with Gilroy the more accurate of the two. In the eighth, he did slip down for a count of two, but at the end of the round neither man heeded the bell and again the referee had to spring in between them to stop the exchanges. Gilroy now realised that the last two rounds meant everything to him; immediately the bell had gone for the ninth he stormed into the attack, swinging punches from all angles. D'Agata took some of them on the arm, but others obviously hurt him. In the last round, there was no doubt that Gilroy was well on top and the Italian's only hope of gaining victory was by a knockout. The record books show that that this didn't happen and Freddie went on to win comfortably.

As happened frequently, Gilroy suffered badly bruised hands and both were immersed in an ice-box for a long period after the fight. His left eye was also badly damaged but Jimmy McAree said that the injuries were "purely superficial". He added, "I cannot see how he can fail to be given a chance for the world title now."

Freddie didn't get a crack at the world title for his next outing, but did get the next best thing – a chance at Piero Rollo's European bantamweight title. Rollo, who was born in Cagliari, Italy, on 9 February 1927, and was nine years Gilroy's senior, had won the crown with a win over Gilroy's last opponent, Mario D'Agata, on 12 October 1958, retaining it by drawing with Juan Cardenas and winning, on a disqualification, against Federico Scarponi. Before stepping into the ring with Gilroy, Piero had contested fifty-four fights, winning forty-three, losing five and drawing six – a pretty useful record by any stretch of the imagination.

Rollo did well against Freddie, giving his all in defence of his title and, in a thrilling final round, the fighters stood toe-to-toe and exchanged punch for punch. The London crowd went wild with excitement at the finish as Freddie Gilroy, the pride of Ireland, lifted the European crown.

After the fight Freddie remarked that "Piero was certainly a tough one, but then you expect that from a European champion with his record. He was fit and took everything that I threw at him. But to tell the truth, he didn't trouble me as much as Mario D'Agata."

In his final contest of the momentous year that was 1959, Freddie knocked out the South African Bantamweight Champion, Bernie Taylor, out during a defence of his Empire bantamweight title in the King's Hall. Before the bout, and unknown to everyone except Jimmy McAree and the doctor who administered it, the champion had to have a cortisone injection. This was to relieve a recurrence of pain in his left shoulder that had been wrenched in his clash with Rollo the previous month. Despite this, Gilroy administered some bad medicine to Taylor, culminating in a tranquiliser dart of a left hook that sapped the South African of all energy in the fifth round. The courageous Taylor did manage to get to his feet at nine, but referee Frank Wilson counted him out. Bernie had been undefeated in his previous eight contests, but the calibre of his opponents didn't compare to the classy Gilroy.

Billy Rafferty, a twenty-seven-year-old Glaswegian, was never going to take the boxing world by storm, but he was a tough and courageous little man who gave his all from the first bell to the last. By courtesy of a win over Welshman Len Rees in a final eliminator for Gilroy's three titles, his big day duly arrived on 19 March 1960.

In the King's Hall that night, Billy's performance was better than the majority of fight fans expected, though Gilroy was a clear but weary victor. Rafferty's right eyebrow, first gashed in the seventh, was in a bad state when the referee stopped the contest in round thirteen.

Some three months later in Manchester, Billy would outpoint Mexican Ignacio Pina – the same fighter who, on Monday, 25 April 1960, would be the first opponent to scupper Gilroy's unbeaten record when they met in Belle Vue, Manchester.

Pina's win was no fluke, for he boxed like a master, calmly counter-punching Freddie, whose vision was impaired by an eye injury from the fifth round onwards. Although Gilroy was beaten, the verdict was in doubt right up to the end, with everyone thinking he would pull something out of the bag and save the day. In the ninth, he turned Pina's legs to jelly with a shuddering left hook to the jaw that rocked the Mexican back against the ropes. But Freddie lost his chance; instead of measuring his opponent for the kill, he went berserk. A left hook crashed into Pina's jaw and made the crowd roar but the punch didn't carry its usual lethal dosage of venom, and Pina, boxing cleverly on the retreat, kept away from trouble, holding off a fierce Gilroy onslaught in the tenth and last round. Although Ignacio was repeatedly hurt he kept calm.

Freddie had done his utmost to save his unbeaten record and keep his world title ship afloat but the Mexican just about deserved the decision. After the fight, Jimmy McAree said, "We can't grouse. All I can say is that a sharp Gilroy would have beaten him. Yes, we were a trifle put out by the upsets in our travel arrangements [Freddie and his manager had missed the Manchester plane by two minutes], but I am not offering that as an excuse."

There would be more glory for Freddie Gilroy, but it wouldn't come on Tuesday, 25 October 1960. At Wembley's Empire Pool, he was so unlucky in his quest to win the vacant world bantamweight title (European version) against French-Algerian Alphonse Halimi. Not one British journalist was of the opinion that Halimi deserved to win. In fact, the *Boxing News*' headline declared NO LUCK OF THE IRISH FOR GALLANT GILROY, continuing:

> But how on earth Belgian referee M. Philippe managed to arrive at the decision will remain, for us, one of the fistic mysteries of all time. In the last round, with Gilroy forcing Halimi on to the ropes in his own corner, in Halimi's corner, and in neutral corners, slamming away freely, the vast crowd were certain that Gilroy had done it and they began a thunderous stomping of the feet in premature applause long before the final bell.
>
> When Mr. de Backer walked towards Halimi we thought he had made a mistake and expected him to change direction and hold up the hand of the British champion. We were astounded when the Frenchman received the verdict. It seemed incredible... unbelievable. The crowd refused to believe it. They booed the place down. They hooted and whistled. They threw missiles at the ring and when the world championship trophy was handed to Halimi they booed the little champion.

The bible of boxing did credit Halimi for his habit of "touching gloves at the start of every round", adding that "Gilroy... was only too pleased to keep the contest clean".

Freddie most definitely stamped his authority on the bout from the very start, concentrating on Halimi's body and pounding away with rat-a-tat punches on the inside of the French-Algerian's defence. While emerging from the first round with a puffed eye, the Belfast man wrote the script for the second, resisting Halimi's weak advances and upping the tempo to continually wrong-foot his opponent. This was most evident when Gilroy got through and landed powerful two-fisted body blows that completely dumbfounded Halimi. Throughout the contest, Alphonse continually permitted Freddie to trap him in the corners and ropes, subjecting himself to Gilroy's barrages, a situation which led to Freddie being lectured by the referee on having to "break" when immediately instructed to. Perhaps unfairly, those instances where Halimi continued holding when instructed to break went unchecked.

Alphonse did carry the heavier punch and used it to good effect by hurting Gilroy in the seventh, but the bigger the ammunition deployed by Halimi, the more Gilroy seemed to enjoy it. He shook off the big punches he had soaked up in the seventh and eighth, not forgetting an accidental low right in the ninth, to keep coming back to force a fight out of Halimi.

The onslaught on Halimi's body continued into the tenth, and despite being drawn into an "uppercut trap" in the eleventh, Gilroy took every opportunity that the distressed-looking Frenchman offered him, extending his edge in the proceedings into the twelfth and, finally, an incredible thirteenth round.

Halimi's optimistic, but mostly ineffective, upper-cutting handed the lead role to Gilroy, but the Irishman did have the spotlight dragged away from him momentarily when one of Alphonse's uppercuts finally found its target, right to the jaw, crippling Gilroy to the canvas close to his corner and hushing the assembled fight fans. Gilroy was rescued by the bell at the "three" count, but he was still suspect in the fourteenth and somehow managed to stay out of real trouble to regain the initiative in the last round. He unleashed all that he had in the fifteenth, pinning Halimi at one point in the Irish corner to absorb all the punishment, looking every inch a world champion. Unfortunately, the referee must have been looking at a different fight, and the Irish fans' contentions that their man had been robbed could not be disputed.

Halimi would win his next three fights, but in an ironic twist of fate he would lose his world title to another Belfast boxer by the name of Johnny Caldwell, Freddie's 1956 Melbourne Olympic team-mate and fellow bronze medallist.

Freddie put the injustice of the Halimi verdict firmly behind him, notching up points wins over Italian Ugo Milan in London and Sheffield's Billy Calvert in Liverpool, and knocking out Edinburgh's Jackie Brown in Paisley and stopping French-Algerian Boualem Bedourd in Belfast. All of these victories occurred in the early part of 1961.

Freddie would suffer the third defeat of his career when he was knocked out in the mammoth Palais des Sport in Brussels as he challenged Pierre Cossemyns for the vacant European bantamweight title on 27 May 1961. The Belfast man retired after taking terrific punishment. He was down five times in the eighth when he was saved by the bell, and he was down again at the start of the ninth when his seconds intervened.

Gilroy was the master in the finer arts of boxing, beating Cossemyns consistently to the lead. In the second round it seemed as if he could also out-fight his rival, whom he put down for three counts, and he appeared to have an excellent chance of improving on his fourth round knockout over the Belgian three years previously. Always, however, there was the danger to which Freddie was so prone. Gilroy's suspect defence had never been more cruelly exposed; for all of his courage, he was unable to shake off the effects of the really telling punches to which he was inclined, from time to time, to leave himself open to. He had two spells of disaster in his clash with Cossemyns. The first was in the fourth when two crashing rights had him down for counts of six, and he was desperately shaky at the bell. A spell of superb boxing apparently enabled him to weather the storm as he jabbed away to Cossemyns' head and piled up the points.

Then disaster struck again. With confidence regained, Gilroy stormed back in the eighth from the brink of defeat and his rashness proved his undoing. He dropped his hand and threw a left. Cossemyns was in like a flash with a searing left hook that crashed Gilroy to the canvas for a count of eight. There were two more counts from the same punch and nobody could understand how Gilroy managed to struggle to his feet on those three occasions.

His misery was not over. Cossemyns again chopped him down with the left, and this time the eight thousand spectators cheered themselves hoarse. The count of ten was completed without Freddie moving a muscle. Pandemonium broke loose; then it was discovered that the bell to end the round had rung, unheard, when the count was at three and Freddie had to face more torture. It was, however, not for long. He dashed over to Cossemyns' corner throwing punches blindly, but the Belgian landed again with a vicious left hook. Gilroy clutched his opponent's legs as he slumped forward to the canvas. The towel fluttered in from the Irish corner.

This would be Freddie Gilroy's last defeat. Afterwards, Jimmy McAree told reporters, "Gilroy took too many chances when he was leading on points. Cossemyns is a clever boxer. In one knockdown in the eighth round Gilroy's head hit the canvas very hard. That did as much damage as the knockdown. Freddie is to have some rest and he might go to the United States for a holiday."

Freddie did go to the States not only for a well-deserved rest but also to give serious thought to his future. His confidence was at such an all-time low that he wrestled with the problem of whether or not he should remain in the sport that he had graced so magnificently from boy to man.

But an incident, not far from Niagara Falls, in which the Belfast star "decked" a would-be bag thief, who was much heavier than himself, convinced Freddie that he still carried the "dope". He decided there and then that he was not finished with the fight game just yet and headed for New York, where he was well known in boxing circles from his Golden Gloves days. He worked out with a couple of sparring partners against whom he more than held his own.

When Freddie returned from the States he weighed an incredible eleven stone which didn't go down too well with Jimmy McAree. Freddie said, "For years the Press had claimed that I could not make the bantam limit without

Gilroy and Caldwell: local heroes

considerable trouble. If they had seen me then who would have blamed them for crowing, 'We told you so.'"

Under McAree's watchful eye, Freddie shifted the surplus calories, getting to within striking distance of the bantamweight limit, and was soon enjoying training once again.

After ten months of ring inactivity, he returned to the squared circle on 3 March 1962, in a rematch with Billy Rafferty. The two little battlers once more gave the punters their money's worth, but it was the bruised, battered and completely exhausted Scot who succumbed after one minute and five seconds of the twelfth after a savage mauling by Gilroy. He had been down three times before this, twice without a count and once for "five". Up to the fifth round Rafferty was making it a gruelling slogging match. Punch for punch there was little in it with the local boy just a fraction in front. Rafferty had the champion wearing a worried frown in the third when he clipped him with two particularly good right hooks to the head.

Billy began the fourth well. Again he connected with two right hooks to the head, prompting one to wonder why Gilroy was being so foolish and fighting Rafferty's fight at close-quarters. But towards the end of the fourth it was clear that Billy was out of touch. When he grabbed the initiative he could do little with it. His chances came and went because he was slow on his feet and slow with his punching. When he cut Gilroy's left eye in the sixth, it was the beginning of the end. Cornerman Jackie McHugh did a wonderful job on the long slit, which, later in hospital, took eight fine stitches to close, and the eye was really no bother after that.

In the sixth, with blood pouring from his eye, Gilroy slammed at Rafferty with a series of swinging blows that would have mowed down a lesser fighter than Billy, but it was the last of his really wild moments. From the seventh onwards, Freddie began boxing much more coolly. He right-jabbed his way to the front by a clear margin and, in the ninth, he had Rafferty tired and groggy after one pulverising left hook to the jaw.

It was a right jab that put Billy down at the start of the eleventh, but he got up without taking a count. Gilroy could have finished the scrap in this round if he had stepped back and picked his spot. But the finish was not long delayed. Staggering out with his eyes vacant and his legs a dead weight, Billy was set up for the kill in the twelfth. He took "five" in a neutral corner from a right and left hook to the head and, when he got up, he was battered right across the ring to the other neutral corner where Gilroy finally chopped him down with a short right hook to the head that few people in the body of the hall could have seen.

Billy was so punctured that he could make no effort at all to beat the count. He just sat with his eyes staring and both arms draped over the bottom rope as Welsh referee Ike Powell counted him out. Rafferty could hardly stand when photographers asked him to pose for pictures. Gilroy was so full of bounce that he danced and jigged around the ring, lifting his manager and cornermen into the air one after the other with the joy of being the first Irishman to win a Lonsdale belt outright.

Afterwards, in his dressing-room, the little "braveheart" from Scotland announced his retirement from the ring. The ferocity of Gilroy's punching had been a major factor in Peter Keenan making a similar decision three years earlier.

Belfast boxing fans were thrilled to bits when it was announced that Freddie would clash with Johnny Caldwell, with Friday, 29 June touted as the likely date. Their happiness was short-lived when Dublin was mentioned as the venue; many felt there was only one place that such a potentially exciting encounter between two world-class Belfast fighters should take place, and that was right on their own home turf.

Before the Caldwell bout, however, Freddie had to face Frenchman Rene Libeer in a contest at the Empire Pool in June. Gilroy won on points but sustained an injury to his right hand. This delayed the mouth-watering fight against Caldwell for Gilroy's British and British Empire titles until 20 October. The venue for this hugely-anticipated confrontation was also changed to the King's Hall in Belfast, which proved a lot more palatable to the local fans.

In light of Gilroy's justified reputation as a murderous, double-barrelled slugger, it was thought that Johnny would try to keep the fight at long range. However, from the start, the excitement was electrifying as both boys locked horns, trading punch-for-punch. Gilroy then stepped back and threw a vicious left which caught Johnny on the side of the face. He went down, but only for a split second, and no count was taken up.

The next four rounds saw the pendulum of victory steadily swinging back and forth but Caldwell was probably in front by the most microscopic of margins. In the sixth, Gilroy's left eye was opened by an accidental clash of heads. This was no real surprise given the ferocity of the in-fighting. So it continued into the seventh round – bitter, ruthless but scrupulously fair fighting. Freddie's cut eye reopened, but as it was on the side of the eye, there was no imminent danger of the fight being stopped.

Going into the eighth it was close. There were so many twists and turns, the whole thing could have been promoted by Alfred Hitchcock. Gilroy sank two vicious hooks of such ferocity into Caldwell's body that they would surely have hospitalised a lesser mortal than Johnny. Caldwell merely grimaced and fought back. The crowd was in a frenzy: never had they witnessed such excitement, and they roared even harder when Johnny emerged from yet another mêlée with claret dripping from his right eye. In Caldwell's corner was Danny Holland, a man famed for his expertise in repairing cuts, but trying to stem the profuse flow from Johnny's eye was like Joan of Arc trying to hold back the flames.

In the ninth, Gilroy really went to town on Caldwell's injured eye and both men were covered in blood. Despite this, everyone present seemed to love every minute, every second, and every breath of this spectacle. Even Baroness Edith Summerskill, a fervent opponent of boxing who died in 1980, might have found herself hanging on every swing of the glove in this contest. It was clear when the round ended that Caldwell had no chance of continuing. Holland called over referee Andy Smyth, but the decision was the responsibility of the corner during the interval. The Board of Control doctor was asked to inspect the damage and manager Docherty, who had been watching from ringside, retired his gutsy little battler. Both men had given more than their all.

In the aftermath of this great bout, a contractual dispute arose which resulted in Freddie and his manager being fined £1,000. A satisfactory conclusion could not be reached and their respective licences were withdrawn. Gilroy never fought again.

Although this latter incident provided a sorry end to Freddie's career, it should never be forgotten just *what* a career it was. A powerful puncher and a supreme craftsman at his rugged trade, among the "band of brothers" who comprise Ulster's outstanding glovemen of yesteryear, he was never anything less than world class.

PROFESSIONAL CAREER
1957-1962: 31 contests, won 28, lost 3.

Johnny Caldwell

Courage beyond the call of duty

Many years ago, I wrote a piece for a Belfast newspaper on the Johnny Caldwell versus Eder Jofre World bantamweight title fight, the headline for which was: AGAINST JOFRE, JOHNNY CALDWELL SHOWED COURAGE BEYOND THE CALL OF DUTY. The same banner could equally

Johnny Caldwell and Jackie Brown after their bout in Paisley

have been used for Johnny's heroics against Freddie Gilroy, a fight which old-timers still discuss with bated breath, and against Alan Rudkin, where Johnny was making a first defence of his British and Empire bantamweight titles.

Forty years or so after these great battles, Johnny was still displaying great courage when he began his fight against throat cancer – a fight in which Johnny could count on his large family circle, as well as his many friends, fellow pugilists and fans being in his corner.

Johnny was born on 7 May 1938 to Brigid and John senior, a joiner, and grew up in 63 Cyprus Street, off the Falls Road in Belfast. He attended St Comgall's, not far from his home, where he was a bright pupil. Around the age of ten, while other kids were sucking iced lollipops and playing marbles, hide-and-seek, or leap-frog, he joined the famous Immaculata Boxing Club. The club is steeped in history with many "gentlemen of clout" having passed through its doors, such as Barney Wilson, Bernie Meli, Jim McCourt, John Breen, Eddie Shaw, Peter Sharpe, Paddy Moore, Paddy Maguire, Jim McAuley, Paddy Graham, Hugh Gilhooley, Spike McCormick, "Fra" McCullagh, Tommy Madine, Paul McCullagh, Gerry Fitzpatrick, Jimmy McGivern, "Nugget" Nugent, Stephen Gibson, Patsy McCusker, Harry Enright, Vinty McGurk, Ned McCormick, Maurice McCusker and Jack McCusker, a trainer of champions, whose prowess in imparting his vast knowledge to young hopefuls was legendary. His death in 1960 was a devastating blow to the Ulster fight scene, both at amateur and professional levels.

Johnny studied hard at school and passed his leaving certificate, which enabled him to further his education in Hardinge Street School. With his education complete he obtained a job as an apprentice plumber with John Dowling Central Merchants in Upper Queen Street. He was fortunate to have learned a skilled trade, for he would return to it when his boxing career was over.

Johnny trained diligently every morning, seven days a week, running for miles up the Springfield Road. With the likes of Jack McCusker, Harry Enright and Ned McCormick at the helm, coupled with his own natural ability, the cognoscenti weren't in the least surprised when he won amateur titles at every level. These included, in 1956, the Ulster Senior and National Senior flyweight titles, which he retained in 1957. The highlight of his amateur career came when he represented his country at the 1956 Olympic Games in Melbourne, where he won a bronze medal at flyweight. The winner of the gold medal, incidentally, was Terry Spinks from Canning Town. Before embarking on his Olympic adventure, John had won in Chicago, Montreal, Dublin and Glasgow. In January 1957, in an international against England in the Royal Albert Hall, which Ireland won 6-5, he lost to Derek Lloyd from New Buxton; in subsequent internationals the same year, he had victories against Italy, Scotland and England.

From boy to man, Johnny learned his trade exceptionally well in the

Immaculata and had the tools to go a long way in the most gruelling of all professions. On Wednesday, 15 January 1958, in a packed St Mary's Hall in Belfast, Captain T D Morrison, President of the Ulster Council, brought gasps from fight fans who had gathered to watch a big Down and Connor amateur tournament, when he announced that Johnny was to make the switch from amateur to professional. There was a deathly silence, then an almighty burst of applause for, although amateur boxing was losing its brightest star, the fans knew that a rare talent was about to enter the professional ranks.

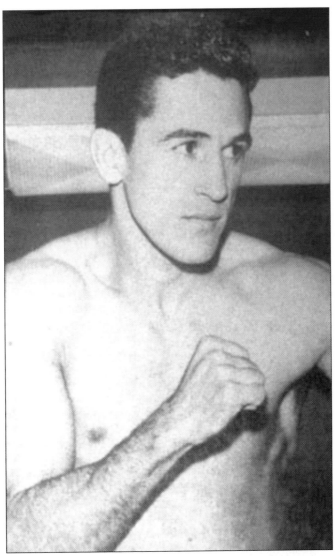

Eder Jofre

Johnny was managed by Jack McCusker, but always hovering on the fringe of the action was a Scottish-based bookmaker and promoter called Sammy Docherty, who eventually took over the managerial reins. Johnny later said that he would "always regret" this change as it was a partnership that led to bitter acrimony, culminating in a court case which Johnny lost.

Caldwell was initially based in Glasgow and was to have his first six contests in that great boxing city. He made his debut on 5 February 1958, getting his career off with a bang by knocking out Bill Downer of Stoke Newington in two rounds. He had a similar victory over Rotherham's Eddie Barraclough, beat Frenchmen Moncef Fehri (pts 8) and Michael Lamora (rtd 4) and, in the autumn of that same year, in only his fifth contest, he had a points victory over the South African British Empire Flyweight Champion Dennis Adams. Adams had won his title when he knocked out Frankie Jones

DISPUTA DO TÍTULO MUNDIAL DOS PESOS GALOS NO GINÁSIO ESTADUAL DO IBIRAPUERA

FEDERAÇÃO PAULISTA DE PUGILISMO

16 de Janeiro de 1962, as 21 hrs.

PROMOTOR Jack Solomons

EDER JOFRE
CAMPEÃO MUNDIAL VERSÃO E.U.A.

VERSUS

JOHN CALDWELL
CAMPEÃO MUNDIAL VERSÃO EUROPA

Cr$ 100,00

LUTA EM 15 ASSALTOS DE 3 X 1 Ms.

of Plean in three rounds in Glasgow on 23 October 1957. Before the autumn leaves had settled on the ground, Johnny kayoed Spain's Juanito Cid in five rounds in Glasgow, and had a points win over Esteban Martin from France in what was Johnny's first Belfast appearance since turning professional.

His winning streak continued in 1959 with victories over Simon Carnazzo (France) (rtd 5) in Belfast, Henry Schmid (France) (pts 8) in Glasgow, Francisco Carreno (Spain) (rsc 4) in Belfast, Piere Rossi (France) (pts 8) in Glasgow, and Giacomo Spano (Italy) (pts 10) in Glasgow. In the space of twenty-five days, he defeated Salvatore Manca (Italy) twice – in Belfast (pts 10) and in Glasgow (rsc 6).

On 9 February 1960, in his London debut, the fans at Streatham Ice Rink knew that they were watching a future champion when Johnny disposed of Spain's former European flyweight king, Young Martin, in three rounds. Martin, who had been down on five previous occasions in the fight, never looked like beating the count. It took him two minutes to recover.

Johnny then met the man who had taken Martin's flyweight crown, Finland's Risto Luukkonen. Caldwell gave another polished performance, winning on points over ten rounds at Wembley, a venue to which he returned on 31 May to secure another points win, this time over Frenchman Rene Libeer. He was awarded the accolade of Ulster's "Boxer of the Year", being the unanimous choice of the committee that, every year, awarded the Dalzell Memorial Shield, a trophy which was instituted in 1952.

On 8 October 1960, on a George Connell promotion in the King's Hall, Johnny wrested the British flyweight title from Frankie Jones, who had won it from Welshman Len Reece in Porthcawl in July 1957. Johnny was just inside the flyweight limit for the fight, which might have indicated that he was having trouble making the 112lbs maximum. You wouldn't have guessed it, however, and the Jones boy had his lease on the title terminated when he was knocked plain out in the third. There was now more than just a little speculation that Johnny might fight World Flyweight Champion Pone Kingpetch from Thailand, who had won the title from Argentinean, Pascual Perez, but the fight never materialised. Nevertheless Caldwell, now proudly wearing the flyweight diadem, brought a year of outstanding achievement to an end when he stopped French-Algerian Christian Marchand in seven rounds at the King's Hall.

On 31 January 1961 at the Royal Albert Hall, Johnny stopped Italian Angelo Rampin in eight rounds and, exactly two months later in Bristol, he stopped the Frenchman Jacques Jacob in five. His next fight was to be against the former World Bantamweight Champion, Alphonse Halimi.

By the time he entered the ring at the Empire Pool in Wembley on the evening of 30 May 1961 to listen to instructions from referee Ben Brill, Johnny Caldwell was unbeaten in twenty-one fights, held the British flyweight title, and was about to engage in his first bantamweight confrontation by going for the European version of the world title. Brazil's Eder Jofre was recognised as champion by *The Ring*, the National Boxing Association of the USA and the South American Boxing Federation, but the British Boxing Board of Control and the European Boxing Federation had both given the nod to the man who now faced Caldwell, Alphonse Halimi, after the French-Algerian was on the right side of a hotly disputed decision over Johnny's Olympic team-mate, Freddie Gilroy. With the bell about to get the contest under way, the politics of the fight game were the last thing on the minds of the combatants.

It was an interesting contest for at least seven rounds; then, in the eighth, a gash opened over Halimi's left eye and the blood came in a cascade. From that moment on, Alphonse was on a survival mission and, in the last round, he was sent reeling from a left, followed by a right, which saw him sprawling against the ring post. He was glassy-eyed as he rose, swaying on rubbery legs. Johnny moved in for the kill but Ben Brill protected the champ until the eight count was completed. It was a hell of a round, and Ireland had its first world champion since Rinty Monaghan. The next day Johnny received a hero's welcome, and banners proclaimed the new champion through the parish of St Peter's. He later made an appearance from an upstairs window in his parents' home in Cyprus Street. He had been given the tag of "Cold-Eyed Killer", but was modest in the extreme and simply said, "Thank you, friends."

Following his great victory, Johnny took care of France's Pierre Vetroff (pts 10) in Carmarthen, and Juan Cardenas (ko 8) in Cardiff. Halimi must have been as sick as a turkey by Christmas at the sight of Northern Ireland boxers: he had already lost to Jimmy Carson, was amazingly awarded the previously mentioned decision over Gilroy, and had taken a mauling from Caldwell. When he faced Johnny once again, a mere five months later, his confidence

Gilroy and Caldwell sign up for their legendary confrontation. Promoter George Connell looks on (second from right at the back)

could not have been too high. Although Johnny won, this scrap was as dull as the first one had been lively. The crowd had come to see dynamite but had to settle for a muted fireworks display instead. Coming into the last round, Halimi needed a knockout to win and that just wasn't going to happen. The Belfast boy was still champ.

By now, Johnny had relinquished his British flyweight title. The vacant crown was contested between Edinburgh's Jackie Brown and Birmingham's Brian Cartwright, with Brown winning on points.

The complicated political mess which had blighted the world bantamweight scene was now as clear as the arc lights above a boxing ring. There were two main players – Johnny Caldwell and Eder Jofre – and they would meet on 18 January 1962 in Sao Paulo, Brazil, to decide once and for all who the rightful claimant to the bantamweight throne was. The bookies had no doubt whatsoever on whose head the crown would sit. In Brazil, Jofre was a 1/5 shot and in Belfast, a generous, or so it seemed at the time, 3/1 against Johnny could be got. There were rumours that Jofre was having trouble making the weight, giving a glimmer of hope to the Caldwell camp.

Jofre had real celebrity status in Brazil and was idolised by young and old, rich and poor. He was unbeaten in forty-four fights, thirty inside the distance, and had gained NBA recognition by knocking out Eloy Sanchez in six rounds in November 1960. He successfully defended his portion of the title by stopping Venezuelan, Ramoan Arias, in six rounds and was acknowledged to be champion everywhere except Britain and Europe. Jofre had obtained so many wins inside the distance because, despite being a bantamweight, he punched with the power of a welterweight.

This unification encounter had all the makings of a classic. The outcome appeared to hinge on two things: the Irishman's lightning speed and ring know-how against the Brazilian's sledge-hammer punching. Leaving nothing to chance, Johnny arrived in Sao Paulo about three weeks ahead of schedule, giving himself plenty of time to get acclimatised. Local sports journalists were impressed with the way he performed against indigenous sparring partners, and his trainer Danny Holland was of the opinion that, if the fight went the distance, Johnny would be successful. Plenty of roadwork was the order of the day.

When Jofre wound up his training, he told waiting journalists of his great respect for Johnny, and that he [Jofre] would have to be at his "very best to win".

Johnny stepped on to the scales in his hotel to find he was well inside the limit, but when he was weighed for a second time on different scales there was consternation in his camp: he was found to be just under a pound overweight. On the advice of Tony Petronella of the National Boxing Association of the USA, Caldwell was given an extra thirty minutes to jettison the offending surplus. He did a few laps around the grounds of the building where the weigh-in was to be held and everyone breathed a sigh of relief when he shed the weight before the deadline. Jofre, meanwhile, just managed to scrape through the weigh-in by the width of the laces in his boxing boots, thus confirming the previous rumours about his own weight concerns.

Sao Paulo was in the grip of a bitter, 66°F cold spell, which some felt may be to Johnny's advantage, but a serious epidemic of fight fever prevailed to counter the shivering temperature. The fight replaced football as the main topic of conversation, and the names of Jofre and Caldwell were on everyone's lips.

Johnny's march to the ring in the Ibirapuera Stadium that January evening all those years ago was something akin to a prisoner taking the walk to the gas chamber or a crocodile passing a handbag factory. Sections of the seventeen thousand Brazilians who packed the arena were screaming for their boy to "Kill him, kill him!" Caldwell looked fit and determined as he made his entrance against this venomous background. Needless to say, Jofre was given a reception fit for royalty. And so the scene was set: the Champion of Europe versus the Champion of North and South America in a clash that would determine who was the undisputed Bantamweight Champion of the World. Overseeing the proceedings was the former Flyweight Champion of the World, Willie Pep.

Clash of the titans: Gilroy versus Caldwell

Both boys were ultra-careful in the first round, showing each other the greatest respect. The crowd, however, even at this early stage of the bout, wanted action, and there was a lot of booing and jeering. In the second round, Jofre landed two heavy body shots and, in an effort to keep out of trouble, Caldwell began to bob and weave. When the round ended, his face was slightly bruised. The booing resumed in the third because Caldwell was holding but it soon turned to cheers when Jofre caught Johnny with a vicious left. Caldwell stepped up a gear to put Jofre on the back foot, doing well in the fourth and silencing the vociferous Brazilians when he punished their hero with hard punches to the body.

The fifth marked a turning point in the fight. Jofre trapped Caldwell on the ropes and drilled home a savage left to the stomach. Caldwell hit the canvas and took an eight count. Although Johnny had the occasional success he was punished relentlessly by a flawless ring mechanic and, in the tenth, he went down from a sizzling right to the jaw. He got up but Jofre tore into him with crunching lefts and rights. He went down once again and manager Docherty signalled the end of the fight. If there was to be any consolation for Johnny in defeat, it was that the same fate would undoubtedly have befallen any of the other top ten contenders had they been in the ring with the Brazilian.

Next was the encounter which is still talked about as if it were one of the "wonders of the world": Gilroy versus Caldwell. Although Gilroy emerged the winner from the proceedings, it was an even contest in the sense that both men had given more than their all to produce a fight that is nothing short of a classic, and which is still spoken of today with awe by many fans who were there – and many who weren't. As a consequence the names of Freddie Gilroy and Johnny Caldwell, who was retired in the ninth round because of concerns over his injured eye, are irrevocably linked in the minds of all local boxing enthusiasts because of that night in October 1962.

In February 1963 in the Royal Albert Hall, Johnny was unlucky to lose to Frenchman, Michael Atlan. Caldwell was ahead by the proverbial mile but the fight was stopped when he sustained an eye injury brought about by a clash of heads.

At the ABC Cinema in Belfast in March 1964, Caldwell taught George Bowes from Hesleden a lesson (rsc 7) to win the vacant British and Empire bantamweight titles, which had been relinquished by Gilroy. This victory had added significance as it meant that Johnny was the first Irishman to win both the British flyweight and bantamweight crowns. In the 1980s Hugh Russell would go on to achieve a similar feat in reverse order.

Johnny went on to beat Raphael Fernandez from Spain (pts 8) in London, and had "Lady Luck" on his side when he was awarded a draw against former champ Jackie Brown in Paisley. He also defeated Nigeria's Orizu Obilaso (pts 8) in London. But his fabulous career was drawing to a close. He wasn't losing any of his brilliance, but was plagued by nose problems which affected his breathing. This was manifest when he defended his titles against Alan Rudkin in Nottingham on 22 March 1965. During the bout, Johnny was swallowing lots of blood which was making him ill. He took severe punishment in this fight and was relieved of his titles in the tenth round. Attempts were made to rectify the nose problem and Johnny had several operations.

Seven months after losing his titles, Johnny faced Monty Laud from St Ives, who was the Southern Area Bantamweight Champion. The fight took place in Brighton's Metropole Sporting Club. With no disrespect to Laud, Johnny was expected to wipe the floor with him, before dusting him off. But it was just not Caldwell's night and he lost on points. Not only was this a shock defeat for Johnny, it was also the final curtain being lowered on the career of an outstanding amateur and professional fighter.

Johnny returned to his old job as a plumber. This may not have been as exciting as listening to the roar of a Belfast fight crowd urging him on or the hysterical screams of a Brazilian crowd baying for his blood, but it was a living. In the course of his remarkable professional career, he had twenty-nine victories and marked himself out as one of the greatest champions that Ireland has ever produced.

PROFESSIONAL CAREER
1958–1965: 35 contests: won 29, lost 1, drew 5.

Henry Turkington

The ultimate crowd-pleaser

Henry Turkington looked more like a choirboy than a fighter. But amid those angelic features was a chin as solid as Aberdeen granite and a steely determination to give of his best. In eighteen years as an amateur and a professional he was never counted out.

He was a crowd-pleaser of the highest quality, who would relentlessly stalk an opponent, eating up jabs and punishment, but who was more than capable

of meting out his own particular brand of retribution. He could deliver vicious, meaty, left and right hooks to the body, which would see his opponent sink painfully to the canvas, gasping for breath like a claustrophobic in a confined space. "Kill the body and the head will die," Henry was heard to say.

No matter if he was topping the bill or on the under-card, Henry had drawing power and a full house was nearly always guaranteed when he was fighting. He always aimed to please his fans and was seldom found wanting.

In his ring days, the pundits thought of more handles to Henry's name than possibly any other boxer's: the "Terrible Turk", "Terrible Henry", "Homicide Henry", "Handsome Henry", "Smilin' Henry", and "Hammerin' Henry" were but a few.

He was born on 4 December 1943 in Massareene Hospital, Antrim, to builder's labourer William Turkington and his wife Joanna, both of whom hailed from near Doagh. Henry would be an only child for but a short duration since, on 14 April 1945, his brother William came along. The two young

"Turks" were educated in Parkgate Primary School, where Henry was awarded a silver medal for never having missed a day. He may have been as good as gold during his lessons but when the bell tolled for the end of the school day, Henry and his brother were always getting into scrapes, the majority of which they won. This gave the two of them a reputation as fighters and tearaways; they were in hot water so often they must have felt like tea bags.

The Turkington boys came to the attention of a seasoned boxing trainer called Coe McConnell, a publican and farmer who was constantly on the lookout for lads who were useful with their mitts. Coe had been taught all there was to know about ring warfare by his good friend Terry Milligan, one of Ireland's greatest ever amateur boxers. Henry and William's father, grandfather, and uncle Norman had all been smitten with the boxing bug, so when Mr McConnell invited the youngsters to join his Doagh stable, it was like carrying on a sporting tradition for the family.

The brothers took to boxing like a shark to an injured seal, and their amateur careers accelerated with such speed that they were eliciting rave notices not just locally, but from across the water. They were also receiving offers to turn professional with monotonous regularity. Henry won the Ulster Junior welterweight, All-Ireland Junior middleweight and Ulster Senior light-middleweight titles. Going for the All-Ireland light-middleweight title he came unstuck against Terry Joyce of Arbour Hill in what was a bitterly disappointing result for the kid from Doagh. He had been winning the fight with comparative ease when, with a minute remaining of the final round, a momentary lapse of concentration spelt disaster: Joyce caught him with a good punch and the referee stopped the fight.

In an international fixture against Wales in Prestatyn, which Ireland won 6-4, Henry stopped Eddie Avoth in the first round; he also knocked out George Aiken in forty-five seconds while representing Ulster against a Scots' Select squad. However, in a match against Hungary, which the Magyars won 7-3, he was deemed very unfortunate not to get the decision over Janos Erdely. In forty-seven amateur outings, Henry only lost three times.

Billy meanwhile won the County Antrim Junior, Irish Juvenile and Ulster welterweight titles. When he stopped T Murphy from the Lourdes stable in Drogheda in the second round, he added the All-Ireland welterweight mantle to his tally. In an international meet against England in the Royal Albert Hall, which finished 5-5, Billy closed down R Taylor in the third; and on 11 February 1965 in Swansea's Drill Hall, he had a magnificent win while representing Ulster over V Stanton, whom he kayoed in the first. However, he was knocked out by Jerzy Kulej in the second round of his bout during another international against Poland on 6 March 1965. Poland won the match 6-4.

When Billy turned professional he was managed by Bert McCarthy, and made his debut on 12 October 1965 in the Ulster Hall. Here he shared the

points with Chris McAuley from Larne but, in a topsy-turvy career punctuated with inactivity, he had only thirteen more fights. The final one was in Islington on 7 February 1978 against hard-hitting Welshman Colin Jones, who stopped him in the first. Jones would go on to win the British, Commonwealth and European welterweight titles. In a challenge for the vacant WBC welterweight belt, he boxed a draw with Milton McCrory. One notable victory in Billy's career was a points victory in his fifth contest over Jamiacan Bunny Sterling, a future British, Commonwealth and European middleweight champion.

When Henry made his eagerly awaited professional debut on 11 February 1964 in Derry's Guildhall on a Jack Solomons and Mike Callaghan promotion, he stopped Manchester's Charlie Grice in four rounds. Four days later, he was walking up the aisle to marry his number one fan, Virginia McClean. Billy acted as best man and Virginia's sister Linda was bridesmaid.

Henry assists in the judging of a local beauty contest

Henry, who was employed as a builder's labourer with Wilson's Masonry, was on the road every morning from 5.30am, running for more than six miles. On returning from work he would go to the Doagh ABC, where he would work out vigorously on the punch-bag. Once home, he would retire for the night no later than 10pm. Compared to today's luxurious training facilities, things were pretty primitive for Henry, but he loved every minute of it.

In his second fight, at the ABC Cinema in Belfast, on the night that Johnny Caldwell beat George Bowes for the vacant British and British Empire bantamweight titles, he knocked out Greenock's Adam Robertson in the third. Henry wasn't one hundred per cent ready for this fight as he had injured his thumb sparring with Gerry Hassett. But one hand was all that he needed and the unfortunate Robertson took several minutes to recover after being counted out. Thankfully, he wasn't seriously hurt.

Just over three weeks later at Wembley Pool, Henry was stopped in the fourth with a cut eye by Eddie Avoth, whom he had previously seen off in one round while on international duty for Ireland against Wales. Avoth, who was a protégé of Eddie Thomas, the former British, British Empire and European Welterweight Champion, would go on to win the British and Commonwealth light-heavyweight belts.

On 30 April 1964, Henry beat Louis Onwuna from Nigeria on points over eight rounds in Larne. The sheen was taken off the win when Onwuna's manager, Billy McDonald, protested to the Northern Ireland Area Council of the British Boxing Board of Control. He said that the contract he had signed was for 8 x 2 minute rounds and not 8 x 3 minute rounds, adding that his fighter had only trained for the former. "Three minutes was too much for me," Onwuna complained. If he had been honest, he would have admitted that it was Henry who had been too much for him.

Henry next cemented his superiority over Charlie Grice (rsc 2) in Manchester, beat Doncaster's Pat O'Rourke (ko 1) in the same city, and gave himself a great birthday present when he beat Berkhamsted's Joe Somerville (rsc 3) in Belfast.

Wearing his famous boyish grin, Henry has told of the night he fought Clem Winchester in Manchester's Free Trade Hall. He was winning comfortably against the Jamiacan without really having to put his foot on the accelerator. However, referee Wally Thom, the former British, British Empire and European Welterweight Champion, was having none of it. Thom told Henry in no uncertain terms to "get the finger out" or he would be disqualified. In the next round, which was the fourth, Henry showed no clemency to Clem and promptly knocked him out.

Henry and Coe McConnell would go their separate ways in the winter of 1965 with Henry's affairs being taken over by Billy Frame, a Belfast greyhound trainer. Henry would have other trainers and managers, including Patsy Quinn (Gerry McAllister), the former Northern Ireland Welterweight Champion, John McBride, and that other great little scrapper, Jackie Briers, the former Northern Ireland Flyweight Champion.

1965 saw Henry stop Fitzroy Lindo from Jamaica in two rounds in Belfast, and he took a significant step up in class when he was matched with the experienced Peter "Al" Sharpe for the vacant Northern Ireland welterweight title. Peter was a veteran of more than one hundred fights and was a former holder of the Northern Ireland lightweight and welterweight belts. Henry came in at $2^{3/4}$lbs over the limit and lost the catchweight fight on points in what turned out to be a thriller.

His next four fights took place in Belfast, where he had wins over Birmingham's Sid Brown (pts 8) and Ghana's Bob Coffie (pts 8), but was beaten by the Nigerian Johnny Angel (pts 8). On 12 October, he faced Peter Sharpe for the second time to decide for the Northern Ireland Middleweight Championship. It was on this same bill that Henry's brother would make his professional debut. The *Boxing News* described the second Sharpe versus Turkington encounter thus:

> From as early as the third round, when he stopped Turkington dead in his tracks with a great right hand to the chin, an inside-the-distance win for the older man was always on the cards. Sharpe emphasised this again in the fourth when he cut loose with a barrage of punches just before the bell, and

Turkington, wobbling at the knees, headed for a neutral corner when the round ended, obviously in a dazed condition. But the Doagh boy recovered well and was soon back forcing the fight and in the seventh had a real punch-up with Sharpe. The round ended with honours even. A quiet eighth round, which Turkington shaded, gave the youngster fresh hope, but the wily Sharpe had been only biding his time and, in the ninth, he hit Turkington with some superb punches to the head with both hands which brought a timely intervention by referee Billy Duncan. Henry spent the night in hospital, where he had six stitches inserted in a mouth cut, but he was discharged the following morning.

With this victory, Sharpe carved himself a niche in Irish boxing history, becoming the first Irishman to win three area titles at different weights.

Henry had barely digested his Christmas dinner when he recorded a second points victory over Louis Onwuna in Dungannon on 27 December, bringing 1965 to a close on a high note.

On 26 January 1966, at the Reo Cinema in Ballyclare, Henry fought Les McAteer from Birkenhead, but lost on points. Les would go on to garner the vacant British and British Empire middleweight titles in 1969 by beating left hand specialist, Wally Swift. He remarked that Henry was an "outstanding prospect".

The Turk then beat Pat Vernie (St Lucia) (rtd 2), Oliver Lyttle (Belfast) (pts 8) and Dennis Pleace (Cardiff) (rsc 6) in London, but lost to Terry McTigue (Belfast) (rsc 6). This last fight was an eliminator for the Northern Ireland middleweight crown. Henry had another points win over Lyttle but, on 26 January 1967, in a packed AEI canteen in Larne, came the final Sharpe-Turkington confrontation. It was close and, in an all-action fight, Sharpe got the decision by half a point, thus completing a hat-trick of wins over Henry. It was commented that the bouts between the two men were so exciting that if they had fought every night of the week the hall would still be packed.

On a Bob McCammond promotion in the Ulster Hall on 4 March 1967, Henry stepped in at short notice to replace Sharpe, who had injured his shoulder. His opponent was hard man Harry Scott from Bootle, who was ranked number three in the British middleweight ratings. Scott had caused a bit of a storm when he took the wind out of Rubin "Hurricane" Carter's sails with a points victory on 20 April 1965 in London. The "Hurricane" had blown away World Welterweight Champion Emile Griffith in the first round of a non-title fight in 1963. Scott had shared the ring with some top-class fighters, including Griffiths: men like former World Junior Middleweight Champion Nino Benvenuti, former European Middleweight Champion Laszlo Papp, Yolande Pompey (who Harry kayoed in the first round), former British and European Middleweight Champion John "Cowboy" McCormack, former British Welterweight and Middleweight Champion Wally Swift, and former British Middleweight Champion Mick Leahy, among others. Harry probably was of the opinion, like everyone else, that with his vast reservoir of experience all he needed to beat the Doagh slugger was a haircut and shave. But when the referee lifted Henry's arm in victory, Scott's manager Arthur Boggis protested vehemently and Joe Jacob's famous cliché, "*We wuz robbed!*" was resurrected.

Much was now expected from Henry but he suffered setbacks against Cardiff lad Carl Thomas (rsc 2) in Newcastle, Nottingham's British Middleweight Champion Johnny Pritchett (rsc 2) in Manchester, and Jamaican Bunny Sterling (pts 8) in Belfast. From 16 January 1968 until 6 October 1969, Henry had only two fights, losing to both Mark Rowe (rsc 6) and Harry Scott (rsc 1) in London, giving the latter his revenge after his defeat at Turkington's hands in Belfast.

Henry was inactive for about six years, due to what he called "a decline" in boxing promotions. Then, in May 1975, at the age of thirty-two, he made a comeback and stopped Karl McCarthy from Belfast in three rounds.

He had two fights in 1977, beating Belfast's John Breen (pts 6) and being beaten by Merthyr's Gareth "Tashy" Jones (rsc 6) in Ebbw Vale. He had his last fight on 7 February 1978, losing to Mick Mills from Islington (rsc 3) in Southend. Ironically, on the same night, after losing to Colin Jones in Islington, Henry's brother Billy also retired.

Even today, likeable Henry is constantly in demand for interviews, and fan mail continues to drop through his letter-box. One such fan, who resides in Frankfurt, wanted a picture of Henry but did not have a proper address; the request was sent to *Henry Turkington, Professional Boxer, c/o The Lord Mayor of Doagh*. Suffice to say, there was as much chance of the Lord Mayor of Doagh receiving that letter than there was of Lord Lucan playing for Ballyclare Comrades.

Henry is as popular an individual today in the East Antrim area as he was in his heyday and, in 2004, he was inaugurated into the Newtownabbey Hall of Fame.

PROFESSIONAL CAREER
1964–1978: 34 contests: won 19, lost 14, drew 1.

Jim McCann

A short but memorable career

By the time Jim McCann junior entered this world on 1 March 1944, his father had participated in eighty-three professional boxing bouts since his debut in 1935, in the course of which he had won the Northern Ireland bantamweight and featherweight titles. In an amazing eighteen-year career,

Jim McCann senior won seventy-three out of his one hundred and forty-two contests, and this in an era when beer money was paid for champagne fights. A butcher by trade, he hailed from Joy Street and was married to the former Lily O'Neill.

Jim junior was born in his grandmother's house at 17 Quinn Street in Belfast's Short Strand area. By his own admission, he had "no love for school", but managed to go the distance at the Christian Brothers' School in Oxford Street. On leaving, he assisted his mother and father in their fruit and vegetable shop on the Newtownards Road, but would eventually obtain a position with Jim Rice, a bookmaker and boxing promoter. Rice coined the phrase, "Without the small hall shows, there would be no big ones", and was the first promoter to bring boxing to the King's Hall, on Wednesday, 20 November 1935. The main event that night was a ten-round heavyweight contest between Pat Marrinan and Canada's Ed Wenstob, with the latter winning in the fifth round.

From when he was in short pants, Jim boxed for St George's, where the star attraction was his dad, who, when he wasn't getting himself into peak condition for a fight, would be looking after the interests of the other boxers, encouraging and advising them as only a fighter of his experience could. Throughout their lives, the two Jims were not only father and son, but also the best of friends. Jim senior, who was a founder member of St George's, retired from boxing on 19 May 1952, going out in style with a win (rtd 6) over Leamington's Jackie Turpin, the brother of former World Middleweight Champion, Randolph Turpin.

One of Jim junior's best ever performances was when he beat the English Bantamweight Champion Brian Packer from Dartford in an Ulster versus England match in the Ulster Hall on 2 March 1964, which finished 4-4. In a full international, staged the previous week in Dublin, Packer had out-pointed Ulster Bantamweight Champion, Jimmy Henry from Hollerith. Anyone looking forward to reading about the McCann-Packer clash in the next day's newspapers were in for a big disappointment since journalists and photographers had boycotted the match after being denied ringside seats. They claimed they could not report from seats some forty feet away from ringside.

A month later, there was uproar in the Ulster Hall when Jimmy Henry was awarded a majority decision over Jim in the Ulster Senior Bantamweight Final. The St George's boxer certainly put on a terrific show and had the holder in trouble several times, but the decision went against him. In the following year's championships, Jim would again suffer bitter disappointment when Henry was awarded another controversial decision over him. McCann thought that he "had done enough to win" and his father agreed that "Jim got a raw deal. Could anyone blame him if he decided to join the paid ranks?" The Henry versus McCann fight was one of the best on the bill and not a second of the scrap passed without a punch being thrown. In the end, there was little in it with the judges marking it in favour of Henry: 59-59, 58-59 and 60-57.

Henry's snappy left hand was impressive in the first round, but it was hard to separate the two men. In the middle round, McCann showed steadiness as he countered Henry's thrusts and evened up any advantage the Hollerith boxer might have initially gained. The third round was also very close, but the decision in favour of Jimmy Henry angered Jim so much that he said goodbye to the amateur ranks.

As a professional Jim would be looked after by his dad and the former Northern Ireland Bantamweight Champion, Tommy Madine. He made his debut in the Ulster Hall on 30 March 1965, a mere six weeks after his second loss to Henry, doing all that was asked of him when he clearly out-pointed Simon Tiger from Nigeria. McCann showed all the touches of class that marked his career in the amateur ranks, winning every round for a clear-cut decision.

For his second outing, Jim out-pointed another Nigerian, John Adebisi. On his last two outings, Adebisi had stopped Brian Smyth in two rounds and

Jim McCann
senior

knocked out Mancunian Sammy McIlvenna in five. Nevertheless, McCann punched his way to a points win in a tough contest. The Nigerian was an active little battler but spoiled a lot of his work by persistent hitting with the inside of the glove; in the final analysis, this must surely have weighed against him.

Jim's best rounds were the second, when he rocked Adebesi with a solid left hand to the head and moved inside to score with good shots to the body, and the third, when he had Adebisi wobbling after crashing in a good right hook to the chin. Both boys lost a lot of their sparkle from the fourth round on and Jim's misguided tactics of attempting to move in close at every opportunity allowed Adebisi to gain respite. The Belfast lad was much superior when he jabbed with his left and threw over the right. Overall, it was another good performance by Jim, a durable, compact fighter, and fight fans were undoubtedly looking forward to seeing the little bantamweight in action again.

In 1965, the Northern Ireland area of the British Boxing Board of Control declared several titles to be vacant, including middleweight, which had been relinquished by George Lavery, and bantamweight, which had been given up by Billy Skelly. The outcome was that Peter Sharpe and Henry Turkington would battle for middleweight, and Jim McCann and Alex O'Neill would fight for bantamweight. Both contests were scheduled to take place in the Ulster Hall on 12 October.

Three weeks before Jim was due to meet O'Neill, his weight was 10st 7lbs. Needless to say, there was plenty of exceedingly hard work to be done before 12 October. During preparatory sparring sessions, Jim was at times so weak that he could barely lift his hands and sparring partners were "hitting him at will". Eventually, he managed to shed the surplus weight while remaining strong – so strong, in fact, that sparring partners were unable to stick the pace and one by one they dropped out.

O'Neill, who was managed by John McGuinness, had fourteen fights under his belt, seven of which he had won. In his last contest before meeting McCann he boxed a draw with Tony Barlow from Manchester. Barlow was number two challenger for Walter McGowan's British flyweight title, and O'Neill was number three. It was difficult to take these ratings seriously, however, as Barlow and O'Neill were the only challengers due to a dearth of flyweights. The classy McGowan had won his title by knocking out Edinburgh's Jackie Brown in May 1963.

So, on a night when Peter Sharpe belied his years with a magnificent win (rsc 9) over the hard-as-nails Henry Turkington to win the vacant Northern Ireland middleweight crown, Jim McCann made his father a very proud man indeed by stopping O'Neill in the ninth to win the local bantamweight mantle. Although the fight was stopped as the result of O'Neill sustaining a badly-cut eye, McCann was well ahead at that stage, having forced the fight throughout. He punished Alex with solid hooks to the body and head, and was always doing a lot more work at close quarters than his opponent.

The Ulster Hall on 2 November 1965 witnessed Sharpe having a great win over leading middleweight Nat Jacobs, but McCann was very unlucky to be disqualified by referee Jim McCreanor for hitting low against Scottish Bantamweight Champion, Jackie Brown. It was an unfortunate end for Jim as he had been very much on top when the bout ended with Brown writhing in agony on the canvas. Brown showed touches of class in the first round

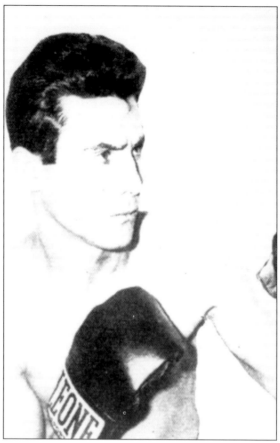

Tommaso Galli

when, with brilliant footwork, he slipped all that Jim threw. After this the non-stop aggression of McCann shook the Edinburgh man out of his stride. Jim's eagerness almost brought success when he connected with some solid left hooks and, despite his disqualification, his performance had been excellent.

Compared to McCann, Battersea's Don Weller (thirty-one fights, twenty wins and three draws) was a very experienced fighter. He was eight years older that the Belfast boy, but was still considered good enough to be rated number five for Alan Rudkin's British bantamweight title. Weller had won the Southern Area bantamweight belt in November 1960 when he beat Dennis East, and had defended it successfully on four occasions with wins over Danny Wells, Mick Hussey (twice) and Brian Bissmire. However, on 18 May 1965, he lost his area crown to Monty Laud from St Ives. When the courageous former area champion from Battersea was stopped in the fifth round of a one-sided contest by McCann, he looked much older than his twenty-nine years. Although it was the age-old bogey of a cut eye which caused the fight to be halted it would have made no difference, for McCann had given a five-star performance, commanding the driving seat throughout.

With a successful first year in the professional ranks behind him, Jim began 1966 at his very best when he stopped Welsh champion Terry Gale in the third round of an Ulster Hall contest, the Cardiff boxer sustaining a badly damaged right eye.

Later, on a night when Billy and Henry Turkington did Doagh proud with wins over Brendan Ingle and Pat Vernie, and there was controversy when Terry McTigue was awarded a draw against Pat Dwyer, McCann did a very professional job against Barcelona's Angel Chinea, winning on points over eight rounds. Against a gangling and ring-wise opponent, the local champion made a cautious start but in the final minute of the first round he trapped the Spaniard on the ropes and let go with both hands to the head and body in a fierce toe-to-toe exchange. In the second, it was McCann again looking for his man and finding him with stiff shots to the body. On two occasions, the Spaniard picked up warnings from referee Billy Duncan for slapping.

The third saw McCann slam home a good left hook to the head and the Spaniard's right eye was cut. A short right stopped Chinea in his tracks and the Belfast boy was beginning to forge ahead; his work was cleaner and his punches sharper. Chinea adopted the tactics of world champion Cassius Clay in the fourth, with his hands at hip level, as he waited for the incoming McCann. But he got little change out of Jim and only succeeded in picking up another warning for slapping.

By the end of the fifth, the verdict was never in any doubt. In the sixth, Jim threw his best punch of the fight, cracking in a great right hook to the body, which brought a gasp of pain from Chinea, and another right to the face, which opened up a cut on the bridge of the Spaniard's nose. Then, in the seventh, came the amazing sight of the referee removing a broken needle and thread from Chinea's glove. There was no explanation as to how it got there, but the Board officials were themselves obviously needled, with the incident still being discussed long after the last fight was over. There was no disputing the merit of McCann's performance. It was workmanlike and thorough and proved beyond doubt that he was right up there with the best of the British bantams.

Jim, who had been fighting once a month, enhanced his growing reputation even further by stopping Nigerian Sammy Abbey in the fifth, after Abbey sustained a badly-gashed eyebrow in a fall from the ring. The Nigerian seemed to be holding his own until Jim exploded midway through the fifth round and sent his opponent reeling through the ropes on to the time-keeper's bench. Abbey scrambled back into the ring, but with blood streaming ominously from an inch-long cut over his right eye, his corner had no option but to retire him.

McCann's calibre was really put to the test in the Empire Pool, Wembley, on 14 June 1966 against Argentina's Ernesto Miranda. Nine years earlier, Miranda had twice drawn with one of the greatest world bantamweight champions of all time, Eder Jofre. Jofre had held the world title (NBA and World) from 1960 until 1965 when he lost it to Japan's Masahiko "Fighting"

Harada. In 1960, Ernesto had boxed Jofre twice for the South American bantamweight title, going fifteen rounds with the great Brazilian on the first occasion, while on the second, being knocked out in the third round. But the little bantam from the Markets was up for this one and he gave a great display to win on points in this, his first fight outside Belfast. Jim triumphed with sheer determination and aggression. He put his head down and walked forward for the whole eight rounds, spending punches like a sailor spends money buying drinks, and Miranda was never allowed to settle. The Italian-based Argentinian did most of his scoring on the retreat, catching McCann as he came in with hooks and uppercuts, but he did not land often enough to tip the balance, and there were no arguments when the Irishman's hand was raised at the end.

After the fight, Jim and his dad were on the tube heading back to their hotel in Piccadilly Circus. The tube was packed to capacity, and Jim had a strange feeling that he was being stared at. He thought that people recognised him from the fight at Wembley and asked his father, "Why are people staring at me?" Jim senior replied with a grin that all would become clear when they got back to the hotel. Sure enough, while preparing for a shower, Jim looked in the mirror and saw that his face was black and blue.

A very tasty domestic contest was lined up for fight fans on 13 December when Jim put his Northern Ireland bantamweight title on the line against the very talented Sean McCafferty, a former amateur star from the St John Bosco Club in Belfast. As an amateur, Sean had won Ulster Youth titles at six stone, and in 1963, he annexed the Ulster Senior flyweight crown and the All-Ireland Junior and Senior flyweight titles, which he retained the following year. In international matches, McCafferty had notable wins over E Pritchard from Wales, whom he'd stopped in two rounds, and C Bovey from England, whom he'd stopped in the third. The Bosco star was particularly impressive when he out-pointed the Hungarian Imrie Harangozo in a Dublin match, which Ireland lost 7-3. Like McCann, McCafferty had turned professional in 1965, and to date had won all of his eight contests, six of which were via the short route.

In the second round of their encounter, McCann opened up well to the body. McCafferty came back but ran into two sizzling left hooks from the champion. In the third, Sean tied up the bustling McCann, but couldn't keep him off all the time, especially his quick combinations. McCann was dictating the proceedings but at the start of the fourth he was caught with some stiff shots on the ropes. However, he came back strongly to the body and, in the fifth, the crowd sensed a quick win when McCafferty, who had slipped, went down on one knee.

In the sixth, Sean came more into the fight with some neat boxing and, in the seventh, he shook Jim with a right cross after taking some stiff straight rights himself in the most thrilling round so far. A more confident McCafferty took the fight to the champion with hefty body punches and, momentarily, it looked as if McCann might be slowing down. At the start of the ninth McCann showed real class when he dropped southpaw Sean with a perfect right to the chin, before trying desperately for the finish. But McCafferty fought back gallantly to survive the round.

The tenth was a thrilling slam-bang affair with the champion never letting up, a pattern which continued into the eleventh. The crowd rose to their feet in a magnificent last round as both boys stood toe-to-toe, slugging constantly for the full three minutes with McCann's hand raised in victory by referee, Billy Duncan. The buzz around the hall after the fight was that it would take a "good one" to prevent McCann from winning the British bantamweight crown. When asked about which fight had been his most difficult, Jim would reply without hesitation, "Sean McCafferty".

Jim's next opponent was Italian Tommaso Galli, a former European Bantamweight Champion, who had won the title from Mimoun Ben Ali on 19 August 1965 in San Remo. In two defences of his title, he drew with Walter McGowan in Rome and defeated Frenchman Pierre Vetroff in Marseilles, but Ben Ali snatched the title back from Galli on 17 June 1966 in Barcelona. On 20 August 1969, Galli would win the European featherweight title in round fifteen from Manuel Calvo in Barcelona, but would go on to lose it on 26 June 1970 to the former World Featherweight Champion, Jose Legra, in Madrid.

Jim's strict training regime of running seven or eight miles morning and night obviously stood him in good stead for his encounter with the Italian on 17 January 1967. He seemed to have an endless supply of energy as he kept moving forward, throwing punches all the time. Galli, a classy fighter and a fast mover, absolutely refused to be drawn into a fight and his spoiling tactics must have been frustrating not only for Jim, but for the fans as well. The clean blows delivered were few and far between and Galli picked up a couple of warnings for holding at close quarters and also for punching with the inside of the glove. It was inside that Jim did his best work and the Italian didn't relish his punching to the body. McCann opened up a cut over Galli's left eye in the third round and cut him again, this time above the right eye, in the sixth. Early in the ninth, however, McCann also sustained a nasty gash just above his right eye. He stated afterwards that he "couldn't see out of it in the final round".

Galli had opened in confident style and his longer reach threatened to pose problems for McCann, but the Belfast battler got his left hand working in the second. By the end of the third, his non-stop tactics were easing him ahead. McCann continued to hammer away at close quarters in the fourth, before a change of tactics was adopted by Galli. He opened the fifth by shooting out his left hand at speed and moving around the ring. Jim just couldn't catch him up, but the cut that Galli received in the sixth round above his right eye caused the Italian to lose his composure and he was now prepared to trade punches with McCann. Jim's cut right eye in the ninth was the only uneasy moment the home boxer experienced. He weathered the storm and gave as good as he got in the final round to merit the decision.

Galli and his manager, Luigi Proetti, disagreed with the referee's verdict, complaining that McCann was permitted to "lie-on" and "use his head". Their European agent, Bobby Diamond, nevertheless was prepared to accept the referee's decision. He commented that "It was close, and McCann's strength and willingness to make a fight of it made him difficult to beat. McCann is very fit and strong and that means a lot among the bantamweights."

Jim said, "Galli is a very fast and experienced fighter. He was difficult to catch and at no time did he want to have a fight. I learned a lot from this fight and am very happy with the result."

On a Peter Keenan promotion on 11 May 1967, in his third year as a professional, Jim McCann stood in the ring at Paisley Ice Rink prepared to do battle against Evan Armstrong in a final eliminator for the British bantamweight belt. In contrast to Jim's first professional purse of £30, the take-home pay on this occasion would be £3,500. But, regardless of the money, Jim's real desire was to join that illustrious trio of Belfast former British bantamweight champions: John Kelly, Freddie Gilroy and Johnny Caldwell. Jim's uncle, George O'Neill, had also challenged for the bantamweight crown on 11 December 1954 in the King's Hall but lost on points to Peter Keenan. Of course, further down the line, Paddy Maguire (1975-1977), Hugh Russell (1983) and Davy Larmour (1983) would win the title.

Armstrong was a year older than Jim and had won twenty-two of his twenty-six contests, seventeen of them inside the distance. Three boxers who had failed to stay with him were John Adabesi (ko 7), Angel Chinea (rsc 2) and Jackie Brown (ko 4). Adebesi and Chinea had both stayed the course with Jim, while Brown had beaten Jim on a disqualification, but McCann wasn't too concerned about Armstrong's reputation as a big hitter. Before the fight he commented, "I hear all this talk about Armstrong being a big hitter. This doesn't worry me, as I have fought big hitters before."

But Jim's dream of getting a chance of joining his illustrious predecessors ended abruptly when, before a crowd of only six hundred, he was stopped in the fifth with a badly cut left eyebrow. The cut, which needed two stitches, was opened in the dying seconds of the fourth and, in the next session, it became so bad that Jim's father, who was chief second, was forced to signal his son's retirement. Until this unfortunate incident Jim had been doing extremely well and, in the dressing room afterwards, he said that he was "bitterly disappointed" at the way the fight had finished. Jim senior, however, said it was better to retire him and give him the chance to "fight another day".

This was Jim's second defeat in a dozen fights and, as with his first, it was at the hands of a Scot. From the start, Jim had been forced to concentrate his attack on Armstrong's body, and these tactics paid dividends in the first two rounds. Armstrong relied mainly on the use of his left jab at long range but the game little Irishman refused to allow him to dictate matters and constantly lunged forward to score heavily with hooks to the Scotsman's body. Armstrong tried hard to finish the contest and caught Jim with several strong right hooks to the head, but Jim retaliated immediately with powerful left hooks to the body.

In the fourth, it was a real "slugfest" as both boys neglected jabs to battle it out toe-to-toe in the centre of the ring. With only seconds to go, disaster came for the Belfast boy. As he came out of a clinch, blood was streaming down from his left eyebrow. His seconds worked furiously on the cut at the interval, but after only moments of the fifth, blood once more began coursing down Jim's cheek. Spurred on by this opportunity to win inside the distance, Armstrong attacked hard but this only brought more frenzied efforts from McCann and, when the end of the round came, Jim's face was a gory mask. As the bell sounded, he made to walk to his opponent's corner, then turned and went to his own stool. After about thirty seconds of feverish work, Jim senior signalled to the referee, Roland Earin, that his boy was unable to continue.

Needless to say, Jim was bitterly disappointed at the outcome and commented, "He is a fair puncher, but at no time did he hurt me and I felt he was beginning to weaken midway through the fourth round. I am certain I would have stopped him."

Evan Armstrong's win didn't bring him an immediate shot at the bantamweight title, but when his opportunity did come on 9 June 1969, he was stopped by Alan Rudkin in the eleventh. On 5 July 1971, Armstrong won the British featherweight title by knocking out Jimmy Revie in the twelfth at the World Sporting Club.

In view of Jim's fine performance and the circumstances of his defeat by Armstrong it is very unlikely that this setback would have affected his status as a genuine title contender. Even if he had been victorious, McCann would never have boxed again because he already had his future plans mapped out. In 1970, he moved to Dundalk where he established himself as a successful businessman. In 1981, he married his girlfriend Anita at Dromiskin Chapel, and the couple would go on to have nine children.

It is likely that, if he had continued with his boxing, Jim would at the very least have challenged for British and European titles. It was not to be but, despite having a short innings in the fight game, McCann junior, as with McCann senior, certainly left a lasting impression.

PROFESSIONAL CAREER
1965–1967: 12 contests: won 10, lost 2.

Paddy Graham

Let down by amateur and professional bodies

There are two mysteries which have baffled people in local boxing circle for many years, and they both involve the great Paddy Graham. Firstly why was Paddy not among the seven boxers chosen to represent Northern Ireland at the Empire Games in Jamaica in 1966? Secondly, how could a fighter such as Paddy, who was never out of the top three for five years, be denied a crack at the British bantamweight title? Why these questions have continued to tax Irish fight fans will become clear in due course, after considering Paddy's record.

Paddy was born on 27 June 1947 in 17 Garnet Street, off the Falls Road to parents Agnes and Peter. Peter hailed from Carrick Hill and was employed

in that famous old place of entertainment the Diamond Cinema. Agnes was from Falls Road stock. Paddy's mother and father would have eight children in all four girls and four boys. Paddy recalled that one brother, David, who is now unfortunately deceased, painstakingly accumulated every press cutting and photograph that he could from Paddy's career and put them into a scrapbook. This was meant to provide a perpetual reminder of Paddy's ring battles but ironically, has lasted as a treasured reminder to Paddy of his brother. Another of Paddy's brothers, Laurence, won an Ulster 5st 7lbs schoolboy title and although he didn't pursue his boxing career, went on to become a highly respected and valuable international senior coach with St Agnes's ABC.

Paddy attended St Peter's School in

Raglan Street and when he was aged ten he joined the Immaculata ABC. After Jack McCusker's death, he switched to Hollerith ABC under Barney Campbell and from 1961 to 1964 he won Ulster Juvenile titles: Boys' 5st 7lbs, and 6st 7lbs pounds; and Youths' 7st 7lbs, and 8st. In his first venture in the National Championships in 1961 he reached the semi-finals, and the following year he lifted the Boys' 6st 7lbs title. He was runner-up in the 1963 Youths' 7st 7lbs class, losing to Mick Cullen from Wexford CBS. In the 1964 County Antrim Championships, Paddy won his first major title at flyweight and, in 1965, won the Ulster and the All-Ireland Junior flyweight titles.

On 11 February 1965, at the age of eighteen, Paddy gained his first representative vest when he boxed for Ulster against Wales in Swansea's Drill Hall, but lost to A Williams from Dowlais in a match which Ulster won 6-5. After his fight Paddy was taken to hospital with a suspected broken thumb.

In Ballymena on Monday, 18 January 1966, when England beat Ulster 5-4, Paddy beat Tony Humm from Harris Lebus, a 1965 ABA semi-finalist. This was a fight which Humm, an eighteen-year-old apprentice butcher, was expected to win. However, Paddy nicked it on a split decision in a contest which had the crowd on its toes. In an international against Poland in Dublin in February that year, Paddy gave an outstanding performance to beat K Czempik on points. The match finished all-square at 5-5.

Despite winning the Ulster Senior flyweight title and the All-Ireland Senior flyweight title in 1966, a shadow was cast over his outstanding performances by his exclusion from the Northern Ireland team selected to participate in the Empire Games. What made Paddy's failure to make the list of fighters bound for Jamaica especially difficult to comprehend was the fact that he had been rated third on the panel of boxers submitted by the Ulster Council to the Empire Games Selection Committee. His record, which included his recent wins over Humm and Czempik as well as a victory over the 1966 ABA champion Paddy Maguire from Vauxhall Motors in Luton, was second only to the brilliant Jim McCourt, who incidentally won the gold medal at light-welter in Jamaica. Many fans wrote letters to the press, highlighting what they regarded as Paddy's unfair omission from the squad. But the situation was made all the more distressing for the young Falls Road man by a telegram he had received from the Honorary Secretary of the Ulster Provincial Council, Ernie O'Regan, which congratulated Paddy on his "selection for the Games. The Council will meet the team on Friday, 24th June, at Paisley Park after training. Make sure of this date." If any lesson was to be learned from the whole debacle, it was surely that there was a grain of truth to be found in the old adage, "Don't believe everything that you read."

On 2 February 1967, Paddy, fighting out of the Holy Family, represented Ireland against England at featherweight and had a brilliant victory over ABA finalist Tony Cunningham of Mayfair in the Royal Albert Hall, with the overall result being 5-5. Just over a month later in an international against Scotland in The Stadium in Dublin, he out-pointed S Ogilvie from Dundee,

IRISH AMATEUR BOXING ASSOCIATION

Ulster Provincial Council

| Vice-President | President: | Hon. Treasurer |
| MR. J. BLACK | MR. E. THOMPSON | MR. J. DOWEY |

Hon. Legal Adviser: MR. D. P. MARRINAN, B.A.   Hon. Medical Adviser: DR. F. C. COYNE, M.B., B.CH., D.P.H., D.C.H.

All Correspondence should be addressed to the Hon. Secretary: MR. E. O'REGAN, 64 HIGHBURY GARDENS, BELFAST 14. PHONE BELFAST 748775

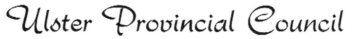

Dear Paddy,

Congratulations on your selection for the Games

The Council will meet the team on Friday 24th June at Paisley Park after training. Make sure of this date

yours Sincerely

Ernie O'Regan

with the Scots being annihilated 10-0. Paddy knew the significance of these victories: the European Championships were to be held in Rome at the end of May, but there were still a few hurdles to be crossed before a trip to that historic city was guaranteed.

On Friday, 15 April 1967 in Dublin, Paddy lost to Immaculata's Jim McAuley in the featherweight final. McAuley, in the "fight of the night", was at his brilliant best, but neither man deserved to lose.

In an international against Italy in the Ulster Hall, which the Italians won 6-3, Paddy overcame the handicap of two damaged hands to outpoint the Italian champion, Elio Cotena. Gerry Storey had pleaded with Graham to retire at the end of the second round but Paddy was adamant that he would finish the fight. This fine performance virtually clinched a place in the Irish team for Rome. The final Irish line-up for the "Eternal City" was: Flyweight Brendan McCarthy (Dublin Arbour Hill); Bantamweight, Sammy Vernon (Holy Family); Featherweight, Paddy Graham (Holy Family); Lightweight Sammy Lockhart (St John Bosco); Light-Welterweight, Jim McCour (Immaculata); Light-Middleweight, Eamonn McCusker (Banbridge)

Heavyweight, Dan McAlinden (Edgewick Trades Hall, Coventry). The Irish manager was Superintendent Phillip McMahon. Paddy progressed to the second round in the championships when his opponent, Jerome Denebourg from Belgium, was disqualified for hitting south of the border. In the next round he lost to the big hitting Romanian, C Staney. Of the six Ulster boxers in the team the only man to live up to his reputation was Paddy Graham.

The year 1968 proved an important one for the twenty-one-year-old because, as well as discarding the amateur vest, which he had worn with distinction on 135 occasions (losing about fifteen), he would marry his pretty girlfriend, Irene. The marriage would produce five children.

On Tuesday, 27 February 1968, at a dinner, boxing and cabaret show in Belfast's Fiesta Ballroom, held under the auspices of the Sporting Club of Ireland (whose motto was "Every Seat a Ringside Seat"), Paddy made his eagerly-awaited professional debut against Coalisland's Pat Joe Quinn. As expected, he got off to a great start with a points win over six rounds. After the fights, Rinty Monaghan entertained the crowd with his rendering of "When Irish Eyes Are Smiling".

Exactly a month later, Paddy returned to the same venue, but this time it was a cloth-cap affair as the bow-ties and dress-suits were discarded, and he demolished the tall South African Brady Barlow in the second round. The punch which sent Barlow into the twilight zone was a short right to the chin, and was described in the local press as one of the best punches seen for some time. On the same bill Willie Rea (Belfast) beat John O'Neill (Glasgow) (pts 8), Gus Farrell (Dublin) beat Jackie Pow (Glasgow) (rsc 4), Jim McAuley beat Pat Joe Quinn (pts 6) and Dave McCooke (Antrim) beat Brian Smyth (Belfast) (pts 6).

On a Mike Callaghan promotion in the Ulster Hall, Paddy beat Glasgow's John Kellie on points over six rounds. On 6 April 1971, Kellie stopped Johnny Clark in two rounds in a final eliminator for the British bantamweight title, so Paddy wasn't doing too badly to see the Glaswegian off in what was only the Belfast lad's third professional fight.

Due to the political unrest in Northern Ireland, Paddy was inactive in 1969, but he continued his winning ways on 10 February 1970, when he stopped Rotherham's Nick Kennedy in the fifth in the Ulster Hall. Paddy boxed mainly as a southpaw and was – surprisingly after such a long lay-off – very sharp, but perhaps a little over-eager. After a brilliant first round, which had twenty-year-old Kennedy bewildered, Paddy became a little careless and suffered a nick on the bridge of his nose in the second. The sturdily-built Kennedy, with weight advantage, did well in the second and third rounds, but Paddy put his foot on the pedal in the fourth with vicious uppercuts and short rights to Kennedy's chin. In the fifth, Kennedy showed plenty of courage but had no answer when Graham went for the kill. Shortening the delivery stance, Graham dropped his opponent with a right to the jaw. Up at the count of eight, the Rotherham-born heating engineer

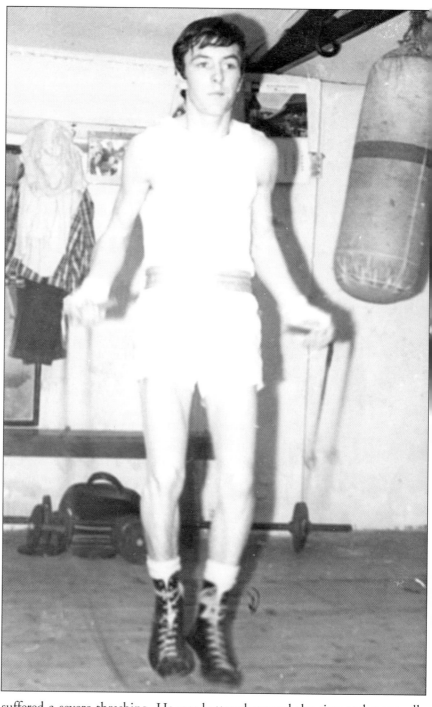

Paddy Graham in training

suffered a severe thrashing. He was battered around the ring and eventually went down on one knee in Graham's corner. Up at seven, he was duly trapped against the ropes and hammered until referee Hart intervened in two minutes and twenty seconds of the round. On the same bill, Belfast's Sean McCafferty lost on a fourth round disqualification to Sammy Lockhart from Lisburn in a controversial fight for the Northern Ireland Junior lightweight title. In a contest for the All-Ireland welterweight mantle, Des Rea knocked out Dublin's Gus Farrell in round eleven. Although Rea was born in Belfast and had thirty-one contests under his belt, he was remarkably making his Belfast debut.

Paddy had been scheduled to fight Kircaldy's John Mitchell, but when Graham failed to make an appearance in the Ulster Hall a bitter war of words erupted between himself and promoter, Mike Callaghan. "He will never box for me again," threatened Callaghan, and for a while it looked as if the Boxing Board of Control would withdraw Paddy's licence. But Paddy was also incensed and retorted, "It sounded as if I'd withdrawn at the last moment. In fact, it was nothing like that. I was only offered this fight twenty-four hours before the show. I wasn't fit, so I refused, but they kept on at me and persuaded me to go to Mike Callaghan's office. Eventually I was talked into signing. Overnight, I realised that I had made a mistake and my father contacted the promoter first thing in the morning. There were several reasons why I didn't fight: firstly, I had started a job after a year out of work. I didn't dare take time off to rest on the day of the fight, and I didn't fancy mixing plaster till six o'clock then rushing into the ring. I was also thinking of my reputation. What was the point in fighting without any preparation? Nobody would have been interested in excuses if I'd been hammered." This was shrewd thinking by young Graham, for Sammy Vernon stepped in as a substitute to face Mitchell and was stopped in three rounds. There is no problem so serious that cannot be resolved, and Paddy and Mr Callaghan settled their differences amicably.

For a while Paddy became disillusioned with the fight game and was out of action for eight months. "There didn't seem to be anything doing in Ireland, and I couldn't see a future in boxing. I stopped training and put it out of my mind," he remarked. However, on 20 October 1970, Paddy honoured an agreement which he had with Mike Callaghan to fight John Mitchell and he kept his unbeaten record with a points victory over six rounds.

Up to this point, Paddy had managed himself, while receiving business advice from Billy Frame, a director of the Sporting Club of Ireland, but he decided to sign up with English manager Jack Burns. At different stages of his career Paddy would be managed by Al Phillips, the former British Empire and European Featherweight Champion, Sid Ross, and Mike Callaghan. Three weeks later, in the Midland Sporting Club, Solihull, Paddy lost his unbeaten record to Leamington's Joey Wright when he was disqualified in the second of a scheduled eight-rounder. In the first week of December, in his seventh contest, Paddy had a return with Wright in Wolverhampton. So one-sided was the contest that not only did Joey retire at the end of the fourth round – he retired from boxing.

Paddy was in action against Nigeria's Orizu Obilaso on 13 January 1971.

Orizu's record was thirty-seven contests, won twelve, drew three and lost twenty-three. He would add another loss to his record for Paddy stopped him in round seven in Solihull. On 5 May in the Midlands Sporting Club, Paddy beat Eric Elderfield, with the Hammersmith lad retiring in the second.

On 3 June 1971 in Glasgow's Govan Town Hall, Paddy was the victim of an outrageous miscarriage of justice. When referee George Smith from Edinburgh decided that John Kellie, who was number two contender (Graham was number three) for Alan Rudkin's bantamweight title, had done enough to win, even Kellie's own supporters were stunned, and jeered, cat-called, booed and stomped their feet in disgust. Some of Kellie's supporters even threw coins into the ring.

The *Boxing News* were also of the opinion that Graham had won, as was Denis O'Hara of the *Irish News*. Denis wrote: "Not for some time have I seen such a blatantly biased verdict as that dished out by referee Smith … This was a stinker to beat all stinkers." Even Billy Rafferty, an old foe of Freddie Gilroy, muttered, "This was a disgrace to boxing," and promoter Peter Keenan, the former British, European and British Empire Bantamweight Champion, told the stunned crowd that he would "definitely feature Graham on his next bill".

Kellie had taken a hammering in the ninth and it was obvious that the contest should have been stopped. After the fight, a dejected Paddy said, "What have I got to do to earn a decision?" But asking Paddy to discuss his hard luck was like asking a resident of Pompeii what he thought about lava.

Three months later, Graham travelled to the West of England Sporting Club in Bristol to meet Tonyrefail's Colin Miles, who had won thirteen of his eighteen bouts. Paddy forced the fight at the start but emerged from a spot of in-fighting at the end of the second with a bad cut on the side of his left eyebrow. Referee Adrian Morgan allowed the fight to go on after Graham's seconds had done good work in patching up the injury. Paddy made strenuous efforts to end the proceedings quickly and shook Miles with some solid right hooks in the third and fourth rounds. Miles, however, fought back well and, as Paddy tired, the twenty-two-year-old Tonyrefail boxer earned the points for a well-earned draw.

Paddy had his final contest of 1971 in the Civic Hall, Solihull, when he beat the former Welsh champion Gareth Howells on points over eight rounds.

The Belfast battler had only one fight in 1972, and that took place on 19 June in Nottingham against the outstanding Dave Needham. Needham, who was fighting on home soil, was rated number three contender for the vacant British bantamweight title (champion Alan Rudkin had retired). He was undefeated in fifteen fights. Paddy, at this particular juncture of his career, was number seven in the ratings, with nine wins in twelve fights. This was always going to be a difficult task for Paddy, especially as he was suffering from back and neck pain, and Needham won on points.

Paddy's discomfort kept him out of action for nine months but when he returned to the Midlands Sporting Club he dismantled Merthyr's Les Pickett in the first round. Graham was at the wrong end of yet another diabolical decision in his first venture into the featherweight division. According to the referee, he was out-pointed by Bingo Crooks from Wolverhampton, but the reaction of the crowd, who loudly booed, perhaps gave a more accurate picture of who should have been awarded the fight. On 14 November 1973, Paddy was in Solihull once again but this time he left much happier after his victory (pts 8) over Charlie Parvin of Wishaw.

On his first 1974 outing, Paddy lost to unranked Wandsworth fighter Barry Harris on points over eight rounds in Solihull. This was a shock set-back for Paddy. The only consolation was the defeat didn't affect his number two rating in the bantamweight division, which was ruled by Dave Needham, as the fight was made at 9st 11lbs. Paddy's manager, Al Phillips, thought that the decision was a poor one. Less than two weeks later, in the Bedford Sporting Club, Paddy produced a fine display of aggressive boxing to out-point Bedford's Mario Stango over eight rounds. On Stango's next outing, he won the vacant Southern Area featherweight title by stopping Jimmy Revie, the former British Featherweight Champion, in two rounds. This was an indication that when Paddy was having a good day he was difficult to beat.

In September 1974, Paddy came in as a late substitute to fight Bobby Dunne, the former British Commonwealth Featherweight Champion, and had to fly to Melbourne for the encounter in the city's Festival Hall. He put up a sterling performance before losing on points over ten stanzas and even the Australian's own fans were of the opinion that Paddy had been unlucky with the decision. So impressive was Paddy on this, his first visit down under, that he was asked to stay for two more money-spinning fights. Paddy just smiled and said, "No, thanks. I must get back to my wife and kids." He did return to Australia on 29 November for a contest with Paul Ferreri, the former Commonwealth Bantamweight Champion, but he lost on points over ten rounds.

It was nearly a year before Paddy fought again, and he repeated a previous win (pts 8) over Mario Stango in Bedford. On 7 June, Paddy travelled to Accra to fight Ghana's Sully Shittu, who had won a gold medal at flyweight at the Jamaican Commonwealth Games in 1966; he had also, on turning professional, won the Commonwealth bantamweight title in Accra by beating Paul Ferreri on points over fifteen rounds. In the second round, Paddy felt a twinge of pain in his right arm, which intensified to such an extent that the doctor called a halt to the proceedings at the end of the fourth. This was unfortunate since Paddy was ahead at the time.

On 14 June in Portsmouth's Guild Hall, Paddy lost to Wayne Evans of Waterlooville in a final eliminator for the British bantamweight title. Paddy had now been a professional since he was nineteen and, with the exception of the early part of his career, had always been a leading challenger for the bantamweight title. It was, therefore, most unfair that he had to wait until he was almost thirty years of age before he even participated in a title eliminator. In this he was surprisingly beaten by the twenty-one-year-old Evans, who had been given no more than a puncher's chance.

On 7 October 1977, after an absence of sixteen months from the ring and in his first fight under new manager Mike Callaghan, Paddy, who was now officially boxing as a featherweight, beat Spaniard Luis Rodriguez on points over eight rounds in the Ulster Hall. Considering the ring rust, which must have accumulated after such a long spell of inactivity, it was a sound performance by Graham.

On 28 February 1978 in Derry's Templemore Sports Complex, the Maiden City's native son Charlie Nash won the vacant British lightweight title by beating Johnny Claydon from West Ham. On the same bill, Paddy beat Strabane's Billy Rabbitt, with the referee stopping the fight in the eighth. That April, in London's Albert Hall, Paddy lost (pts 8) to Wapping's Jimmy Flint. Flint was the Southern Area Featherweight Champion and had won fourteen of his fifteen fights. He was also rated at number two for Dave Needham's featherweight title. As always, Paddy fought gallantly but on this occasion experience had to bow to youth.

In his final contest of 1978 he was out-pointed by Warley's Pat Cowdell in Solihull's Midland Sporting Club. Cowdell would go on to win the British featherweight title, the European featherweight title and the European Junior lightweight title. On 25 September 1979 in Hammersmith, Paddy was out-pointed by Hartlepool's John Feeney, who was undefeated in fifteen outings and would go on to lift the vacant British bantamweight crown in September 1981 by beating Londoner Dave Smith over eight rounds.

Paddy Graham, who rarely got the rub of the green in the course of his professional career, quit the fight game after beating Birmingham's Jarvis Greenidge on points over eight rounds in Belfast's Beechmount Leisure Centre on 20 November 1979. He had tangled with some fine performers and, from the time he first donned the gloves at the age of ten until his retirement at the age of thirty-two, he was never kayoed or stopped as an amateur or a professional. Quite an achievement by a talented and courageous little boxer.

PROFESSIONAL CAREER
1968–1979: 29 contests: won 16, lost 12, drew 1.

Francie "Fra" McCullagh

A tough-as-teak pressure fighter

Boxing is a fascinating, intoxicating, magnetic and riveting spectacle. When the lights in the arena dim and the music blasts out, beckoning the brave combatants to the squared circle to give a public account of themselves before a critical audience, the toughest sport of them all gets under way. Serious injury can be only a powerful jab, or a short left or right hook, away. Some fighters who are clever enough can keep out of trouble with good lateral movement, back-pedalling and counter-punching; others, who are in possession of that envious explosive punch, are often the favourites to have an easy night of it. If your opponent had been Francie McCullagh, however, the chances were that you would not have had an easy night.

Once the bell went for the action to begin, McCullagh, a tough-as-teak and powerfully strong fighter, who had a "macadamised" jaw, would stalk his prey in a style reminiscent of Rocky Marciano, torturing his opponent with unrelenting pressure, which tested their spirit and resolve to the limit. Even if he was hurt, Francie would come back even stronger, crowding and smothering his man, and never taking a backward step.

McCullagh had a huge fan-base, even though he had a mere seven professional fights. He was a throwback to the old days, a good old-fashioned crowd-pleaser, for whom standing ovations were par for the course.

He was born on 22 March 1953 in Pound Street, Belfast, to Francis and Kathleen McCullagh. He had four brothers and a sister. Francie's father, a welder, was popularly known as "Keeler" and played football for Belfast Celtic's second string. Such was the standard of the Belfast Celtic squad that getting a game for the reserves was considered something of a major achievement.

Young Francis' early education was in St Brendan's on Milford Street, from where he progressed to St Peter's Secondary School in Britton's Parade. Striking out into the workplace, he was to obtain a position as a motor mechanic. He was introduced to boxing by his brother Paul, an outstanding trainer, who prepared Darren Corbett for his fights. Darren would go on to win the All-Ireland, Commonwealth, and IBO Inter-Continental cruiserweight titles, as well as the vacant IBO Inter-Continental light-heavyweight mantle.

Francie's first club was the Hollerith ABC, which he joined when he was sixteen, and his first contest as an amateur was against a young man with a very famous name, Joseph Louis, who was stopped in the second round. It is with the Immaculata Boxing Club, however, that McCullagh will always be associated, joining the legendary club's distinguished roll of honour alongside the likes of Eddie Shaw, Peter Sharpe, Sean Canavan, Spike McCormick and Paddy Maguire, to name but a few.

In 1972 he married his sweetheart, Christine Connolly, from Belfast, in St Patrick's Church, Dundalk. The couple would have four girls.

Francie dropped out of amateur boxing for a considerable period but, when he returned, he brought even more honour to the Immaculata in 1978 by beating Terry Ward of Holy Family for the Ulster Junior light-heavyweight title and Gerry Diamond of Bellaghy for the Ulster Senior light-heavyweight title. It may have been St Valentine's Night when McCullagh met Diamond but there was no love between the two men in what was undoubtedly one of the most exciting Ulster finals ever witnessed. So enthralling was the contest that, for the first time in the annals of local amateur boxing, "nobbins" cascaded into the ring as a token of the crowd's appreciation for two outstanding gladiators.

Francie not only retained his titles in 1979 and 1980, his victim being Draperstown's Chris Speers, but he added the All-Ireland light-heavyweight crown to his achievements in 1979 with a magnificent win over Kilkenny's Ben Lawlor. When McCullagh was announced as the new champion, the crowd's rapturous response singled him out as the most popular winner of the night. The lion-hearted Belfast man fought as if his very life depended on it, absorbing everything that Lawlor could throw at him, before coming and displaying real strength and character. The decisive factor was probably his ability to jab effectively with his left in the closing round. The judges made it four-to-one in Francie's favour, although for a time victory seemed very much in the balance.

Jumping back to 1978, the twenty-five-year-old Immaculata pupil was in such tremendous form that it came as no great surprise when he was selected to represent Ireland in a tour of the United States in March. In Louisiana, on 17 March, St Patrick was definitely not looking after his own as the Irish squad was thrashed 8-1, their sole victor being welterweight, White City's Ken Beattie. Francie had not been called upon that evening since his opponent was injured. Five days later in Texas, Francie boxed against a US-Mexican Select and stopped Wade Walker in the second round in a match which ended 4-4. In a fixture against an American AU Select in New Jersey, unfortunately, he lost to Kelvin Anderson, with the Irish visitors losing 6-5. Anderson was later tragically killed in a plane crash, which also claimed the life of the brother of Mexican Carlos Palomino. Palomino had won the World welterweight title on 22 June 1976 from Bethnal Green's John H Stracey, and defended it six times before losing to Puerto Rican Wilfred Benitez on 14 January 1979. A successful television and movie star, Palomino's triumphant defence of his title on 21 January 1977 against fellow-countryman Armando Muniz is notable in that it marked the first time in boxing history that two college graduates had met for a world title.

One of Francie's favourite memories was formed during another US tour when he boxed in Pennsylvania for Leinster against an American team called Muhammad Ali Promotional Sports, or MAPS. Ali himself took a particular interest in the MAPS squad, wanting them to do well and progress in the game with a view to maybe turning professional. One member of the US team who did turn professional was Tony Tubbs, from Santa Monica, California, who would go on to win the WBA heavyweight belt by beating Greg Page from Louisville, Kentucky – Ali's birthplace – on 29 April 1985.

At that time, Ali was training at his camp in the village of Deer Lake, Pennsylvania, for his return with Leon Spinks, who had sensationally relieved him of his world title on 15 February 1978. The camp, situated in a beautiful and peaceful setting, contained log cabins, a gym, dining hall, barn and, probably most importantly of all, a building used by Ali to pray and meditate in. Another great attraction in the camp were the large boulders on which Ali's father had painted in large letters the names of former world champions Rocky Marciano, Willie Pep, Joe Frazier, Joe Louis, Kid Gavilan, et al.

During the Leinster/MAPS encounters, the only winner on the Irish team was McCullagh, and his victory was witnessed at close hand by Ali, who was commentating on the match. When the Leinster lads visited Deer Lake, prior to their departure from the States, Francie was approached by "The Greatest", who told him, "You made a mistake which could have lost you the fight. You kept looking out of the ring at me." Francie quickly retorted, "And you nearly got knocked out by Henry Cooper because you kept looking out of the ring at Elizabeth Taylor and Richard Burton."

Action from Francie's first fight with Paul Newman

On 15 December 1978, Francie was part of an Irish team which travelled to Liverno in Italy, where they lost 7-4. Francie himself was beaten by G Cevoti on points.

In January of 1979 in Dublin's National Stadium, Ireland very nearly repeated a 1967 whitewash of Scotland, their only loser being Michael Holmes of Phoenix. In the ninth contest of the evening, McCullagh stopped Tommy Ross in the third round when he caught the Scot with chopping lefts and rights to the head. Ross, who had already sustained a nasty cut under his left eye, suffered another at the side of his mouth which prompted the referee to send him back to his corner. While it lasted, McCullagh was on top in the close-quarter exchanges. He was sharper to jab and hook coming out of the clinches and was well ahead on points when it ended.

Perhaps the finest performance of Francie's outstanding amateur career was against Detroit's Tony "TNT" Tucker in 1979. The encounter took place in the Cal Neva Lodge, Nevada, which at one time had been owned by Frank Sinatra. Francie lost the bout and took some heavy punishment in the process, but impressed those present enough to be approached after the fight by Tucker's father. Dressed immaculately in a whiter-than-white suit, Tucker senior was full of admiration for the young Irishman, telling him, "You took some great shots. What do you eat over there in Ireland?" Francie said simply, "Irish stew." "TNT" Tucker would go on to win the vacant IBF heavyweight title by beating James "Buster" Douglas in ten rounds on 30 May 1987. When Mike Tyson relieved him of his title the following August he was only the fourth boxer to go the distance with "Iron" Mike, the other three being James Tillis, Mitch Green and James "Bonecrusher" Smith. Francie would meet Tucker again, in the King's Hall, when the American boxed an exhibition bout on the Chris Eubanks versus Ray Close world title bill in May 1994. Eubanks won that one on a split decision in very controversial circumstances.

When Ireland had a great 9-3 win over Canada on 2 November 1979 in the National Stadium, the hero of the night was Francie McCullagh. He had been dropped in the opening moments by the giant Tony Morrison and there was real doubt over his chances. But Francie shook off the effects of the early barrage along the ropes and, by sheer grit and punching power, he proceeded to take Morrison down a peg or two. The crowd loved every minute of it and were on their feet as McCullagh waded forward, throwing a variety of punches. Morrison was very skilful and varied his stance from orthodox to southpaw, but it did not bother Francie. Despite seemingly running out of steam, he dug deep to find fresh reserves and fought his way to a fine win.

Three weeks later at the same venue, Francie came up against P Totka, a tough Hungarian, and lost on points in a match which finished all-square at 4-4. Francie had rallied admirably in the latter stages of the third round after soaking up a lot of punishment but it wasn't enough to clinch the verdict.

He was back in action on 5 December in Cardiff, where the Irish routed Wales 8-2. The Welsh were trailing 7-1 when their light-heavyweight Aneurin Williams scored a surprise second-round knockdown against McCullagh. The Immaculata fighter recovered sufficiently to take a unanimous decision.

In 1980, Francie had to withdraw from the Ireland and Ulster teams through illness and injury, and in 1981, he chose not to defend his light-heavyweight title which was eventually won by E McKenna from Kingscourt.

The big light-heavyweight with a heart as big as Divis Mountain decided at the age of twenty-eight to take the professional road. Managed by Barney Eastwood and trained by the late Eddie Shaw, Francie made his debut on Monday, 3 August 1981, in the Brighton Corn Exchange against Glenroy Taylor from Chiswick, a fighter who had yet to register his first professional win in nine outings. Taylor would eventually obtain a victory but it wouldn't be against the powerful, hard-hitting McCullagh, who won five out of the six rounds against a back-pedalling opponent whose main object was to stay the course. On the same bill, Barry McGuigan lost in controversial circumstances to local boxer Peter Eubanks.

On 22 September in the Ulster Hall, Francie had his second contest, his opponent being debutant Dwight Osborne from Nigeria. At the outset, Osborne looked stylish, but once McCullagh had settled down, the end was inevitable. Meaty punches from the Belfast boy brought the contest to a close when Dwight was bleeding from a gash just above the nose.

By the time Paul Newman ducked between the ropes and into the Ulster

Hall ring to meet Francie, the Bognor Regis scrapper had already won six out of thirteen contests, his best performances being against Harry Pompey Allen (ko 2) and Billy Warner (rsc 2). But at the end of six thrilling rounds, McCullagh had chalked up his third consecutive win as a professional. Newman was punished severely in the first two rounds and, at times, had to dig deep to survive the onslaught. In the third, Paul came out like a new man and caught the local boy with short hooks. However, when McCullagh started to use his powerful left jab he succeeded in keeping the Bognor boxer at bay. This was the kind of action which Francie thrived on and, when it was all over, he had won the contest with two rounds to spare.

Francie ended the year on a high when he out-pointed Clint Jones from Crawley on a Barney Eastwood promotion in the Ulster Hall on 8 December. Jones, who had turned professional in 1977, had ninety-five rounds of boxing (eighteen fights, seven wins) under his belt compared to McCullagh's fourteen rounds (three fights). He must therefore have felt reasonably confident about his chances of notching up the eighth win of his career. But so comprehensive was McCullagh's superiority that it looked like he was the more experienced of the two.

From the opening bell, Francie looked sharp, menacing and very fit. He scored repeatedly with left jabs and hooks, worrying Jones who went into survival mode. This tactic didn't pay off and the Crawley lad took a count of four in the third when stunned by a left-right combination. Although Francie failed to stop his opponent it was, nevertheless, an impressive performance. On the same bill, Barry McGuigan out-pointed Peter Eubanks.

Francie brought his unbeaten run into 1982 when he stopped Gordon Stacey in the second round on 27 January. Stacey, from Battersea, had won nine of his nineteen fights, and had triumphed over the likes of Paul Newman, Steve Goodwin, John Vaughan, Pharoah Bish, John Joseph and Dave Turner. In the initial fencing, Stacey looked useful when he caught Francie with accurate left-handers, but from a close-quarter exchange he suffered damage to his left orb and the writing was on the wall. The injury worsened in the second round and the referee wisely called a halt to the proceedings.

On a 23 March bill, which saw Barry McGuigan stop Italian Angelo Licata, and Hugh Russell hinder Keith Foreman, McCullagh and Newman came face to face for the second time. When it was all over, money showered like confetti into the ring. McCullagh recalled that none of it went into his pocket. As early as the second round, Newman's right eye was cut, and a right by McCullagh in the third left the courageous Bognor Regis boxer standing on shaky pins. The non-stop action thrilled the crowd and, at the bell, Francie was awarded a hard-earned but thoroughly deserved decision.

He had the last of his seven professional fights on 5 October 1982 in the Ulster Hall when he boxed a draw with Bootle's Steve Goodwin. He had turned professional because he had fallen "out of love" with amateur boxing and, at twenty-nine, his love affair with the professional code also came to an end. There is absolutely no doubt in many fight fans' minds that, if he had discarded the amateur vest years earlier, he would have done well in the professional ranks.

Francie, however, did not completely sever his connections with the fight game and is today a respected member of the Boxing Union of Ireland.

PROFESSIONAL CAREER
1981–1982: 7 contests: won 6, lost 0, drew 1.

Jimmy Carson Junior

A chip off the old block

When Jimmy Carson junior was born on 25 August 1958 in 23 Newport Street on the Oldpark Road to Lily and Jimmy Carson, he bore an uncanny resemblance to his father. In fact, Junior would go on to tread the same path in life as his dad, becoming expert at fishing, hunting and clay pigeon shooting. It was in boxing, however, that the most striking similarities between father and son became apparent. Both won Youth, Junior and Senior titles: Jimmy senior represented Ireland against England on 9 February 1953, while Jimmy junior represented Ireland against England on 9 February 1977.

For their efforts, each of them was presented with beautifully inscribed silver tankards.

While growing up in the Oldpark area, Jimmy junior went to Sacred Heart School. He was no different from any of the other kids, except that he could boast about a father who was a professional boxer who had once beaten the world champion, French-Algerian Alphonse Halimi.

Jimmy junior had three brothers, one of whom, Henry was an outstanding amateur with the Holy Family ABC, winning Ulster Juvenile, Irish Juvenile, Boys' Federation and County Antrim Junior titles. On a charity show for the late Johnny Owen, who died after a fight with Mexican Lupe Pintor for the World bantamweight belt in September 1980 in Los Angeles, Henry knocked out J Lewis, the Welsh Senior Champion and ABA finalist in the first round.

It was not Jimmy's dad who encouraged him to join the Sacred Heart ABC but a parish priest, Father McAllister. At first, Carson's mother Lily was reluctant to give her son permission, but a little bit of persuasive dialogue about all that was good about the club caused her to relent.

When the Carson family moved to Newington Street, Jimmy was attending St Patrick's College, or "Bearnageeha". It was around this time that he joined the distinguished Holy Family ABC, where he was in the capable hands of the inimitable Gerry Storey, whose son Sam would win the vacant British super-middleweight title at the expense of Croydon's Tony Burke.

Knowing how good his father was, there must have been a lot of pressure on Jimmy as he embarked on his amateur career. But his own particular talent for the squared circle came to the fore and he just got better and better. He was Down and Connor Champion in 1971, Ulster Juvenile Champion from 1970 to 1975 inclusively, Irish Juvenile Champion from 1971 to 1973 inclusively, and again in 1975, County Antrim Champion in 1975, Ulster Junior Flyweight Champion that same year, Irish Junior Light-Flyweight Champion and Ulster Senior Light-Flyweight Champion in 1976, Ulster Senior Flyweight Champion in 1977, Irish Senior Light-Flyweight finalist in 1976, 1977 and 1978, Irish Senior Flyweight finalist in 1980, Irish international representative (twenty-six Senior Vests), Northern Ireland representative at the Empire and Commonwealth Games in Edmonton, Irish representative at the Multi-Nations Games in Holland (where he was a silver medallist), Irish representative at the Multi-Nations Games in Romania (taking home a bronze medal), and Irish representative at the Multi-Nations Games in Hungary (bronze medallist).

One notable victory in Jimmy's amateur career was against Richard Sandoval on 26 November 1977; a year after their encounter, Sandoval would win the Golden Gloves light-flyweight title, and as a professional in 1984, he won the World bantamweight title by knocking out Jeff Chandler in round fifteen. Richard was due to defend his title on 10 March 1986 against Gaby Canizales. Sandoval had not fought as a bantamweight for over a year and, with the fight fast approaching, was an unbelievable ten pounds over the limit. Two days before he was due in the ring, he all but went on "hunger-strike" in a last-gasp effort to shed the extra weight. Hours before the fight, he still retained four pounds of offending surplus but somehow he made it. When the fight started he was as weak as water and trying to hold off Canizales was like trying to stuff toothpaste back into the tube. In all, Sandoval was down five times – in the first, the fifth, and three times in the seventh. When he went down for the fifth time, he lay still. His breathing stopped for more than a minute. Thankfully he survived but his boxing career was over.

On 22 February 1980 in the Ulster Senior Flyweight Final, Jimmy lost to Dave "Boy" McAuley, who, when he turned professional, would take the IBF flyweight title from Duke McKenzie and go on to defend it five times. A few

A 8 (3min.) Round Flyweight Contest at 8 st. 6 lb.

EXITING ALL ACTION FIERY   IRISH FLYWEIGHT CHAMPION

KEITH WALLACE v JIMMY CARSON
Islington & Prescot   Ireland

	1	2	3	4	5	6	7	8	Total	Ref's Sc.
WALLACE										
CARSON										

Referee:

An 8 (3 min.) round **LIGHT-WELTERWEIGHT CONTEST** at 10 st 6 lbs

The unbeaten "MARINE MACHINE"   A CAPABLE OPPONENT

TERRY MARSH v LLOYD CHRISTIE
Basildon & Stepney   Coventry

	1	2	3	4	5	6	7	8	Total	Ref's Sc.
MARSH										
CHRISTIE										

Referee:

TIMEKEEPERS:	T. RICE	FOR FUTURE PROMOTIONS WHY NOT BE ON OUR MAILING LIST AND HAVE DETAILS SENT TO YOU.	MEDICAL OFFICERS:	DR. G. CARP
	W. FLEMINGTON (trialist)	FILL IN THIS FORM AND SEND IT TO: NAME.		DR. B. MONK AREA REP. W. SHEERAN
INSPECTOR:	C. THURLEY	F. WARREN	REFEREES: APPOINTED BY B.B.B.C.	
WHIP:	D. HOLLAND	1/5 LONG LANE LONDON E.C.1 ADDRESS.	M.C.: DICKIE WATERHOUSE	

weeks later, Jimmy met McAuley again in the National Senior final, but the outcome was the same, with Jimmy losing on points.

The centrepiece of the Carson family home is the beautiful trophy cabinet. It is an Aladdin's cave of silverware, trophies, plaques, cups, et al, a reminder of the achievements of a father and son in an exacting sport. However, there would be no more amateur trinkets adorning the cabinet with Jimmy junior's name engraved on them since, on 22 September 1980, he had his professional baptism in the Ulster Hall against Newport's Steve Reilly. Coached by the indefatigable Paddy Maguire, who won the British bantamweight title from Dave Needham in October, Jimmy gave a thoroughly efficient display of punching and ran out an easy points winner over six rounds.

On 30 March 1981, Jimmy boxed a draw with Eddie Glencross in Glencross's home city of Glasgow, and on Sunday 10 May, at Dalymount Park in Dublin, he beat George Bailey from Bradford (pts 8). This was the same bill on which Charlie Nash lost his European lightweight title to Italy's Joey Gibilisco (ko 6), and Barry McGuigan made his professional debut against Manchester's Selvin Bell (rsc 2). A return with Newport lad Steve Reilly on 22 September saw Jimmy once again better the Welsh boxer (rsc 6) in Belfast.

On an Ulster Hall card on 27 October, where McGuigan again featured, Jimmy accounted for Derry's Neil McLaughlin (pts 8); then, on 30 November, he had a points win over Glencross in Enniskillen, going one better than the draw he had managed against the Glaswegian eight months earlier.

In the London Bloomsbury Centre Hotel, on 5 April 1982, Jimmy was paired with the Liverpool lad Keith Wallace, who was managed by Frank Warren. Like Carson, Wallace had been an outstanding amateur and was a dual ABA champion in 1981 and 1982. Although he had come home from the Moscow Olympics without a medal, he'd made such an impression that professional managers were queuing up for his signature. In the end he settled for a move to London under the guidance of Warren. Wallace had won his first three fights inside the distance and Jimmy, the Irish Flyweight Champion, was undefeated in six. If Jimmy were to win this one, it was almost certain that he would get a shot at the flyweight crown, which had been vacated by Charlie Magri from Stepney.

But the script didn't go according to plan and Jimmy was completely overwhelmed by the red-headed Liverpool terrier. A vicious hook to the head from Wallace in the first round put Jimmy in dire straits, and this was followed up with a fusillade of punches which dropped Jimmy for five. On rising, more punishment awaited him, but he gamely finished the stanza on his feet. In the second, Carson caught Wallace with punches to the head and, momentarily, it looked like Jimmy might just stem the tide of Wallace's fistic ferocity. In the third, Carson tried his utmost to get back into the fight, but Wallace was too strong and when the end came it was dramatic – if not unexpected. Wallace caught Jimmy with a barrage of hard punches which saw the Belfast boxer sink to the canvas by the ropes. Courageously, he got up at eight, but when Wallace hit him again referee Sid Natham stopped the fight. After the contest Jimmy announced his retirement, a decision which, in view of circumstances which would unfold, would prove to be very wise.

Wallace, who would go on to win the Commonwealth flyweight title by stopping Kenyan Steve Muchoki in the ninth round on 3 February 1983, died in the year 2000 at the age of thirty-nine. He was a marvellous little fighter who won twenty of his twenty-five contests. When Jimmy heard about Keith's death he was visibly upset.

Jimmy junior would have his own share of misfortune health-wise when he collapsed as a result of a brain haemorrhage while playing soccer for Downpatrick Rec. He had only participated in seven professional fights and had never taken the full count. As he lay critically ill in hospital, the Carson fighting spirit, coupled with prayers from his family and friends, enabled him to go the distance. He made a complete recovery and he and his wife, Cathy, now run a busy newspaper and confectionery shop in west Belfast.

Jimmy Carson junior never got a crack at the British flyweight title but he did get a crack at something infinitely more important. Life.

PROFESSIONAL CAREER
1980–1982: 7 contests: won 5, lost 1, drew 1.

David Irving

Hand trouble put paid to promising career

Seconds out. Round one. Like master dancers Sugar Ray Robinson and Sugar Ray Leonard, David Irving glides effortlessly around the ring, hands slightly ajar and held low. There's plenty of lateral movement, and his concentration – like a surgeon performing a delicate operation – is one

hundred per cent. As would be expected from a top fitness instructor and lifeguard, he is extremely fit and, as he focuses on the job at hand, he is prepared for any eventuality. Then, suddenly, he shouts, "Break!"

The description above is of David Irving, the highly respected boxing referee. It could equally have described David Irving in his fighting days as a hard-hitting light-welterweight, looking for an opening to land one of his big right-hand "bombs" on his unfortunate opponent. In fact, the same skills that David employed as a boxer, in accurately finding a chink in the other man's armour so as to deliver a conclusive blow, are employed by him as a referee, where his sharp eye ensures that the fights under his watch go off fairly and squarely.

On 8 June 1985, at Loftus Road in London, after his second loss (rsc 3) to Paisley's Dave Haggarty (their first contest in the Ulster Hall in October 1984 was an absolute thriller with "nobbins" being thrown into the ring), on the same bill that Barry McGuigan won the WBA featherweight belt from Panama's Eusebio Pedroza, Irving was absolutely distraught and his hands were hurting, as they nearly always were after a contest. David was always his own harshest critic and he didn't take defeat lightly, so on returning to the Eastwood gym in Belfast's Castle Street, he told Paul McCullagh, an outstanding trainer, that he was thinking of "packing it in". Paul replied, "Fair enough, but why not remain in the game? Why not think about becoming a referee?"

Nobody comes in for more unwarranted criticism than the "third man" in the ring. Before a licence is granted by the British Boxing Board of Control, the applicant must undergo a brain scan, and his knowledge of the fight game is put to the test. He also has to prove his skill before the critical eyes of experienced senior referees. David passed with honours, clearing the relevant hurdles and is now a well-respected referee who, when the occasion arises, is entrusted with overseeing every fight on a promotion.

David was born on 20 February 1962 in Belfast's Turf Lodge area to Robert and Theresa Irving. David has two brothers and four sisters. His dad, a former bus driver, was a keen fan of both the amateur and professional boxing codes and, as soon as his young son, who attended Gort na Mona School (now St Gerard's Resource Centre), started to stretch a bit, they would both go to the fights on a regular basis. It wasn't long before David, too, became hooked by the spectacle of the boxing ring and, at the age of ten, he joined the Dominic Savio ABC. Here, he remained for a year under the tutelage of Sean Canavan, who has been involved in amateur boxing for most of his life. As Ireland's manager, Sean was in Limerick boxer Andy Lee's corner at the 2004 Olympic Games in Greece.

David moved to Holy Trinity, adjacent to his home in Turf Lodge, and when his schooldays were over, he worked as a motor mechanic on a youth training scheme in Northumberland Street. He was also employed as a sales assistant in a well-known gent's outfitters called Austin's.

At Holy Trinity, under the supervision of coach, Michael Hawkins, David trained twice a day and every night until he was as fit as a fiddle. His dedication paid off handsomely for, between 1977 and 1980, he was unbeaten in inter-club fixtures.

25 January 1980 in the National Stadium was a momentous occasion in that, on one memorable evening, seven out of eleven titles came north. David won the All-Ireland Junior lightweight title by beating Patsy Ormond of Donore in Dublin on points, and was voted Best Boxer of the Championships. More icing was added to the cake when Holy Trinity got the Best Club award. On his way to All-Ireland glory David had disposed of Frank Connolly from Curragh, whom he knocked out in the second round; and in the semi-final he stopped Sean Barnes of St Joseph's in Wexford in the third. Michael Hawkins declared that "there was never a sweat about David winning the overall award for the best boxer. It was a unanimous decision – it just had to be. He's a boy of great promise, a fantastic prospect for the future." On the stage of amateur boxing, Irving was now one of the leading young players.

*Irving with some
of his silverware*

David truly enjoyed training in the gym. He also loved the runs six nights a week that brought him down the Monagh Road, up the steep Glen Road, down the Shaw's Road into Andersonstown, and concluding with the agonising and energy-sapping jog up the 'Rock and Upper Springfield Road, before returning to base.

In his efforts to win the Ulster Senior lightweight title in February 1980, David suffered a little heartache when he lost to classy, twenty-five-year-old Ballymena butcher, Gerry Hamill, who was a Commonwealth Games gold medallist in Edmonton in 1978. On his way to the final, David had been very impressive when stopping Carrickmore's Kieran Horisk, and many boxing aficionados thought that he was in with a shout against the vastly experienced and talented Hamill, who had achieved enormous success as an amateur. It was not to be, however, and the Turf Lodge boy, despite putting up stubborn resistance after taking two counts in the third, lost on points.

David was selected to represent Ireland at welterweight in the European Junior Championships in Rimini in May 1980. He probably could have made lightweight with some effort but Ireland already had a representative in Martin Brereton of Edenderry in Offaly. Since the inauguration of the championships in 1970, when they were held in Hungary, until 1978, when they were held in Dublin, the gold medal at welterweight had been won mainly by Russians. Therefore, the omens were not good for David as he prepared to face the Russian champion, Alexandre Mitrosanov. Immediately, the man in the red vest went after the young Irishman and landed some punishing lefts to the head. David, who was facing a much more experienced opponent, could find no room to avoid Mitrosanov and was forced to take a standing count midway through the round. Having got off to such a disastrous start there was no way back for Irving. After taking some more punishment, the referee sent him back to his corner. David claimed later that he had "difficulty keeping his feet" on the slippery canvas and that had upset his rhythm in those vital opening seconds. The gold medal at welterweight was won by T Holonics from Germany, and Barry McGuigan and Brereton won bronze medals for Ireland.

Keeping Irving out of the spotlight was no easy task. The young amateur star would shine brightly once more when he defeated Kieran Horisk on points to win the Ulster light-welterweight title in the Ulster Hall in March 1982. Horisk was forced to take two standing counts in the second round and was the architect of his own downfall, continually leaving himself open. Three weeks later, David garnered the All-Ireland light-welterweight title when, in the "Fight of the Night", he defeated Martin Brereton on points. The road to the final had seen Irving defeat Irish internationalist Peter Murphy from Drimnagh, who in January had defeated English internationalist Renard Ashton in Coventry. These fine wins earned David a dream trip to America but his night of joy was tinged with sadness. A hand injury, which he had always been susceptible to, came back once again to haunt him, forcing him to withdraw from the trip which would have seen him in action in Mississippi and Louisiana.

With the 1982 Commonwealth Games in Brisbane fast approaching it was imperative that David kept winning. In June, at the luxurious Abbey Lodge Hotel, just outside Downpatrick, he knocked out Alistair Laurie inside two minutes of the first round during an Ulster versus Scotland match. Irving looked awesome as he delivered sickening body blows to the unfortunate Scot. In trying to protect his body, Laurie left his chin exposed to the elements and when Irving connected, all that remained for him to do was pack his bags for the sunny climes of Australia.

He got off to an amazing start in the twelfth Commonwealth Games when he knocked out Papua New Guinea's V Anipina in the second. However, the Holy Trinity boxer failed to reach the semi-finals when he lost on points to Charles Owiso from Kenya. Owiso was a Roy Ankrah type of boxer, with fast, skilful hands and David was in a spot of bother from a right hand in the first round. He did manage to survive the opening stanza without taking a standing count, and in the second the Kenyan was the one with problems when the referee inspected his eye. He was allowed to continue and went on to win on points. Roy Webb from Larne was the victim of a bad decision but came home with a silver medal after losing to Nigerian Joe Orewa. Another Northern Ireland boxer, Tommy Corr from Clonoe in County Tyrone, came home with a bronze.

When David returned from Australia he represented Ireland against England in the National Stadium, but in a match that ended 6-6, he lost to the opposing nation's best boxer, Clyde McIntosh of Bell Green in Coventry. Prior to the 1983 Ulster Seniors, David performed brilliantly to stop Scotland's Ian Cameron in the third during a contest in the Andersonstown Leisure Centre.

On 17 February 1983, Irving won the Ulster Senior welterweight title by knocking out Jim Colvin of Midland in Belfast in the second round. In one of the finest performances of his entire amateur career, he stopped ABA Welterweight Champion Bob McKenley from Cavendish ABC in the first round at the Antrim Forum in September of that same year.

The ABA champion had started off confidently enough, prodding out a few lefts, when, like a bat out of hell, over came Irving's right, catching McKenley on the button and sending him through the ropes. Seconds later, a left hook to the body forced another count; then a left hook to the chin dropped McKenley on his knees. After the mandatory eight-count expired, the shattered champion was led to his corner. This would be Irving's last fight in the amateur ranks.

Managed by Barney Eastwood and trained by Eddie Shaw, David made his professional debut on 25 January 1984 in the King's Hall on the undercard of the Barry McGuigan versus Charm Chiteule fight. His opponent, Colin Neagle from Merthyr, had fought fifteen times as a professional, winning seven, losing six and drawing two. In a fight that was shorter than the introductions, Irving stopped Neagle in the first, catching him with a short right hook. The Welshman took a count of eight, but when he got up he was in no position to defend himself and the referee called a halt.

Leicester's Tony McKenzie had begun his career with three wins, two inside the distance, but Irving had him in trouble in the second when the two met in Birmingham a month after the Neagle fight. McKenzie recovered to drop David twice in the third, and the referee intervened and stopped the fight.

The Belfast scrapper put things straight on 4 April in the King's Hall by stopping Hull's John Murray in the third. David was always in control and, to be honest, the fight could have been stopped seconds earlier as Murray was being subjected to unnecessary punishment when the result was never in question.

On 5 June 1984 in the Albert Hall, David met Danny Shinkwin, one of three fighting brothers from Watford. Shinkwin had fought seven times, winning three and losing four. In one of his wins, he had stopped Tony McKenzie inside a round, a fact that may have caused some concern to the Irving camp. Equally, Danny must have felt reasonably confident about meeting the former Irish amateur star.

Any worries on the Belfast side of the ring were allayed fifty seconds from the end of the second of six scheduled rounds. A right dropped Shinkwin for five in the first but he fought back stubbornly. He came storming out for the second but was then hurt by a right. Another right to the head knocked him flat on his back near his own corner where he was counted out by referee, Tony Walker.

On another big night of boxing in the King's Hall, which saw Barry McGuigan beat Paul De Vorce (rsc 5), David beat Ray Price from Swansea, with the referee stopping the contest in the fourth. Price, who was a year younger than Irving, had boxed thirty times as a professional, and regardless of a career which had been submerged in a sea of defeats, he still managed to win the vacant Welsh light-welterweight mantle from Geoff Pegler, also from Swansea. Nevertheless, Ray paid the price for trying to mix it with the dynamite-fisted Irving and was stopped in the fourth.

When Barry McGuigan was in action there was a good chance that David Irving would also be on the card, and that was the case on 17 September 1984 in the Corn Exchange in Brighton. McGuigan was boxing a three-round exhibition with Croydon's Pat Doherty. Irving also gave a fine exhibition of body punching by stopping Leicester's Les Remikie in the third.

One month later, in the King's Hall, David came face to face with a tough hombre from Paisley called Dave Haggarty. In a fight that made an execution look like a Sunday School picnic, the Belfast boxer twice crawled off the canvas in the last two rounds to finish what the late Harry Mullan, former editor of *Boxing News*, called "one of the fiercest six-rounders I've seen for years".

Within the space of two months, David was twice in action in the Ulster Hall. He disposed of Plymouth's Joe Lynch in no uncertain manner one minute into the second round. However, Irving himself was then knocked out in the seventh by Geoff Pegler. David was in trouble as early as the third, sustaining a cut under his right eye. It was also ominous that the Welshman was able to take David's best shots without flinching. By round six, Pegler was getting through with lefts and rights to the head and Irving was in danger of being stopped as the round ended. The end eventually did come in round seven when a left hook to the Irishman's chin left him stretched on his back, unable to beat the count.

In the penultimate contest of David Irving's colourful career, he returned to form when he knocked out Brighton's Mark Simpson in the third round at Wembley.

On the night that Barry McGuigan won the world title – 8 June 1985 – David had another absorbing, "slam-bang" encounter with Haggarty but was stopped by the tough Scot in the third. With his hands aching, Irving decided that, at the age of twenty-three, he was going to call it a day.

In the years after that last fight, David married his girlfriend Angela and became a father to two children. His own father sadly died on 2 November 1994. Nowadays, the only aggression that David is inclined to show in the ring is when, as a British Boxing Board of Control Class "A" referee, he has to warn one of the boxers for some infringement of the rules.

PROFESSIONAL CAREER
1984–1985: 11 contests: won 7, lost 4.